THE PHILIPPINES:
Fire on the Rim

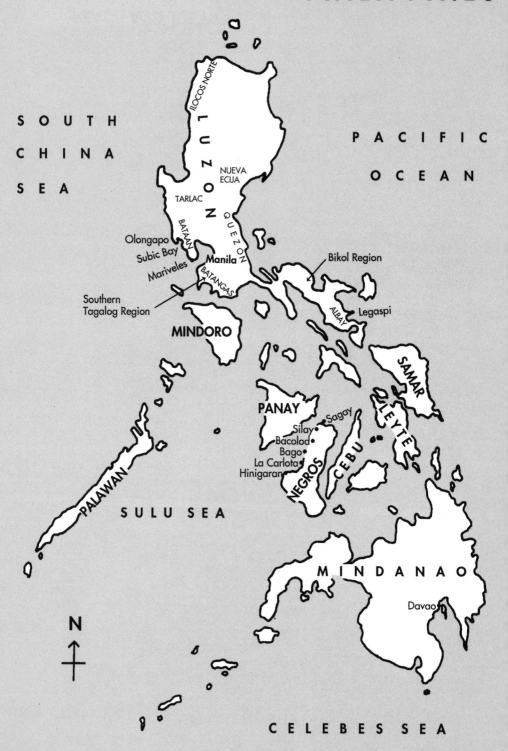

PHILIPPINES

SOUTH CHINA SEA

PACIFIC OCEAN

ILOCOS NORTE

LUZON

NUEVA ECIJA

TARLAC

QUEZON

BATAAN

Olongapo
Subic Bay
Mariveles

BATANGAS

Manila

Bikol Region

Southern Tagalog Region

ALBAY

Legaspi

MINDORO

SAMAR

PANAY

Silay · Sagay
Bacolod
Bago
La Carlota
Hinigaran

LEYTE

NEGROS

CEBU

PALAWAN

SULU SEA

MINDANAO

Davao

N

CELEBES SEA

THE PHILIPPINES:
Fire on the Rim

Joseph Collins

A FOOD FIRST BOOK

The Institute for Food and Development Policy
145 Ninth Street, San Francisco, CA 94103

Library of Congress Cataloging-in-Publication Data

Collins, Joseph, 1945-
The Philippines: Fire on the Rim / Joseph Collins
p.   cm.
"A Food First book."
Bibliography: p.
Includes index.
ISBN 0-935028-50-1 : $18.95. — ISBN 0-935028-51-X (pbk.) : $9.95
1. Philippines—Politics and government—1986- 2. Philippines—Economic
conditions. 3. Philippines—Social conditions. 4. Interviews—Philippines.
I. Title.
DS686.614.C65 1989
959.904'7—dc20   89-34331   CIP

Printed in the United States of America

10 9 8 7 6 5 4 3 2 1

To order additional copies of this book, please write or call:

The Institute for Food and Development Policy
145 Ninth Street
San Francisco, CA 94103
(415) 864-8555
Please add 15% for postage and handling ($1 minimum).
California residents add sales tax. Bulk discounts available.

Photos at opening of chapters:
p. 2 Jeanne Hallacy; p. 18 Robert Gumpert; p. 68 Robert Gumpert; p. 112
Robert Gumpert; p. 148 Jeanne Hallacy; p. 204 Pat Roque; p. 238 Robert
Gumpert; p. 290 Jeanne Hallacy

Design: Constance King

Contents

Word to the Reader

The heart of this book is fifty "voices." Each voice speaks a life's story, in her or his own words. Together they describe the social turmoil that makes their country one of the most explosive in the world; a turmoil generally unreported in our daily "news."

My opportunities to learn from Filipinos span more than a quarter of a century. Visits to their country have deeply shaped my life's work: probing the root causes of hunger, and joining with others working to overturn the obstacles to the changes necessary to free our world from hunger.

In the Philippines, as in virtually every other country where the majority go without enough to eat, the cause of hunger is not a lack of food. Rather, hunger is rooted in inequalization, in the absence of equitable and democratic control over food resources, locally, nationally, and internationally. In few other countries is the contrast between wealth and misery, surfeit and hunger so conspicuous as in the Philippines. Burgeoning quantities of food and other agricultural products are shipped out of the country in the face of hunger, even the hunger of those by whose sweat the sugar, fish, coconut oil, bananas, and pineapples are produced.

Every time I visit the Philippines I encounter women, men—even children— who know that their suffering is needless and how it is generated. They have discerned a myriad of ways, little and big, in which they can act, often at great risk to themselves, to end needless suffering for themselves and others.

Many Filipinos have tactfully taught me a painful lesson: my own country's policies and institutions are deeply intertwined with the roots of much of the suffering in their country—and with the obstacles to change. Accordingly, they have given me the gift of mission: to make more of my fellow Americans aware of what is being done in our name in the Philippines, so that we comprehend our common stake in thoroughgoing change.

This book is intended to bring to life several key issues that are tumultuous and pervasive. It focuses on what most would agree is the fundamental conflict in the Philippines, which happens to be the one I know best: the conflict between the land-rich and the land-deprived. In addition, the book incorporates inter-views on the export-oriented light industry zones developed in the 1960s and '70s for multinational corporations. Finally, as an American primarily writing for Americans, I thought it vital to convey the impact of the U.S. military bases in the Philippines. After all is said and done, these bases have become the central rationale for the continuous interference of the United States in Philippine national affairs.

In September 1986, I visited the Philippines for the first time since the overthrow of Marcos earlier that year. I visited Manila and rural areas in Mindanao, Mindoro Occidental, Negros Occidental, and Nueva Ecija in central Luzon.

I returned to the Philippines in December 1986, having thought out my plans for the book. I stayed until the following April. I visited different areas of the country, tape recorder in hand, interviewing nearly one hundred fifty individuals. I returned to the Philippines in September 1987 and in January 1988, to record a few interviews that I had been unable to arrange before. During each visit I talked with many more people than I taped; many conversations that do not appear in this book nonetheless shaped my perceptions.

Everywhere I went I sought out a representative diversity of class, perspective, and position on major issues. More than half the interviews were conducted in English; with the others I was able to find interpreters to translate from Tagalog, Ilongo, Visayan, Cebuano, and Bicolano. In addition to the greater Manila area, I was in three provinces of the Bikol region; Negros Occidental province; the banana plantation areas near Davao on Mindanao; the provinces of Mindoro Occidental; Nueva Ecija, Laguna, and Tarlac (the site of President Aquino's enormous sugarcane hacienda); the Bataan peninsula (particularly, the Bataan Export Processing Zone in Mariveles); and Olongapo City (alongside the U.S. Naval Station at Subic Bay). I visited most of these areas two or more times over an eighteen-month period. In a number of areas I was able to visit the "underground" New People's Army and National Democratic Front. Most of the photos were taken by Filipino photographers a short time after my visit, so as not to detract from the conversational tone of the interviews.

I located most of the people I interviewed through Filipinos I knew from previous research visits for the Institute for Food and Development Policy/Food First, or through their friends and relatives. Others I met by chance. Generally, I introduced myself as a writer helping outsiders better understand the Philippines. Filipino culture is not tight-lipped, and being known as "the author" (several books of mine have been published in the Philippines) gave me easy access to seemingly anyone with whom I wanted to talk. A few persons I interviewed in the countryside asked me to change their names for fear of reprisals and, of course, the names given by members of the underground are *noms de guerre*. A typical interview lasted an hour and a half, although some were much longer and some much shorter.

I winnowed a mountain of transcripts down to fifty interviews. Even then, for the purposes of this book, it was necessary to make extensive cuts. In cutting, I sought to preserve the principal thrust of each interview. Given the large number of voices, I also sought to avoid excessive repetition.

A challenge in preparing the text was how to handle the Filipino-vernacular English of most of the voices and the interpreters. My editor and I made sure that the interviews read intelligibly and smoothly to American readers, while preserving whenever possible the actual words and manner of speech of the person interviewed. The glossary includes a number of words used frequently by Filipinos speaking English that are either from their own languages or are coined from English terms. My own words are in italics.

Most Filipinos know a great deal about the United States. By contrast, most Americans know virtually nothing about the Philippines. If this book does anything to narrow the chasm, I will have succeeded.

Joseph Collins
August 1988

Acknowledgments

This book, an ambitious undertaking spanning two years, would not have come to fruition without the collaboration of many people both inside and outside the Philippines.

First, there is the obvious collaboration of fifty people who spoke with me candidly and for the record. In doing so, some took great risks. I trust that even those with whom I have great differences will find faithfulness to their meaning. I also interviewed many more people who do not directly appear in this book. Often I had wished this were a two-volume edition. Each person I interviewed broadened and deepened my understanding.

Many generous individuals and organizations in the Philippines, behind the scenes, taught me and pointed me in the right direction. I hope this book lives up to their expectations. *Utang na loob*! A heartfelt debt of gratitude to: Edgar Cadagat; Michael Tan of the Health Action Information Network; Francisco Lara and Cynthia Hallori of the Philippine Peasant Institute; KMP; Philippine News and Features; Jun Cañete; EPIC; IBON Databank; Raul Segovia of the Association of Concerned Teachers; Brenda Stoltzfus of the Mennonite Central Committee; Jim Goodno; Nonoy Pedragosa; Randy David of the Center for Third World Studies; Agnes Quisumbing of the University of the Philippines; Renato Constantino; Kit Palomera of the Popular Bookstore; and—for dedicated, all-around assistance day in and day out during these two years—Delfin Cleofas.

For help with the difficult task of transcribing the hundreds of hours of interviews in several languages, I thank Dani Gutierrez, Maria Tanchuling, Keith Wood, and the staff of Robert Ocana—Linda, Jun, Sarah, Jackie, and Aling.

There are several persons in the Philippines I can thank only anonymously, for fear of placing them in jeopardy. I hope they know who they are.

I was touched by the generosity of a number of Filipino and other photographers to whom I turned in my search for photographs for this book. My thanks also to Jonathan Best for sharing his collection of historical photographs and art books.

I am grateful to all my colleagues at the Institute for Food and Development Policy for their collaboration in many forms. Special thanks go to Walden Bello; in writing this book, it was a real plus to have a colleague who is not only Filipino but brilliant, indefatigable, and generous.

For ideas and materials from the earliest to the final stages of this project, I am grateful to Sergi Floro, Joel Rocamora, and to the Philippine Resource Center in Berkeley, as well as to John Cavanagh of the Institute for Policy Studies. Thanks also to Bruce Koppel of the East-West Center.

Special thanks to Gary Covino and Alan Berlow of National Public Radio, for a month of memorable collaboration and its satisfying results.

In developing the analysis of this book, I benefited from conversations with hundreds of people in the Philippines and the United States. Even though many had no idea they were helping with this book, I hope I never failed to communicate my gratitude for things big and small. I also acknowledge my intellectual debt to those whose works I list in "Sources Consulted."

Those who kindly read and commented on the manuscript in whole or part include: Gary Hawes, Melba Vidal, Walden Bello, Frances Lappé, John Silva, Tom Ambrogi, Marilyn Borchardt, Alan Berlow, Michael Tan, David Rosenberg, Medea Benjamin, Viola Weinberg, Monte Kim. Each one contributed; no one, of course, bears any responsibility for the final result.

Once again, Larry Rosenthal has been my editor. His willingness to do so was heartening. Beyond his usual fine editorial contributions, he stimulated the conceptualization of the shape of this book. He challenged and yet supported me to the end, which is the most anyone can ask of an editor.

Peggy Lauer, a superb copy editor, has saved me from countless embarrassing errors and oversights. My thanks to her and to Food First Publications Department director Ann Kelly and her assistant, Susan Galleymore, who oversaw the production of this book.

This book would not be possible without the 20,000 members of Food First. Their contributions, small and large, make ambitious endeavors conceivable. Food First membership information is in the back of the book.

Glossary

amo—Spanish for "master"; still used on haciendas to refer to the owner.

abaca—Hemp.

Alsa Masa—"Masses Arise," a vigilante group promoted by the military, initially in Davao, Mindanao, in 1986. The government has promoted the spread of Alsa Masa and similar vigilante groups throughout much of the country. According to Amnesty International, numerous extrajudicial executions ("salvagings") and other grave human rights abuses are committed by these paramilitary organizations "under the command or with the sanction of the regular armed forces."

Armalite—M-16 automatic rifle.

barangay—Lowest-level unit of local administration; in rural areas, roughly equivalent to a village.

barong—Loose-fitting, hand-embroidered shirt; national formal dress for men. Also called *barong tagalog*.

Bayan—The largest nationalist-radical coalition, founded in 1985; Tagalog for "nation."

BCC—Basic Christian Community, grassroots Catholic communities. "Basic" means "at the base." *Kristianong Katilingban*.

calamansi—Small green citrus fruit.

camote—Sweet potato; also *kamote*.

carabao—Water buffalo, principal work animal of the Philippine peasant farmer.

cavan—A measure of *palay* (rice before it is milled). One cavan is approximately 44 kilograms or 97 pounds.

CHDF—Citizen's Home Defense Force, civilian paramilitary organization established under Marcos.

copra—The dried, oil-bearing meat of a coconut.

CPP—Communist Party of the Philippines, founded in 1968; initially Maoist in inspiration, proscribed by law.

dumaan—Resident worker on sugarcane hacienda.

encargado—Overseer on a hacienda.

gabi—Leafy vegetable.

guayabo—Guava fruit.

gutom—"Hunger," in Tagalog.

hacendero—Owner of a landed estate or hacienda.

hectare—2.47 acres.

Hukbalahap or Huk—The People's Army to Fight Japan, a Filipino guerrilla organization during World War II.

IMF—International Monetary Fund.

ka or kasama—Traditional peasant honorific; Communists use as title, meaning "comrade."

KM—*Kabataang Makabayan*, or Patriotic Youth; established in 1964, a leading organization in opposition to the Vietnam War and to the U.S. bases in the Philippines. Outlawed in 1972, it is the oldest organization affiliated with the National Democratic Front.

KMP—*Kilusang Magbubukid ng Pilipinas*, or National Peasant Movement; a nationwide alliance of militant peasant organizations founded in 1985.

KMU—*Kilusang Mayo Uno*, or May First Movement; established in 1980, it is the nation's largest and most militant labor federation, with affiliates among industrial and plantation workers.

Malacañang Palace—The Presidential Palace; previously the residence of American and Spanish governor generals.

NDF—National Democratic Front, a coalition of revolutionary organizations; founded in 1973 by the CPP leadership and leftist priests. It claims a popular base of ten million Filipinos.

NFSW—National Federation of Sugar Workers; founded in 1971 under the auspices of the Catholic Church. Organizes both plantation and mill workers; affiliated with the KMU. Over 80,000 members, mostly in Negros Occidental.

NFSP—National Federation of Sugarcane Planters.

nipa—Palm leaf; the principal material for huts in rural Philippines.

NPA—New People's Army, the guerrilla force of the CPP/NDF; founded in 1969, the NPA is thought to number approximately 20,000 and to be operating in 67 of the country's 73 provinces. Term also used for individual NPA soldiers.

OIC—Officer-in-Charge; designation applied to governors and mayors appointed by President Aquino, under the decree-making powers she assumed following the ouster of Marcos.

palay—Unmilled rice.

peso—Unit of Philippine currency; 1 peso equals 100 centavos. The peso sign is "P." In 1988, the peso traded at about 21 to 1 U.S. dollar.

picul—Measurement of sugar; one picul equals approximately 125 pounds.

PCFC—Philippine Constabulary Forward Command, anti-leftist vigilante organization established by the military on Negros in 1987.

PKP—*Partido Komunista ng Pilipinas*; the old Communist Party, founded in 1930, with Soviet links; surrendered to Marcos in 1974.

sacada—Migrant; seasonal sugar worker.

sala set—Living room furniture.

salvaging—Kidnapping and summary execution by the military, the national police, or a paramilitary organization.

SFAN—Small Farmers Association of Negros.

U.S. AID—United States Agency for International Development; manages U.S. foreign aid program.

Philippines Social Index

Number of Filipinos in the Philippines
  1960: 27.4 million
  1970: 36.8 million
  1980: 48.6 million
  1987: 59.3 million
  2000: 85.5 million (projected)
Population doubling time at current rate: 25 years
Percentage of Filipinos under the age of 14: 41

❖ ❖ ❖

Percentage of national income of poorest one-fifth of the population: 5.2;
  of wealthiest one-fifth of population: 60.3

❖ ❖ ❖

Percentage of all Filipinos living below the poverty line in 1971: 50;
  in 1985: 60
Percentage of rural Filipinos living below the poverty line in 1971: 48;
  in 1985: 64
Percentage of Manila slum-dwellers born in rural areas: 80

❖ ❖ ❖

Agricultural labor force: 10 million
Owner-cultivators: 1.5 million
Landless: 8.5 million
  Squatters on government lands: 1.5 million
  Tenants (share or leasehold): 2 million
  Farm workers: 5 million

❖ ❖ ❖

Average rice yields in metric tons per hectare (1 hectare = 2.47 acres)
  Philippines: 2.5
  China (PRC): 5.2
  Taiwan (ROC): 3.7
  Japan: 6.4
  North Korea: 6.5
  South Korea: 6.4
  Vietnam: 2.7

Percentage of cultivated land producing crops for export: 55

❖ ❖ ❖

Rainforests and other forests in 1968: 40 million acres; in 1988: 16 million acres

❖ ❖ ❖

Urban daily minimum wage: 64 pesos (21 pesos = $1)
Minimum urban daily cost of living (family of six): 137 pesos
Percentage of the labor force receiving less than the minimum wage: 62

❖ ❖ ❖

Minimum salary of Filipina maid in Hong Kong: $295 per month (plus room and board)
Salary of public school teacher in the Philippines: $95 per month
Number of Filipino maids in Hong Kong: 34,400

❖ ❖ ❖

Per capita GNP in 1981: $790; 1988: $600

❖ ❖ ❖

Foreign debt at start of martial law (September 1972): $2.1 billion;
at time of Marcos ouster (February 1986): $28 billion

❖ ❖ ❖

Percentages of national government budget (1988)
   Health: 3.2
   Defense: 9.1 (not including U.S. military aid)
   Education: 12.1
   Debt service: 45.3

❖ ❖ ❖

Per capita 1989 government expenditure for the military (excluding U.S. military assistance): $17; for health: $2.50

❖ ❖ ❖

Number in armed forces
   1972 (start of martial law): 60,000
   1986 (ouster of Marcos): 250,000

Total U.S. aid (FY 1986): $489 million
Total U.S. aid (FY 1989): $304 million
   Percentage for food aid: 4
   Percentage for development assistance: 13
   Percentage for military assistance: 42
   Percentage for Economic Support Fund (principally projects in vicinity of
   U.S. military bases): 41

❖ ❖ ❖

Percentage of children who die before first birthday: 4.6
Percentage of school-aged children who are malnourished: 70

❖ ❖ ❖

Percentage of Filipinos without access to safe drinking water: 34;
   lacking minimum sanitary disposal facilities: 70;
   infected with tuberculosis: 32; with intestinal parasites: 70

❖ ❖ ❖

Percentage of GNP recommended for health services by World Health
   Organization for third-world countries: 5
Percentage of Philippines GNP allocated for health services: 0.7

❖ ❖ ❖

Percentage of Filipino doctors working abroad: 45; nurses working abroad: 60

❖ ❖ ❖

Number of persons in Negros Occidental per government doctor: 108,000;
   per government soldier: 900

❖ ❖ ❖

Number of Filipinos imprisoned for political reasons in 1986: 76; in 1987: 357

❖ ❖ ❖

Number of summary executions by the military and vigilante groups
   in 1986: 197; in 1987: 267

Chronology

1565—Spain colonizes archipelago, naming it for King Philip.

Mid-1800s—Spain opens Manila and other Philippine ports to foreign trade; principal exports are sugar, abaca, tobacco, and coffee.

1860s—Sugar industry takes off on Negros Occidental, through the impetus of British capital.

Late 1800s—Rise of Philippine nationalist movement.

1896 Aug. 26—Philippine revolution against Spain.

1898 May 1—U.S. Admiral George Dewey defeats Spanish in Manila Bay.

1898 June 12—General Emilio Aguinaldo declares Philippine independence.

1899 Jan. 23—Aguinaldo declares the Philippines a republic.

1899 Feb. 4—Fighting breaks out between U.S. and Filipino forces under the command of General Aguinaldo.

1899 Feb. 6—U.S. Senate votes to annex the Philippines.

1901 Mar. 23—Aguinaldo captured by U.S. Army.

1909 Aug.— Payne-Aldrich tariff establishes free trade between the United States and the Philippines.

1934 Mar.—U.S. Congress (Tydings-McDuffie Act) sets Philippine independence to come after 10-year commonwealth period.

1935 Nov. 15—Philippine commonwealth established with Manuel Quezon as president.

1941 Dec. 7—Japanese attack Pearl Harbor in Hawaii and Clark Air Base in the Philippines.

1942 Jan.—Prominent Philippine politicians organized by Japanese into Philippine Executive Commission.

1942 Mar. 29—The People's Army to Fight Japan (Huk) established.

1942 May—Last of U.S. armed forces in the Philippines surrenders to Japanese.

1943 Oct.—Japanese establish puppet "Philippine Republic" and grant it "independence."

1945 Feb.—Manila cleared of Japanese troops by U.S. armed forces and Philippine guerrillas.

1946 July 2—Philippine Congress accepts Bell Trade Act.

1946 July 4—The Philippines granted independence by the United States.

1946 Sept. 18—Philippine Congress passes "parity" amendment to Philippine Constitution, granting special rights to U.S. investors.

1947 Mar.—Military Bases and Military Assistance Agreement signed with United States for 99-year term.

1950 Nov. 9—U.S. National Security Council authorizes all necessary steps to defeat Huk insurgency.

1965 Nov. 9—Ferdinand Marcos elected president.

1966 Sept. 16—Rusk-Ramos Agreement amends fixed term of the military bases agreement to expire in 1991.

1968 Dec. 26—Communist Party of the Philippines founded.

1969 Nov. 11—Marcos re-elected to second term, the maximum allowed by the Philippine Constitution.

1969 Nov. 29—New People's Army founded.

1970 Jan.-Mar.—"First-quarter storm": massive demonstrations, campus barricades and strikes against Marcos and U.S. Government.

1972 Sept. 21—Marcos proclaims martial law. Five thousand men and women immediately arrested; thousands go underground.

1973—Marcos Constitution ratified by plebiscite.

1974—Marcos given a new six-year term through a referendum.

1978—Elections for National Assembly.

1979 Jan. 7—U.S. Bases Agreement amended: Philippine flag to fly over bases, but United States guaranteed "unhampered" military use of bases.

1981—Presidential elections held; opposition groups boycott.

1982 Sept.—Marcos on state visit to United States.

1983 Aug. 22—Former Senator Benigno Aquino, Jr., assassinated at Manila Airport as he returns from exile in United States.

1983 Sept.—Economic crisis; peso sharply declines. Size of foreign debt made public for the first time.

1984 Apr. 14—National Assembly elections; some oppositionists participate, but fraud minimizes the number of seats they win.

1985—The military and police open fire on demonstrating peasants and sugar workers in Escalante, Negros, killing twenty-seven. Lt. Gen. Fidel Ramos claims the soldier fired in self-defense.

1985 Nov. 3—Marcos announces a "snap election" during interview on U.S. television.

1985 Dec. 2—Marcos-controlled court clears General Fabian Ver and other military officers of complicity in Sen. Aquino's assassination.

1986 Feb. 7—Election held between Ferdinand Marcos and Corazon Aquino, Sen. Aquino's widow; both claim victory.

1986 Feb. 11—President Reagan declares ballot fraud by both parties.

1986 Feb. 15—Philippine bishops denounce election and call for civil disobedience.

1986 Feb. 16—More than a million people join the Aquino civil disobedience rally at Manila's chief park.

1986 Feb. 22—Marcos's Defense Minister, Juan Ponce Enrile, and Armed Forces Chief Fidel Ramos defect to Aquino camp.

1986 Feb. 23—Hundreds of thousands of civilians block Marcos's tanks to protect the reformist faction of the military.

1986 Feb. 25—Corazon Aquino sworn in as president. Two hours later Marcos takes oath of office. That evening Marcos flies to Clark Air Base and then flees to Hawaii.

1986 Mar. 6—600 political prisoners released, including two top-ranking communist rebels.

1986 Mar. 25—Aquino abolishes 1973 Constitution, and declares a Freedom Constitution that gives her decree-making powers.

1986 May 25—President Aquino appoints a 44-member constitutional commission.

1986 Sept. 15—Aquino leaves for week-long state visit to the United States.

1986 Nov. 13—Labor leader and KMU Chairperson Orlando Olalia brutally murdered. Two hundred thousand join in funeral march.

1986 Nov. 27—Government and National Democratic Front sign a 60-day ceasefire agreement, which takes effect on Dec. 10.

1986 Dec. 13—Progressive Labor Minister Augusto Sanchez forced to resign under military pressure.

1987 Jan. 22—Massacre of farmers demanding land reform in front of Malacañang Palace.

1987 Feb. 2—National plebiscite ratifies Constitution by overwhelming majority.

1987 May 10—Congressional elections.

1987 July 22—President Aquino decrees land reform with details to be determined by Congress.

1987 July 27—Congress convenes, ending decree-making powers of the president.

1987 Aug. 28—Bloody coup attempt led by Lt. Col. Gregorio Honasen.

1987 Sept. 18—Leandro Alejandro, chairperson of Bayan, brutally assassinated.

1988 Jan. 25—Provincial and municipal elections held.

1988 June 10—President Aquino signs land reform law passed by landowner-dominated Congress. Law denounced by Congress for a People's Agrarian Reform (CPAR).

One:
BROKEN PROMISES

On June 10, 1988, amid much fanfare, President Corazon Aquino signed into law a land reform bill. Extolling the legislation, the product of nearly a year-long congressional debate, Aquino claimed it would "uplift the Filipino masses from their ancient poverty."

During the more than two years that have passed since Aquino was swept into office, millions of impoverished rural Filipinos have grown disillusioned as they wait for her to act on their behalf. After all, candidate Aquino had pledged that her highest priority as president would be "an equitable sharing of the ownership and benefits of land." Ridiculed by Marcos and his minions for promising land reform while remaining one of the country's largest landowners, Aquino countered that if elected she and her family, the Cojuangcos, would make Hacienda Luisita, their huge sugarcane plantation, "the prime model of what a genuine land reform program should be."

As president, Aquino had an unrepeatable opportunity to lead her nation in bold reform. The uprising that brought her into office gave her a popular mandate for meaningful change—one nationwide opinion poll revealed that roughly two-thirds of all Filipinos strongly favored land reform. They even expressed a willingness to be taxed to help pay for it. Aquino also enjoyed a national and international stature bordering on sainthood, which offered her unparalleled moral leverage to take on the fierce foes of reform—the landed minority. Moreover, during the first seventeen months before a Congress was in place, Aquino possessed full lawmaking powers, something other presidents only dream about.

Curiously, several times during her first two years in office, the major U.S. media trumpeted that she had kept her campaign promise. "Aquino Puts Controversial Land Reform into Effect," announced the *Los Angeles Times* in July 1987, while *The Washington Post* ran the headline, "More Property for the Peasants Under Aquino's Land Reform." In January 1988, UPI put out a story entitled, "Aquino Parcels Her Hacienda to the Peasants."

Like reports of Mark Twain's death, these reports of land reform were greatly exaggerated. The only land reform under Aquino was the ongoing implementation, ever at a snail's pace, of the Marcos-decreed land reform that scantily benefited some tenants on rice and corn farms. Meanwhile, nothing changed for the thousands of workers on the 15,000-acre Hacienda Luisita.

The Urgency of Land Reform

Agrarian reform is long overdue in the Philippines. In a country where more than 70 percent of the population is rural, seven out of ten Filipinos who depend on farming for their livelihood do not own the land they till. More than a third of the country's land-deprived peasants are tenant farmers. Forced to turn over as much as two-thirds of their crops to absentee landlords or to pay steep cash rents no matter how meager the harvest, they are locked into an endless cycle of poverty. They also face credit, farm supply, and produce markets monopolized by merchants, moneylenders, and landlords. Even worse off are day laborers, invariably paid less than a third of what the government cites as necessary to rise above poverty—when they can find work. So desperate are landless laborers that they often do weeding and other tasks without pay for the "privilege" of being hired in the harvest. Most sugarcane plantation workers go without work during the long "dead season" between harvests.

Such widespread impoverishment means that in one of Asia's most fertile countries and the fourteenth biggest food producer in the world, at least 70 percent of the children go hungry.

Despite a respectable 5 percent annual growth in farm output during the Marcos years, the proportion of rural families living in poverty rose from 48 percent in 1971 to 55 percent in 1975, and to 64 percent in 1985. Even the World Bank, a long-time advocate of the theory that overall growth trickles down to benefit the poor, conceded in a May 1987 report on the rural situation in the Philippines that "investments and projects intended to increase agricultural productivity have brought few benefits to those not owning land—the landless laborers and tenants."

Many land-deprived Filipinos will tell you that "children are our only wealth." Not surprisingly, the population is mushrooming at an alarming rate. It is the highest rate in Southeast Asia, and could double in only twenty-five years. By increasing the pressure on the land, the population explosion makes ever more difficult the possibility of distributive reforms needed for the majority of families to enjoy the economic security conducive to family planning. Seen in this context, democratizing access to land, credit, markets, and other productive wealth is frightfully urgent.

Tenant farm families hand over to landlords so much of what they produce that working harder and taking risks to produce more do not seem worthwhile. Anyway, they are too impoverished to afford the fertilizers and other inputs necessary to boost their crop yields—and farm credit rates easily exceed 100 percent a season. Not surprisingly, therefore, Philippine crop yields remain among the lowest in Asia. High-potential "miracle" rice was first developed in a "Green Revolution" research center in the Philippines (set up by the Rockefeller and Ford Foundations, U.S. AID, and multinational farm-input corporations), yet the average output on the largely tenanted rice farms of the Philippines is less than half that attained in Japan, Taiwan, South Korea, North

Korea, and China. In each of these countries, far-reaching land reforms did away with tenant farming. For corn, the Philippine per-acre output is less than a third of that in the Asian countries where land has been redistributed to the tillers. And although the *hacenderos*, or plantation owners, including Mrs. Aquino, boast of "economies of scale," Philippine sugarcane plantations produce on average only about half as much cane per acre as the small (2½ to 5 acres) owner-operated sugarcane farms of neighboring Taiwan.

It is bitterly ironic for many Filipinos that their country, one of the richest in natural resources in a region known for its economic dynamism, and the only nation that was once a colony of the great United States, is now the poor stepchild. But an agriculture dominated by tenant farming and plantations holds back the entire economy. The grossly inequitable distribution of control over agricultural resources impoverishes the majority of Filipinos, thereby blocking the growth of consumer markets and hindering industrialization. Land reform is the essential springboard for economic development that would generate desperately needed off-farm employment.

Land reform also has political urgency. Without it, political stability—the peace for which millions of Filipinos long—is impossible. Widespread and worsening rural impoverishment has provided fertile ground for the growth of a Communist-led insurgency. The sons and daughters of tenant farmers and landless farm workers have swollen the ranks of the New People's Army (NPA), the military arm of the National Democratic Front (NDF). The NPA now numbers 30,000 fulltime and parttime guerrillas, active in sixty-three of the country's seventy-three provinces.

While the NDF has not been able to attract any significant foreign-power support, it successfully relies on the rural poor to provide its base of logistical support. The NDF, in its Fourteen Point Program, promises "a genuine land reform that will liberate the peasants from feudal and semifeudal exploitation," and it has already fostered partial land reform in areas where it has quasi-government control.

Visiting some of the NPA "minimum reform" areas, I found that peasant negotiations with landowners had lowered rents and raised wages. Only owners who refused to negotiate, or who called in goon squads or the military, found their lands seized and redistributed. The NPA often levies a supposedly voluntary tax equivalent to a percentage of the benefits the peasants gain from such reforms.

The 1980s has also seen the formation of the National Peasant Movement of the Philippines, KMP (*Kilusang Magbubukid ng Pilipinas*), which now claims a membership of 750,000 and influence among some 2 million farmers.

Audie de la Cruz

A Grand Deception

However long overdue, has President Aquino finally brought land reform to the Philippines? Tragically, the answer is no.

The 19-page, fine-print land reform law is so full of limitations, exemptions, loopholes, and escape clauses for landowners that it is toothless. Seemingly pro-peasant provisions in the law are cancelled out or rendered meaningless by pro-landlord provisions. That many landlords immediately decried the law—some even threatened to take up arms to defend their properties—perhaps shows only that some landlords have been taken in by the law's rhetoric, while others have learned not to relish their triumph publicly.

Fundamentally, a land reform should transfer land out of the control of absentee landlords and place the control in the hands of the landless, who will become owner-cultivators. The 1987 Constitution recognized that an agrarian reform program should be "founded on the right of farmers and regular farm workers who are landless to own directly or collectively the lands they till." By contrast,

Audie de la Cruz

Jun Cañete

Scenes from Hacienda Luisita, the largest sugar plantation in the Philippines, owned by President Corazon Aquino and her family. *Opposite:* The family of one of 3,000 migrant farm workers who live in these cardboard partitioned barracks during the five-month cane-cutting season. *Top:* Individual shelters house some 6,000 gamecocks; cockfighting is a favorite pastime of Jose Cojuanco, President Aquino's brother and leading member of Congress. *Bottom:* One of the swimming pools inside the family compound of villas. Hacienda Luisita also has its own sugar mill, an airfield, stables for race horses, and an 18-hole golf course.

this law seems on balance formulated to protect the landed rather than to benefit the landless.

This is most evident in the provisions limiting the scope of the law to lands held in excess of a certain amount. The law permits each landowner to keep at least 5 hectares (12.5 acres) and to distribute an additional 3 hectares (7.5 acres) to each child 15 years or older whether he or she is an actual tiller. These retention limits might sound hard-nosed to someone accustomed to American-style farms, but they are generous to a fault in a country where a typical farmer works 1 to 3 hectares. They are much higher than those applied in the successful land reforms in Japan, Taiwan, and South Korea, where the ceilings ranged from 0 to 3 hectares.

Most crucial, even ignoring other serious shortcomings of the law, such relatively high retention limits would mean that far too little land could be redistributed to benefit a significant portion of the estimated 8.5 million landless rural Filipinos. Since the higher the limit the less land is made available for those who need it, Father Antonio Ledesma, S.J., and other leading Filipino land reform experts used the latest agricultural census to calculate how much land would be available, at various possible retention limits, during the congressional debate on the law. These studies revealed that, with the conservative assumption that a typical landlord family has at least two qualified children, this law could affect at most only 2 million hectares or under 25 percent of all the country's agricultural land. If the ceiling were set at 3 hectares, almost 7 million hectares would be available for distribution to tenant farmers and landless farm workers. Moreover, with such a ceiling, there would not be a wide disparity in land holdings between cultivator-beneficiaries and small landlords.

The potential scope of the law is even further reduced by a ten-year exemption of any "commercial farm" devoted to livestock, prawn production and other forms of aquaculture, fruit trees, vegetables, cut flowers, or plantations of cacao, coffee, or rubber trees. Such farms add up to a significant amount of exempted land.

One of the law's most outrageous provisions is that which grants landowners a three-month grace period to transfer land title. Landowners will thus have enough time to parcel out their land in 5-hectare parcels to landless relatives, friends, and retainers, reregistering it in their names but keeping *de facto* ownership of the land themselves. The upshot, of course, is that far fewer landlords than anticipated will "own" land in excess of the amount permitted to be retained by the law. As a result there will be little land to distribute to landless Filipinos. Such "anticipatory transfers" greatly undercut the effectiveness of previous land reform laws in the Philippines.

Some landowners no doubt fear a real land reform someday or for some other reason want to liquidate their land assets. They will find that the law provides for compensation. The amount of the compensation is to be made by the landowner, the Department of Agrarian Reform, and the Land Bank of the Philippines, which suggests, in the opinion of a range of experts on Philippine land issues, that payments to landowners will be generous. In fact, the aggregate compensation could be so high that the government would have to go begging abroad. But a 1987 World Bank report on the land reform issues in the Philippines made clear that the Bank judges as excessively wasteful the granting of loans to governments to purchase land in the name of land reform. And even the U.S. Congress and other donor governments are likely to balk at the idea of passing billions of dollars to Filipino landlords.

The law also provides another way around land reform for the bigger and richer farm owners. In lieu of any of their land being distributed, they can incorporate and sell to their tenants and fulltime farm workers a minority interest in their capital stock, up to the percentage the corporation determines to be the value of the land relative to its total assets. This is likely what Mrs. Aquino and her family will do with Hacienda Luisita. Unlike genuine land reform, which fundamentally has to do with a redistribution of control from the powerful to the powerless, under this arrangement tenants and farm workers would at best become *minority* shareholders with no say in the running of the estate. They could actually wind up worse off: landlords, on the pretext that they are now dealing with "co-owners," will probably move to end paternalistic practices that mitigate the harsh exploitation and desperation of tenants and farm workers, such as occasional free medical care and emergency loans. This provision for stock distribution also entirely overlooks the plight of the *sacadas,* or seasonal workers, who make up a large part of the rural labor force and are among the most impoverished Filipinos.

Every successful land reform has been carried out with dispatch in order to undercut landowners' ability to maneuver, a point emphasized by the World Bank report to the Aquino government. Nonetheless, the law signed by Aquino sets forth an exceptionally lengthy program (ten years) of execution. Even in theory, it defers the affect on much of the privately held agricultural land until after President Aquino completes her term of office in 1992. Long before then, virtually all landowners surely will have availed themselves of one or more of the law's exemptions, loopholes, and—if all else fails—open invitations for court challenges to the law.

CPAR, a 2.5-million-member coalition of peasant and farm worker organizations, joined in denouncing the law as "not even a step forward." A KMP official stated that the law confirmed the "pro-landlord and anti-peasant character" of the Aquino administration. His talk of "disillusionment with the way the Aquino administration has handled the land issue" was echoed in an impassioned attack on the president by Amando Doronila, the widely respected political editor of the *Manila Chronicle*. With the signing of the law, Doronila wrote, "President Aquino formalized her moral cowardice and her surrender to Congress and landed interests."

The rural majority and their advocates plainly see this law as the latest in a long line of ineffectual land reform measures that litter Philippine history. Since the 1930s, land reform has been the subject of no fewer than ten acts of Congress and forty-three presidential decrees, all grandiose in rhetoric about justice and agricultural progress, all failing to make a real difference for the majority of Filipinos. With what is probably more land reform legislation than any other country in East Asia, the Philippines remains the country with the most inequitable land distribution in the entire region.

Colonial Rule

The land problem in the Philippines began with colonial rule.

Before the Spanish colonizers arrived in the 16th century, land in most parts of the archipelago belonged to the community or *barangay*. Tillers generally worked the land individually and enjoyed the fruits of their labors. The community headmen did not own the land but simply administered its allocation to all productive members of the community.

Spanish military occupation instituted far-reaching changes in how agricultural land was controlled. Spanish soldiers and clergy began the process of accumulation of lands by the few and the dispossession of the majority. Lands were purchased for token sums from headmen, even though the parcels were not theirs to sell. The headman often did this without the knowledge of the *barangay* members. All uncultivated lands were declared "reserves" for the Spanish Crown. By royal decree, more and more lands and the *indios* ("natives") living on them were "entrusted" to the care of military officers or the friars of religious orders like the Dominicans. These vast tracts of land were called *encomiendas* ("trusts"). They produced food principally for consumption on the *encomienda*, but the Filipinos who tilled the land were required to turn over part of what they produced as tribute to the Spanish friars or soldiers, the *encomenderos*. As the Spaniards in most of the Philippines governed indirectly, the tribute was usually paid through the chieftains, helping to solidify their elite status as economic and political intermediaries.

Until the end of the 18th century, the archipelago remained outside the world economy. Manila was essentially a transshipment port for the Spanish galleon commercial trade between Mexico and China. Philippine products were not in great demand in Mexico or China, and Spain got all the sugar, tobacco, and coffee it wanted from Cuba and Puerto Rico in the same hemisphere, which are geographically closer.

The development of the Philippines' export-based economy began in the early 1800s. Merchants connected to the large banking and trading companies of the United States, Europe, and China, began to advance money for the production of sugar, coffee, hemp (*manila*), and copra (coconut meat from which oil is pressed), which they would export. In 1834, the Spanish authorities gave in to pressures to open the ports of Manila and other cities to foreign trade. Production of crops for export precipitated a rush for land among the friars, Spanish officials, and mestizo elites, especially the wealthy Chinese mestizo merchants. They expropriated the lands of untold numbers of small native farmers through purchase, donation (to friars), trickery, foreclosure of mortgages, and outright land-grabbing.

The export-crop economy brought with it the hacienda or plantation system of agriculture. Most haciendas were owned by absentee landlords, who leased their lands to an *inquilino* ("lessee") and charged a fixed rent in the form of a share of the harvest. The *inquilinos* in turn parceled out the land to *indio* tenants, for a usually steep share of the produce. Some other haciendas, particularly the large sugarcane haciendas, had administrators and agricultural wage laborers.

The emphasis on export crops, especially the conversion of lands from rice to sugar, resulted in a decline in the acreage planted in rice. Rice became scarce in a country that up until 1850 exported rice to China. Because there was less rice, the price rose dramatically, triggering widespread famine and starvation. As rice prices increased, elites, especially Chinese mestizos, accumulated lands for rice production—with the rice producers, now tenants, paying high in-kind rents.

Incorporation into the world market made the Philippines vulnerable to the vagaries of the international market system. Economic recessions and depressions in the industrial countries set off severe hardships and even starvation in the Philippines, especially in the regions producing sugar and hemp. Exporting also meant that the Philippines had to open up to imports in order to maintain a balance of trade. Local cottage industries, notably a thriving weaving industry on Iloilo, were driven out of business by the flood of industrial imports, such as textiles from Britain. Tens of thousands were deprived of their livelihood.

When the United States took possession of the archipelago in 1898, the transformation of the Philippines was complete. The Philippines was then an exporter of agricultural commodities and other raw materials and an importer of manufactured products—with land and other productive resources increasingly controlled by wealthy Filipinos and foreign corporations.

Reciprocal free trade was enshrined in several acts of the U.S. Congress between 1909 and 1913. Under this policy, the products of each country flow into the other virtually duty-free and without restrictions.

This arrangement had a number of predictable consequences. Philippine growers of sugarcane, tobacco, coconut, and hemp enjoyed a large and assured market. (Many sugar planters on the island of Negros had actively opposed the Republic during the war with the United States.) Wealthy families took over large tracts of farmland and cultivated them with export crops. The land in sugarcane tripled between 1902 and 1918. Dependence on a single market was inherent in the arrangement, because duties would be levied on exports to other countries. By 1941, the last year before World War II, 81 percent of Philippine exports went to the United States.

American political intent behind free trade was to co-opt wealthy landowners into supporting colonial annexation by giving them a vested interest, which would make them see Filipino nationalists as "subversives." The implicit deal with the elites was that, in exchange for their collaboration, the United States would not reform the existing social structures. (The big landowners feared the revolutionary potential of the nationalist Republic.) William Howard Taft, the colony's first American civilian governor-general, cemented this policy by rapidly making the colonial government indigenous. As he did so, the government readily fell into the control of the landed elite—largely the same elite who had emerged to take on the role of political administration for the Spaniards. The identity of the government and this landed elite has remained fundamentally unaltered to this day.

With American rule, certain major U.S. corporations reaped great profits by gaining assured access to low-priced raw materials. Sugar-refining interests saw the virtual annexation of the Philippines (along with Hawaii, Cuba, and Puerto Rico) as a way around tariffs levied to protect American sugar beet farmers. Congress granted U.S. citizens (and therefore American corporations) equal opportunity with Filipinos to own agricultural land in the Philippines. U.S. manufacturers had the windfall of a protected market; competing products from other countries were penalized with stiff duties. By 1941, 84 percent of Philippine imports came from the United States. Efforts at industrialization in the Philippines were profoundly undermined. Despite the rhetoric of "free competition," Philippine industries were in no position to compete with powerful U.S. industries.

In addition to trade policies that reinforced the backward and unbalanced economic system set up by the Spaniards, the U.S. Congress enacted a series of "land reform" laws that wound up working against the interests of the Filipinos who actually tilled the land.

The Philippine Bill (1902), while limiting individual landholdings to 40 acres, gave U.S. citizens the right to acquire agricultural lands and raised the limit on corporate landholdings to 2,530 acres. The road was opened for Del Monte and other U.S. agribusiness corporations to set up plantations. At the same time, landowners were ordered to register their landholdings. Filipino elites found ways around the 40-acre limit, but the vast majority of peasant farmers were either unaware of the new law or too poor to pay the fees for the documentation. Almost all the land titles issued through the Philippine Bill were for large landholdings. Grabbing land from helpless peasants became institutionalized.

Under the Friar Lands Act (1903), the U.S. Congress purchased large agricultural estates—for generations a source of rural unrest—from religious orders. The stated purpose was to resell the estates in parcels to some sixty thousand tenants. But the price (full cost plus interest) was beyond the reach of most tenants. Many could not understand why they had to pay the "rich" U.S. government for land that had been wrongfully taken from their parents or grandparents. Congress amended the act to allow the sale of these first-class lands to foreign nationals. Among the beneficiaries were large U.S. companies.

These and other land reform laws under American rule in fact worsened the land problem for the majority of Filipinos. The percentage of land worked by tenants—a measure of dispossession of peasants—rose from 19 percent in 1903 to 38 percent at the time of Philippine independence in 1946.

A Paper Independence

On July 4, 1946, the United States granted independence to the Philippines with a good deal of self-congratulations. Behind the ideology of the United States as the "good" colonial power, nobly setting the Philippines free after a brief period of democratic tutelage, was the fact that the American Farm Bureau had been demanding immediate Philippine independence since 1929. American sugar beet farmers objected to Philippine sugar imports. Dairy and oilseed farmers feared cheap coconut oil imports. Tobacco growers, cotton farmers, and cordage producers wanted the Philippine competition shut out. Farm workers in California protested the flood of Filipino workers, who would work for lower wages, into their state. The Philippines, remarkably, was attacked almost as if it were an enemy of the United States. One Southern senator captured the sentiment of a growing majority in Congress by calling the Philippines a "millstone" burdening American agriculture. It was the economic coalition of farmers and politicians, in America, in the midst of the Great Depression, that resulted in an act of Congress granting independence to the Philippines in ten years, an act agreed to by Philippine officials in 1934.

The independence granted in 1946 was certainly not economic independence. The Philippines had been devastated by World War II. (Manila was said to be second only to Warsaw in destruction of a capital city.) At levels far lower than had been promised during the war, U.S. Congress tied compensation to sweeping economic concessions in favor of the United States. These compensations were embodied in the Philippine–United States Trade Act.

The Act kept in place the trade and investment benefits that U.S. multinational companies enjoyed during the direct colonial era that were supposed to have been terminated with colonial rule. But now it was one-way free trade. The Act provided for unlimited importation to the Philippines of all American goods duty-free for eight years, after which American goods would be subject to partial tariffs only until 1974. Tariffs and other restrictions would be imposed on goods from other countries. Similar tariff benefits were granted only to some Philippine goods (exceptions included those to which U.S. farmers objected), and the U.S. president was empowered to allocate quotas for Philippine exports to the United States. The U.S. president was also solely empowered to suspend all or any parts of the Act if the president judged that the new Philippine government was acting in a way detrimental to U.S. economic interests. The Act also tied the value of the Philippine peso to that of the American dollar indefinitely; so U.S. investors could always convert peso profits into dollars and take them out of the country without fear of currency exchange losses.

These two measures robbed the Philippine government of the power to regulate imports and currency exchange, essential tools for any government that might seek to develop the country's economic plans beyond exporting low-value, unprocessed agricultural goods and poorly paid labor. (American postwar policy was to make Japan the industrial workshop of Asia and the Philippines the supplier of raw materials.)

Tacked onto the Trade Act was a "parity" provision that guaranteed American citizens, and therefore corporations, the same rights as Filipinos in exploiting the Philippines' natural resources and in owning land and public utilities. American corporations, with their far greater access to capital, technology, and markets than Filipino enterprises, could corner whatever part of the Philippine economy that might become profitable.

While once again most Filipino elites opted to collaborate with the foreign power, nationalist leaders repeatedly denounced these neo-colonial measures. Some years later, their speeches and writings were to have a considerable impact on a new generation of student and other activists. One such leader, Senator C. M. Recto, in lamenting the Philippine government's acquiescence, stated with characteristic sarcasm: "The world was thus presented with the admirable phenomenon of a new nation more dependent, and more willingly dependent, on its former sovereign after independence than before."

Two:
REALITIES

From many "voices" in different regions, I have selected those from two provinces. The interviews in this chapter and the three succeeding chapters come from Albay province in the Bikol region, which makes up the southeastern tail of Luzon, the chief island of the Philippines; and from Negros Occidental province in the central Visayan region of the Philippines.

Albay province is dominated by 8000-foot Mount Mayon, an active, perfectly conical volcano. Around the base of the volcano, and throughout the province, are fields of coconut palms, rice, and corn.

The heart of Albay's economy is coconuts, grown mainly for copra, the dried kernel or "meat" from which coconut oil and dozens of other products are derived. Coconut oil and other coconut products are, in most years, the country's top foreign-exchange earner. Over 30 percent of the cultivated land, on half a million farms across the archipelago is devoted to growing coconuts. One out of four Filipinos depends on the coconut industry for all or part of his family's income. The Philippines supplies an astounding 80 percent of the coconut oil for world trade. (Coconut oil is one of the least expensive vegetable oils, and is therefore widely used in soaps and processed foods, especially candy bars and other junk food.)

Most coconuts in Albay are produced on farms worked by tenant farmers or, to a lesser extent, on plantations with waged farm workers. Most tenant coconut farmers in Albay and elsewhere in the Philippines are forced to turn over two out of three coconuts to their landlords. Farmers husk the coconuts and dry the meat in simple, smoke-filled lean-tos over pits dug into the earth, using the husks as fuel.

Coconuts are harvested approximately every forty-five days. If the weather has been good, a tenant farmer's share can be sold for 500 pesos for every hectare, from which payments for any hired help must be deducted. The government estimates that a rural family of six needs an average income of 112 pesos a day to cover their basic needs. Officially, the plantation worker's wage is now 58 pesos a day, but a farm worker's daily wage in Albay (and nationwide, for that matter) typically runs between 13 and 25 pesos a day. In NPA-controlled areas, "revolutionary land reform" has meant that tenant farmers can keep a greater share of the coconuts and farm workers receive higher wages. Or, as they invariably prefer, the plantation is converted to tenant farms.

Tension between coconut tenant farmers and their landlords is commonplace. One frequent source is whether tenants may plant vegetables, sweet potatoes, and sometimes even rice and perennial crops like papaya between the rows of coconut palms. Farmers want to intercrop to provide food for their families and possibly to gain a little added income. Landlords often prohibit tenants from

Robert Gumpert

Farm workers earn less than two dollars a day, well below a family's subsistence needs. Women and even children work in the fields to add to the family's meager income.

planting additional crops, or want to collect a share of these crops too. Landlords believe that if tenants owned crops between the coconut trees it could be more difficult to evict them. Landlords also fear that if tenants plant food crops their land may some day be subject to reform. (Land reform laws in the Philippines have always exempted coconut, sugar, and other export-crop lands, and targeted, at least nominally, tenanted food-crop farms.)

Negros Occidental, often called simply "Negros," is a province that constitutes the western half of the boot-shaped island of Negros, the fourth largest in the Philippine archipelago. The capital, Bacolod City, is about 240 miles south of Manila.

Negros is an exaggerated microcosm of the whole Philippine archipelago. It is rural, the agricultural land is fertile (the well-watered coastal plains carpeted with deep volcanic soils make for farmland as good as it comes), the economy is geared to production for export, and the disparities between rich and poor are enormous. Even blasé tourists in Negros talk about the ostentatious wealth beside the cruel poverty: the dark windowed Mercedes Benzes driving by listless, emaciated children. To experience Negros is to experience the explosive economic and political inequities that affect the entire Philippine nation.

Inside a bamboo and frond-thatched *nipa* hut of a tenant farmer in Negros.

For over a hundred years, Negros has been "Sugarlandia." Today it produces two thirds of the Philippine sugar crop, both for export and for the nation's domestic sugar market. Most of Negros's work force (some five hundred thousand people in a province of 2 million) are—or were—sugar workers, and virtually every Negrense has become dependent on the sugar industry. More than half the arable land (and much more of the prime land) is devoted to sugarcane. In the 1960s, the sugar acreage more than doubled and new mills were put up when the United States cut off purchases of sugar from Cuba (at fixed, preferential prices). The U.S. turned to its erstwhile colony to supply America with sugar (and drop its plans for diversification).

A careful study by the Catholic Church in 1979 confirmed what everyone knew. Over 98 percent of the people of Negros were totally deprived of land ownership. Eight-two percent of Negrenses lived in extreme poverty. One percent of the 332,000 families in the province owned at least 45 percent of the land planted with sugarcane. In fact, 5 percent of the sugar planters of Negros owned nearly 50 percent the island's arable land, and most of these *hacenderos* belonged to a tight-knit political oligarchy, connected by marriages within the "big families."

Most of the province's sugar land, about 70 percent, is in haciendas, a remnant of the Spanish colonial days. A hacienda—used interchangeably with "farm"—is typically 150 to 300 acres, although some run several times larger.

By contrast, on Luzon Island, Hacienda Luisita, owned by President Aquino and her brothers and sisters, has 15,000 acres cultivated with sugarcane and runs its own mill. In Negros, the original haciendas have been subdivided among many heirs, so that today the largest haciendas now have under 2,500 acres.

The haciendas envelop the entire lives of more than half the people in Negros. Some commentators liken them to the plantations in the American South before the Civil War. The medium-sized and larger hacienda is a self-contained unit with its own store, chapel, school, housing tract, administrative and machinery buildings, and a guarded compound with a large colonial house for the owners or the manager, surrounded by manicured lawn and gardens. The houses for the workers are rough-hewn wood shacks, typically with twenty-five square yards or less of floor space. Most families possess only sparse furnishings, such as thin straw sleeping mats and a few utensils, plus the clothes on their backs. Many haciendas also have a barracks-like structure, partitioned by makeshift cardboard walls, for the *sacadas*, or seasonal farm workers, contracted from the neighboring island of Panay to do the harsh work of cutting cane; they are the poorest of the poor.

There are also some small farmers in Negros, often living at near subsistence level, growing vegetables, sweet potatoes, and rice. Many of them (or their parents) fled hacienda life and squatted on hilly land, mostly in the southern part of the island. Then in the late '60s and '70s, when planters wanted to expand (especially their sugar lands, in response to the higher U.S. sugar quota after the Cuban revolution), these impoverished farmers fell victim to the planters land-grabbing. The New People's Army quickly took hold as guardians and deeply entrenched themselves with these farmers in the south.

Many of the people in Negros I interviewed talk about the "crisis" of the sugar industry. The impact of the crisis, generally said to have begun in 1984, was highly visible: phenomenal numbers of fallow acres and idle people. Following the '84 harvest, much of the land on most farms was left unplanted; by 1986, up to 40 percent of the land originally under sugar cultivation went unused. Two once-prosperous, big sugar mills shut down permanently, and the others were operating well below capacity. As many as two hundred fifty thousand sugar workers (men, women, and children) were unemployed even during the peak milling season. Capital flight (often overseas) stepped up, and Bacolod took on its current depressed and "has-been" look. Many planters stopped lending sacks of rice and money to their workers for necessities like medicines during the long "dead season," during which even in the best of times most workers were jobless. By mid-1986, the Ministry of Health conceded that over one hundred fifty thousand children were starving. In many parishes throughout Negros, families were burying a child every day.

To most planters, the road to ruin began when President Marcos assumed decree-making powers with his declaration of martial law in September 1972. Many wealthy planter families, the traditional landed political oligarchy, had opposed Marcos even before he assumed dictatorial powers. To them he was an upstart, and a particularly greedy one at that. Marcos used his martial-law powers to retaliate.

With his customary rhetoric about long-overdue reforms, Marcos centralized control over the sugar industry under a government agency. He put that agency in the hands of classmate, fraternity brother, and confidant, Roberto Benedicto, scion of a leading Negros planter family. The new agency held a monopoly on the trading of sugar. By selling at one price and paying the planters less, often much less, the government agency (and therefore Benedicto, Marcos, and other cronies) skimmed hundreds of millions of dollars at the expense of the planters. Benedicto and other Marcos cronies even used government monies to acquire plantations for themselves. Benedicto's private fortune grew into one of the country's largest, including ownership of several sugar mills, control of two national banks and one in Los Angeles, and two houses in Beverly Hills. As always, economic power was combined with political power. Benedicto, accountable only to Marcos, dictated most provincial and local appointments on Negros.

In 1974, a forecast of shortages in the world sugar supply triggered skyrocketing world market prices. That same year the U.S.–Philippines treaty expired, which included a sugar quota at a fixed price normally considerably above world market prices. Benedicto and Marcos opted not to pursue a renewal of the treaty, claiming that Philippine sugar would do better on the free market (at a time when the free market price was abnormally high). Without the set price of the U.S. quota system, it would also be easier for the Benedicto-run government agency to deceive planters about the prices their sugar fetched on the world market.

It was not long before the record prices led to increased sugar output in many countries and world prices tumbled. With most of the U.S. quota market foregone, with world prices falling, and the crony government siphoning the lion's share of the revenues (and even delaying payments), the planters certainly felt squeezed. Planters, whose operations had become grossly inefficient during the decades of lucrative sales to the U.S., began cutting back on labor costs. Many purchased tractors and rotary tillers at prices subsidized through a World Bank 100-million dollar loan to help "small and medium farmers." Fewer workers, especially women and children, were employed in weeding. Sugar worker families found their already pitiful incomes drastically dropping.

Robert Gumpert

Sugar workers in Negros. Most farm workers are paid on a piece rate basis.

The economic recession that hit the troubled country in the wake of the assassination of Benigno "Ninoy" Aquino in August 1983 compounded the economic troubles of the sugar industry. As the peso plummeted, prices of all the largely imported inputs in the industry—fuel oil, machinery, spare parts, and fertilizers—soared. In the most inflationary economy in Southeast Asia, banks tightened credit, setting interest rates as high as 44 percent. Many planters were unable to get their customary loans to plant and to harvest. Many had to abandon their farms or leave much of their fields idle, cultivating only the most fertile parts that required little or no fertilizer. Forced to curtail their production and unwilling to sacrifice their exceptionally self-indulgent life-styles, many planters could not (or would not) make payments on their existing loans. Steep bank penalties were imposed. By the 1986 snap election, haciendas accounting for at least 80 percent of the sugar lands in Negros were in default and therefore subject to foreclosure by government-controlled banks.

Most Negros planters were eager to get rid of Marcos. To help foment political unrest, some planters, it has been suggested, even opted to eliminate rice rations, medical help, and other assistance to their workers. Many planters backed, at least privately, the candidacy of Mrs. Aquino, whose family's sugar hacienda had been singled out for economic warfare by Marcos and Benedicto. Yet her campaign pledges of bold reform, and charges by Marcos that Aquino was conciliatory toward the communists, made many planters cautious.

Audie de la Cruz

Truckloads of sugar waiting to be milled on Hacienda Luisita. The sugar industry is largely seasonal, offering employment only four to six months a year. With cane plantations taking up most of the land, little work is to be found during the rest of the year for half a million sugar workers and their families.

These years of crisis in the sugar industry were years of labor militancy, as workers lost much of the earnings and what few benefits they had—as well as any illusions that their *hacenderos* at least would always take care of their minimum needs. Workers organized not only to demand better wages and traditional benefits, but also to demand access to some of the more than three hundred thousand acres of idle land to plant food crops for their survival. At the same time, military and police suppression of labor organizing did much to provoke the sons and daughters of landless workers "to go to the mountains," swelling the ranks of the New People's Army. The NPA force in Negros became one of the strongest and most active in the archipelago, and Negros Occidental became one of the country's most militarized provinces. The NPA claims to have redistributed and helped put into food production over twelve thousand acres in Negros. Most of these lands in the hills had been abandoned by planters, due to fear or for economic reasons.

The interviews in Negros were conducted about a year after the ouster of Marcos. It was a time of healing from an aberration, a time when coalitions united against a common foe were dissolving, a time of uncertainty for many. It was a time when conflicting undercurrents were coming to the surface.

In her first year as president, Mrs. Aquino abolished those aspects of government control of the sugar industry that planters had decried. In another decree, she set forth a plan to return to planters portions of the billions of pesos the Marcos-created sugar agency had stolen from them. Government banks also held off foreclosures of sugarcane plantations.

But the very talk of land reform by the president and her appointed governor, Daniel Lacson, stirred Negros planters to mobilize the powerful landlord forces nationwide before the Congressional elections in May 1987. Planters from Negros also met with the president and cabinet members to lobby against land reform. The most adamant planters talked menacingly of collecting arms and private armies to defend their plantations. They even spoke of Negros seceding from the Republic. Once planters were elected to all six House seats "representing" the province, they were in the front lines of those politicking land reform to death in the Congress.

By the time local government elections were held in January 1988, it was clear to most planters that there was not going to be a land reform. Governor Lacson, once maligned for his talk of land reform, stood unopposed by the traditional planter politicians. The three or four mayors appointed by Aquino who worked for popular reforms encountered heavy-handed electoral opposition by planter organizations and the military. In these elections, traditional planter politicians, and politicians working for them, supplanted virtually all the "pro-people" officials.

The day after the local elections in January 1988, Alfred McCoy, an astute, long time observer of Negros politics, commented to me that the local elections completed the restoration of planter power.

Monsignor Antonio Fortich
Bishop of the Diocese of Bacolod
Negros Occidental

My first meeting with Monsignor Fortich takes place in January 1987. We sit in his narrow, book-lined office next to his bedroom at the Sacred Heart Seminary. He has lived at the diocesan seminary since the episcopal residence and chancery, which adjoin the Spanish-built cathedral on the plaza, were burned in a fire one night in January 1985. A police investigation attributed the fire to faulty wiring, despite the fact it started during an electrical blackout. In the days before the fire, the bishop's office received anonymous telephone calls reviling the diocese's human-rights activities and threatening "retaliation."

The 73-year-old bishop has roused himself from a siesta for my appointment. He is a big man who enjoys smoking his "Havana," the size a Hollywood godfather lights up. As I set up my tape recorder, I comment that I have seen many photographs of him and it seems he is always puffing on a big cigar.

Is that so? Some people ask me why I smoke a cigar. "St. Joseph didn't smoke a cigar," they comment. "You must be richer than St. Joseph." Well, I tell you, young man, if there were cigars in the time of St. Joseph, he would have grabbed one.

The bishop has a national reputation for advocating reforms, so I am especially curious about his social origins.

I was born on the other side of the mountains. We call it Oriental Negros, but it is still the same island. Our family ran a sugar mill—a steam-driven one making brown sugar, not a centrifugal mill. In my family, they will not give you money for candy unless you work for it. So I gathered up the dry leaves of the sugarcane to get just twenty centavos a day. I therefore saw how the people struggle for their lives. But I got into a little corruption. It's very itchy, very itchy work—and for twenty centavos only. My cousin and I thought, how about telling the other boys to work for us and at the end of the week, divide the pie

50/50—50 theirs and 50 ours—that's a good business. Well, we did it, but when we were discovered we were punished. Those old people were really strict with justice!

My mother maintained a free clinic for poor people. She was not a nurse, but the sentiments of my family were really pro-people—and I grew up with that.

Fortich is oft-quoted for calling Negros a "social volcano." What led him to use that phrase?

In 1981, before the coming of the Holy Father, there were many foreign correspondents who came here and asked me, Why is it that Bacolod is not an archdiocese and the Pope is coming to visit Bacolod? I said, Because we are sitting on top of a social volcano.

Robert Gumpert

Monsignor Fortich

What makes Negros so explosive?

I would say that the real crisis of Negros, one that is quite explosive and for years has not been attended to, is our unjust socio-economic structure, with the land belonging only to a few. Seventy percent of the land of Negros belongs to a handful. Then naturally, no matter what you do, there will always be a wave of deep anger and mistrust because the people have suffered for a long time. This so-called sugar-industry crisis is only the effect of the long-standing colonial system where a few own the land and laborers are paid below even the survival level. Right now many planters are still paying fourteen, fifteen, twenty pesos a day—that's a dollar or less a day. Can you imagine a family surviving on that with, say, three children? On top of that, the haciendas have the annual dead season when they hardly pay anyone anything, and now we have over four hundred thousand sugarcane workers unemployed year round. You cannot blame young people for going up to the hills, because they have found out that here in the valley life is really miserable.

You go around on the haciendas, you ask if there is any mother who can afford to buy a can of milk. If you're only receiving twenty pesos a day, do you think a family can afford to buy a can of milk? So, you say, breastfeeding. It's true, the mother is trying to do that. But she is also undernourished. So where is the milk from the body of the mother? You know what they do? They cook rice, put in water and when the rice is cooked, there is a sticky substance that is all carbohydrates. That's what they feed to their babies. You go around there. It's for you to check. That is what is happening. I know because the people and my priests come to me. I listen to the voice of the people. To talk about the truth of the people's situation is not subversion. Everyone should know that the people on the farms are really suffering. The social volcano is really about to erupt.

Land, land, land is the clamor of the people. Marcos made the same promises about land reform as Madame Aquino but didn't follow through on them, and the people rebelled. Cory Aquino will face the same ultimate judgment on the land reform issue. It will be her triumph or her downfall.

Earlier a priest told me that some people were trying to get the Pope to remove Bishop Fortich.

Yes, the landed people here are now very angry with the bishop and my priests because the emphasis of the diocese is justice. They are fed up because even Sundays the priests are preaching about justice—adequate means of livelihood, practice of the minimum wage, land reform, etc. But I am not a troublemaker. I'm a bishop; forget about me becoming a communist. I speak when the flock come to me and tell me their troubles—they are hungry, they are persecuted.

Oh, it's a terrible fight now. The landowners are really fighting to the last ditch. Many have already made pronouncements. There is an association of planters that will have land reform only over their dead bodies. And many *hacenderos* are buying guns. But I told them, wait a minute, is it not better to share a little of what you have than to lose everything? Because the insurgency is becoming stronger and stronger. Three years ago, the military said they were only 12,000. And now, they are already 27,000 fighting units aside from the 5-million supporting cast—the civilians. Because without the help of the civilians, the insurgents cannot continue to exist. Because the civilians will hide the insurgents and give them food, they will continue to exist. So, I said, think it over. After all, you have already benefited for decades from those lands. Now, to buy peace, better share what you have to the tiller of the land. If you don't, then you'll have bloodshed. Unnecessary thing, unnecessary thing!

Fortich thinks land reform would delegitimate the insurgency and be good for business.

Business is lousy. The people have no buying capacity. But once they have buying capacity and houses of their own—never mind if it's a nipa hut, that's still beautiful for the tropical zone—stores here will be reactivated because naturally people will be buying a little sala set, they'll buy spoons, they will buy plates or maybe some clothes.

And what are the bishop's views on his priests who have joined the NPA?

Well, they were working among the poor of Negros, and they found out that they could not achieve what they are conceiving would be a just society. The option is yours, I tell them, but you must bear in mind I have never sanctioned the taking up of arms. But I have to respect your personal options because God has given you freedom of the will and not even God can take back freedom of the will, because to take back what God has given is a sign of imperfection and, as Christians, we know God is absolutely perfect.

Fortich's understanding of his priests' involvement with the NPA fits with the widespread planter's view of him as pro-communist—"Commander Tony," as several planters refer to him. His views, in fact, are strongly anti-communist.

The communists always want to form coalitions with other forces, but when victory is won, these people do not want us Christians because they know that we priests are leaders by nature and these communists want to lead. That is what happened in Cuba and in all other places of the world. In Nicaragua, the Sandinistas, I'm afraid, are a front for the real communists there. Even though there still are priests working with the Sandinistas, don't they fear that they are working for something that is not a real democracy?

But it's the same old story. When you touch the land, the military will always brand you communist because the military is in cahoots with the landed estate. I've come to expect that, you see. When I am put in jail, you should visit me.

Leaving, I notice a large poster on the wall showing a poor child and the Brazilian Archbishop Helder Camara. It says, in English: "When I feed the hungry, they call me a saint. When I ask why are they hungry, they call me a communist."

❖ ❖ ❖

Two months later someone tossed a grenade into Bishop Fortich's residence shortly after midnight; it was deflected by a branch of a tree; so although it exploded outside the bishop's bedroom door, the only casualty was a small bird.

Daniel "Bitay" Lacson
Governor
Negros Occidental

A typically dilapidated Bacolod taxi takes me to Governor Lacson's office. We travel down Lacson Street. As in most of the Philippines, Bacolod's principal streets are named after the handful of families that have dominated the land—and politics—on the island. Lacson Street is named for the great-grandfather of young Daniel "Bitay" Lacson, who was appointed governor by President Aquino. The governor's office is heavily air-conditioned. Governor Lacson is energetic and clean cut, dressed in a simple white barong.

The Governor tells me he is "honored" to meet the author of "that great book on Nicaragua." Flattery from politicians is cheap, but this case is different: he has a stack of forty or so copies of the Philippine edition of my book on the agrarian reform in Nicaragua. He informs me that he has passed out "a couple hundred" copies to planters "as a warning." Nicaragua weighs down on the governor's mind.

Reading your book on Nicaragua, I learned that even as far back as 1968 the Jesuit priests started creating awareness in rural Nicaragua and organizing plantation workers. Well, here in Negros, the Jesuits also started waking up people by coming up with studies that showed the problems of the landless sugar workers and especially the *sacadas*. This was as early as '68–'69 here too. And in your book, you give numbers such as the average wage in Nicaragua. It was about a dollar a day. Well, it's about the same thing here, a dollar and ten cents a day in the sugar industry, and about 70 to 80 percent of our people are involved in the sugar industry. And the land ownership you were talking about—with only 1 or 2 percent of the population owning 50 percent of the land—well here, in the case of Negros, based on a World Bank study, about 5 percent of the population owns 48 percent of the land. Aside from that, you were talking in your book about the situation on the haciendas where you have workers with houses without lights or a water system. Well, that still exists in this province. Although you may have lights, the toilets are still where nature takes you. And most people here don't have homes they could call their own.

Boysie Imperial

Daniel "Bitay" Lacson

And then you told about people as early as 1974 taking over lands, and the reaction of the Somoza government was to send the National Guard to kick them out. Well, last year, 1986, when I was already governor, I did have some similar cases where people would take over some land, and later on to be kicked out by the police or the military. What happens is that they send the military or the police to drive these people out because there seems to be anarchy. When that happens you will have a group of marchers coming to Bacolod City claiming that there is militarization in the countryside. And when I talk to them, I find out that it started because they were just taking over land, with the instigation of the union, because of their condition. So what can I do? We try to talk to the landowners. If they agree to let them use the land, fine. If not, what happens? Then we're in trouble because we have a government that's incapable of providing jobs. You know that in the public sector, we're in a big deficit and we can hardly be the engine for job development. And, as in Nicaragua, we have seasonality of the crops here. The sugarcane is seven months of activity to eight months, and four to five months of dead season.

So that's why I say Negros is very similar to Somoza's Nicaragua. I would say that it may be two or three years before the fall. I tell this to the sugar planters who resist my formula that would sell 10 percent of the land of farms in default to the landless workers, which is a compromise formula between the extreme forces—the Left, which would call for a sweeping land reform, and the Right, which is opting for the status quo.

Governor Lacson prides himself on not being a politician.

I came from the private sector. It's a badge of honor. Politicians are looked upon as crooks, and that's why I accepted when President Cory offered me the governorship. I was president of the fourth largest shipping concern in the Philippines—Bacolod, Manila, Cagayan, all over the country. I used to run the company; the total conglomerate had about eighteen hundred employees, I was president and chief operating officer. Then, my family also owns land. I've been involved in this province, involved in foundations, I've been involved in civic work in the last twelve, fourteen years.

Because I grew up on a plantation with our laborers, I'm aware of their problems. One point in time I told my wife, Look, I grew up together with these guys, and now, after education, I just built myself a home. It may not be a big home, but it's comfortable. But these people are still the same: my friends on the farm, the workers, they still go back to that small shack. And I said to my wife, You and I are talking about more comforts when these guys are missing the basics in life. One day, I told my wife, Look we've got to make a commitment—and this was 1980—I want to spend my life, after I've provided for my children, education, and a little amount for our retirement, helping these guys.

Ramon Nolan
Planter
Negros

*R*amon Nolan *is a tall, big-boned planter, with shocks of thick white hair. I meet him when I'm giving a seminar for the National Federation of Sugar Workers organizers and staff on the agrarian reform in Nicaragua. "I'm very interested in Nicaragua," he tells me. I am intrigued: a planter concerned about Nicaragua and with connections to a militant labor union. I ask to interview him, and we meet the next day at the country club.*

My father came with Admiral Dewey in 1898 and then he was mustered out in the Philippines. He had studied law—I think in Milwaukee. Well, he worked here under a Spanish lawyer, then he self-studied, and then he made it—was admitted to the lawyers' bar.

I inherited land here from my father, but I practiced law. Then I ran the National Federation of Sugarcane Planters from, oh, my gosh, 1957 up to 1966—the time that Marcos became the president. During all this time, my brother-in-law was leasing the land. Then later on I was appointed to take charge of sugar in the government. I was the sugar-quota administrator from 1966 to 1970—only one term, then I quit. Marcos asked me to serve for one year as trade attaché in the embassy in Washington. That was 1971. I worked there for one year, because that happened to be where and when all the sugar legislation took place.

Ramon Nolan is a walking encyclopedia on the history of the U.S.–Philippines sugar trade. He recalls how the planters used to joke that they "owed Fidel Castro a big favor": when the United States decided no longer to buy sugar from Cuba, it transferred to the Philippines much of Cuba's sugar quota (an amount of sugar the United States agrees to import from specified countries at a preferential price). As a result, acreage had to be increased and fifteen new sugar mills built in order to triple overall sugar output.

Nolan sees as "ruinous" the policies of the government sugar monopoly Marcos set up under martial law.

In 1974–75 the price of sugar on the world market shot sky high. The Philippines, instead of giving preference to the U.S. market, made big sales to Russia and China and Japan. Especially in 1975, when the United States really needed the sugar, the Philippines refused to sell, even to a point where we were running out of warehousing capacity. The Marcos government was holding out. Here in Negros we were storing sugar on the tennis courts and in the swimming pools. Even when the price of sugar reached sixty-three cents American per pound, the Marcos government refused to sell to the United States because they wanted more. They gambled and they lost, because eventually they had to sell at less than ten cents. Now that was a big blow to the relationship of the U.S. and the Philippines on sugar, but a bigger blow to the producers here, because the Marcos government gambled on the price of commodities that did not belong to it. We planters were very angry about that.

The United States is gradually going to stop buying sugar from any foreign country. This is brought about by the increased use of high-fructose corn syrup in soft drinks and processed foods, and the U.S. has plenty of corn. That means that the present quota given to the Philippines, which is less now than one hundred fifty thousand tons—less than 10 percent of what it used to be up to 1974—even this one hundred fifty thousand tons will be lost in two or three years. So the only market we will have left is our own domestic market, and we are now saddled with excess land that we do not need anymore for sugar. We have also an excess of mills. Already we cannot operate to full capacity. We have also lots of excess labor.

Nolan thinks that Philippines plantation agriculture is "feudalistic" and that only Filipinos are to blame.

A good market, like what our sugar had with the U.S., is no excuse for us to continue with the feudalistic system. The reason for the existence of the feudalistic system here is not the fault of the United States, or any country who would like to buy our agricultural products. We cannot say that they are responsible for what is going on inside our house. The feudalistic system here has been here even before we had relations with the U.S.

Even without the U.S. market, even now that we are going to produce only for the domestic market, the feudalistic system will still continue, because that is a problem that can be solved only by the Philippine government. It is for the Philippine government and for the individual Filipino planter to change our mentality, our attitude.

What are the chances for a land reform?

There is a lot of resistance from the landowners. These people have the mentality that I inherited the land from my ancestors, I am not going to give

Boysie Imperial

Ramon Nolan

it up. I believe in land reform, but I would give planters an option. Those who cannot accept even the governor's notion of 10 percent of the land in exchange for debt reduction, let them pay the minimum wage.

The objective of land reform is to benefit the masses, and land reform is not the only way. It's only a means. If you have a job and it pays okay, you'll eat, you'll have schooling for your family. In other words, we must put in place the basic principle of survival for everybody in society. Ultimately, land reform will be a solution. But a step would be to have a group [of planters] that would not join you in land reform but would comply with the labor laws.

I believe that the labor union movement is the thing that will improve the livelihood of the whole Philippines, especially the laboring class. Maybe I'm wrong, but I'm willing to bet on this: nine out of ten of the planters who reject even the governor's land reform proposal are also antilabor union. They don't like a labor union and will do anything to prevent it.

If they will just accept an honest-to-goodness labor union, that would take care of 90 percent of the problem, because the labor union, on behalf of the laborers, will always talk to the planter and say, "Look, we cannot live on this." And then they can agree on something workable. The NFSW is quite reasonable.

Are the workers on your hacienda organized?

Yes. Whenever we have to make big decisions—like what should we produce for next year, how much will we leave for sugar, what other new crops to plant, and how do we share the expenses, profits, and all that—all I got to do is call a meeting of the officials of the NFSW. We sit down as equals and we draw up a program and this program is the fruit of our agreement. So we have no problem. That's why, whether they want land reform or not, the decision we make is not mine, it's ours. It's like one family getting together. Now they feel that they own part of the land already.

Do they call me communist? Oh yeah, that's what they call me. But I'm color blind; I don't know the difference between red or yellow. (*He laughs.*) "A free society that cannnot help the many that are poor will not be able to save the few who are rich"—John F. Kennedy said that. Basically the whole philosophy of land reform is within that statement. I explain to those who would call me communist that if they want to fight communism, it's very easy—you fight exploitation. If there is no exploitation, there is no communism.

You're the former head of the National Federation of Sugarcane Planters that now stands against reforms. How did you become so exceptional in your class?

The change in me came after I quit the government. Then I started dedicating my time to visiting my farm. My sons run it, but I take care of the labor policy. My sons can do anything they want, but when it comes to our attitude, our sharing with labor, that's where I come in, that's my only work. What motivates me? You know that statement by Kennedy? We have our own expression here and it means the same thing—"*Sa binisaya nano gani nang di mahimong na kita mong di makaon sila'y gutomon.*" "I cannot comprehend the idea that we will be the only ones eating while everybody around is starving to death." Yes, hunger is what it's all about. How can we continue eating if we are surrounded by hungry people? That's basic.

Nolan seems like a contented man. That makes him rare in today's Philippines.

It's a good feeling when you know that your laborers are well-fed, that they're happy, that you can go to the farm even at the middle of the night and you feel that you can count on them to help you in case you have problems. That's a nice feeling.

I told my laborers that in case there is some kind of violence or upheaval here, in case there is going to be a shooting war, I'd like to live with you people— would you have me? And they said yes. The moment the first shot is fired, I'll leave the city. I'll live with the laborers—so what's wrong with that? (*Laughs.*)

Teresita Mueco
Migrant farm worker, Hacienda Consuelo
La Carlota, Negros

*On Hacienda Consuelo, across the dirt road from the resident farm workers'
houses, stands a long, narrow, concrete barracks. That's where the sacadas
live during the six months of the year they are on the plantation. Night has
just fallen, and the sacadas have returned from the fields. Inside the barracks, lit by
a few naked light bulbs, I find two long rows of five-by-six-foot stalls fashioned out
of old cartons and gunny sacks. My translator, Elma, a resident farm worker, tells
me that the building houses about 120 sacadas and 50 of their children and other
family members. She also says that it is fairly unusual for sacadas' quarters to have
electricity and a cement floor.*

*Filipinos generally handle smoothly what could be awkward situations. Despite my
unannounced intrusion, people smile and even greet me warmly: "Hi, Joe!" (Filipinos
commonly have greeted every foreign white man this way since the days of G.I. Joe.)
Elma introduces me to a young woman sitting on a bamboo platform, with her legs
folded under her. Her name is Teresita Mueco.*

I've been working as a *sacada* since I was 12 years old. This is the third year my
husband and I have been on this hacienda. We've been here almost six months.

We are from Tibiao in Antique [province] on Panay Island. We have a small
farm on the side of a steep hill where we plant bananas and some rice. We have
enough food, so to speak, but very little cash. If we had enough land to produce
crops, we probably would not come here. Most *sacadas* have no lands for
themselves. Here we get an advance of 500 pesos from the *contratista*, which is
deducted from the work that we do.

But we have to buy all our needs—foods, cigarettes, soap, and so forth—on
credit from the *contratista's* wife's canteen. For every peso worth of goods, we
have to pay her back two pesos. Sometimes, when we go back to Antique, we
have a zero balance with the *contratista*, and are left with no cash to take home.

I pray to God that this year we will bring money home to Antique, but as of now we don't know how much we'll have.

This year only my husband has work. He cuts cane and loads it on to the truck. They're paid per ton—fourteen pesos per ton. He usually earns twenty-eight pesos a day. He works the whole day, at least eight hours. In the morning they cut cane and in the afternoon they load cane.

Teresita, Elma, and I visit the common kitchen. It is dirty and blackened with smoke. Without my saying anything, Elma interjects, "They cannot clean because they have to work so long." Several women are stirring pots over fires fed by sugarcane stalks.

We eat rice and vegetables, no meat. Sometimes just vegetables, jackfruit, water, and salt. That is our only food.

When was the last time you had meat?

Well, the last time we ate a little bit of meat was in our province, in Antique. Here in Negros we've had no meat. We only eat meat in the fields because there are plenty of rats and we have gotten used to catching them, taking out the intestines, and drying them in the sun. When we come back here at night we cook them on the charcoal and eat them. That is our meat.

During the night we also used to catch frogs, which we would cook here. We put kerosene in a bottle and old clothes and made a light and then looked for frogs during the night. But now we are too tired. We finished the sugarcane on this hacienda three weeks ago, but the *contratista* is too much of a money-grab-ber, and he takes us to other haciendas to work. When we get home, it's already very late and we are very tired. We have to go to sleep because they will wake us up again tomorrow morning very early. We wake up at two o'clock in the morning and prepare our food, and then we go out at four o'clock. We get home at six o'clock in the evening.

What do the workers eat in the field?

They eat rice, jackfruit with water and vetsin.

Vetsin, I later learned, is monosodium glutamate.

Elma tells me that the contractor prepares midday meals for the laborers, but at fifteen pesos each, that's a pretty steep cut out of daily earnings of twenty-eight pesos.

I use my few phrases in Ilongo to thank Teresita. As Elma and I walk down the corridor, some teenage boys are sitting in a cubicle, their shirts hanging to dry on the bamboo points of the partitions. They are singing, and one plays a guitar. Elma tells me it is a love song for their girlfriends, whom they haven't seen now in six months. Then we come upon a sad-looking older man. "He's very sick," Elma tells me. "Too sick to work. And he cannot get back home because the contractor won't give him any money to go home. The contractor says he owes him money." Outside I give Elma the money to send the man home. It is less than five dollars.

I ask Elma how she and the other resident workers get along with the migrant workers. She replies that the sacadas are hard to unionize, because they are there only awhile and some years on different haciendas.

But, look at my ducks. If we did not have good relations with the sacadas they would steal them. But because they respect us and they know that we are very sincere with them, they do not steal the ducks. Sometimes the ducks go inside their barracks. I say I'm very sorry because my ducks sleep inside there. And they say we will just close the door so that they cannot get inside during the night.

We are looking down the dirt road toward the ten-foot-high cement walls of the owner's compound. Sometimes the owners arrive in a helicopter, Elma says. And whose large modern house is that near the owner's compound at the head of the road?

"That's the contratista's home when he is here."

Victor Puey
OIC Mayor
Sagay, Negros

I happen upon Vic Puey one Sunday in northern Negros near the town of Escalante. It was there in 1985 that the former governor and head of the planters' association ordered the military and the police to open fire on several thousand demonstrators, killing twenty people. The scene this day in 1987 is a wedding, in an attractive bamboo chapel by the sea. Puey and I talk at the reception, which has the feel of a country church picnic.

Born four days after liberation from the Japanese occupation—hence the name "Victor"—Puey is a fit, energetic fellow. He tells me that he is a descendant of a Spanish captain who took control of thousands of hectares in the area. Over the years, the lands have been divided many times among heirs. Nonetheless, as one of the eleven children of his father, he inherited enough land to be a "medium-size" planter.

Victor Puey's appointment as mayor by Aquino, as in so much of the Philippines, represented a restoration.

My family, as far as I can remember, has always been in politics. My great-great-grandfather was the first elected mayor of Sagay. My father was mayor for about twenty years and vice-governor of the province and governor and congressman. And my brother for eight years was the mayor. When Marcos was in power— that is the only time I can remember that we were out of politics. For twenty years we were constantly fighting against the regime of Marcos and the other political war lords in northern Negros.

Vic comes from the jet set of the landed gentry. He is a martial arts champion and a speedboat racer (national champion and No. 2 in Asia). We talk about planters' attitudes, especially toward land reform.

If we sugar planters have a lot of problems, we are partly to blame. When we had a lot of these bounties from Negros and we were all very rich, I don't think we really worried about doing our share for our workers. We were all in Manila, you know. I used to be a member of a very elite social club. We would only think of nice things—cars, yachts, this and that—and not believing that we will have problems back home; not even thinking that our workers were probably not happy with what we were paying them. We always assumed that they were. And we felt that if we employed somebody he was grateful that we were employing him; and at Christmas time, we were giving him a small pack of rice and canned food and we think we are a good employer. All these things, you know, we have never taken into account before. It's only now a lot of people have started to realize that there are problems.

But for me, before a planter can solve his problem, he has to find out what really is his problem. Not conclude what is the solution without finding out first what is the problem: why his people are joining labor unions, why people are even going to the hills, and what's happening here. You know, it's sad to say when planters start hearing that their workers are joining militant labor unions, instead of having a dialogue with their people, of talking to their people, the tendency here is to get security guards and to get the army to come over and take over. You see, this army is not trained to dialogue. They are trained to fight. This is really how problems start, because when you bring the military in, you know, they're not trained for this kind of problem and they create more problems. This is usually when a lot of salvagings happen, a lot of shootings. And who gets hurt? The laborers. And many planters did not intend it to happen like that. Planters thought they were just defending themselves. And so that's very sad. So what I feel that they should do is really get closer to their laborers. A lot of problems should never have started if we, then and now, only cared—that's just it.

A lot of planters still believe in the old days, that those days will somehow come back. A lot of planters just don't want to part with their lands, because they feel they worked very hard for these lands. Even if I inherit it from my father, my father worked hard for us to inherit it. This "I deserve this, I deserve that" is the crucial thing with all planters because the moment we start saying this, of course, we all are very deserving. So it's very hard to argue about those things. The question that should be asked is, Are you willing to share for hunger? So that people can live with a little dignity; so that people will not starve? This is what all planters should answer because we can always argue for years and years whether you deserve to keep that land. One hundred hectares is big. Maybe you can still live with 50 hectares or 60 hectares.

You know, what I cannot understand now is that a lot of sugar planters are spending a lot of money on guns and on security guards when they do not pay their laborers right. If they just used this money that they use for buying guns and for paying eight or ten security guards, if they just used their money for their people, I'm sure they would not need these guns anymore or these security guards. I'm sure their laborers would love them so much then, they themselves will guard them. All over Negros now I see a lot of people training security guards, a lot of people buying guns. I know one planter who bought three or four guns that cost 200,000 pesos—that's more than one year's payroll for all his laborers. But instead of treating their people right, they buy guns. In the north now I know two or three groups training security guards for sugarcane planters. To guard us from whom? From our own laborers? Laborers who have served us for generations. We now all of a sudden are all afraid of our own laborers, of our own people? Why? That's one question that all planters should answer.

Many of these planters are now saying, Hah! The Reds are all over. They will kill us; these people are all communists. And they go to the military and then the military will put a station there. In my part of Negros, one military company is being supported by planters. The planters are the ones feeding them. I don't know if they are the ones paying for the bullets. But these same planters are not paying their own people. That's what's happening in Negros.

Joaquin Villarosa
Planter (retired)
Bacolod City, Negros

As I am leaving my late afternoon interview with planter Tadeo Villarosa, he introduces me to his white-haired father, Joaquin. Getting the viewpoint of a planter-patriarch who recalls "the good old days" could be revealing. Mr. Villarosa readily agrees to talk with me and suggests we make ourselves comfortable in a couple of rattan chairs overlooking a lush tropical garden and lawn. He instructs one of the young maids to prepare coconut-water drinks for us.

Mr. Villarosa sports an Aquino-Laurel T-shirt. He tells me that like many planters during the 1986 "snap election" he opposed Marcos, who "stole billions from us planters." But now he isn't sure he supports Aquino any longer.

I ask him about the history of his family, the Villarosas.

When my grandfather arrived in Negros, nobody owns the land. There were just the Negritos. That was during the Spanish time. My grandfather owned many thousands of hectares, almost one county. He was able to give each of his children more than one thousand hectares.

What I wanted when I was a boy was just to go riding on the horses, the *carabaos*, and on the carts. When my grandmother was sick, I remember, my grandfather supervised the putting up of a *palanquin*—it is a bamboo platform with bedsheets over it—and then my grandmother was placed on it and carried by the workers of our hacienda to our place here in Bacolod where she could receive treatment. I remember how much I loved being carried around on that. Life was simple then. There were no highfalutin ideas like land reform.

Many talk about the haciendas in terms of feudalism.

Maybe my grandparents practiced what they call feudalism. In fact, the word that we are using locally, in our own dialect, is *cacique*—it's the same as a feudal

Boysie Imperial

Joaquin Villarosa

lord—he says you do this, and you do it; he says, do not do this, and you dare not do it.

Maybe my grandfather was a *cacique*. But I never saw him really beating the farm people. He scolded them, but they deserved it. He reasoned with them. Go away, go to other places where you think you can be better off—don't disturb the work here. My grandfather, my father and I, we never tolerate any of our people who bother us because it disrupts the work, the development of the farm, the harmony of the farm.

Feudalism, as it is practiced here now, is more what they call paternalism. But think about this: the paternalism that we practice here is the same as the theory of the Japanese, which enabled them to compete with the industrialized countries. They tell their workers, Okay, we cannot afford to give you as much as in the western countries, but we'll give you security of employment. We will not fire you provided you do your work. You stay with us until you grow old, and then we will give your pension for your work. By doing that, the workers like it so much they stay in the factory. They do not even take their sick leave.

So we protect our workers so that they don't have to worry about anything. That was the way it was before the crisis. The workers were considered part of the extended family. Christmas on the hacienda was a happy occasion.

Lately our people are demanding more and more. You give them so much and then they want more. And finally you cannot work anymore.

Perhaps sensing I was apprehensive of his paternalistic notions, Mr. Villarosa volunteers a theological defense.

If you are a Christian, you will not say that paternalism is not good, because Jesus taught us only one prayer and it begins with "Our Father." How can you say paternalism is not good when Jesus taught us the "Our Father"?

Mr. Villarosa goes on to clarify how permanent and seasonal workers are treated differently.

Our permanent people are called *dumaan*. Their parents have been living there, their grandparents were also living there, they were working for my grandfather, my grandmother. They are all there. We take care of them. We grew up with them.

But the *sacadas*, they are different. They are seasonal workers; they come only during the harvest season. They are contract workers. A *contratista* or contractor, before milling season, will approach the landowner. "I have so many people. How many people do you need for your harvest?" I need so many. "This what I ask for my people," he will say. Okay, you bring your people here. So they cut the cane, then they go home. They do not earn as much as your permanent workers because, as I say, they are contract workers. In fact, we don't even know their names. We only need to know the name of the *contratista*. He takes care of these people. For example, you ask for fifty workers. So okay, they cut so much, so many *piculs* of cane in one week. So the *contratista* is the one being paid. He distributes this money to the workers. We do not deal with the *sacadas*. You cannot be looking over the *contratista's* shoulder while he pays the *sacadas*. In fact, he will tell you that he has already given so much in advances to the workers. That is always the ploy because when the *contratistas* come to us they ask for an advance. They say this is for the families of the *sacadas*. It's really hard to follow up on what the *contratistas* do with the money.

I ask Mr. Villarosa about the impact of the "sugar crisis" on the workers.

On our farm we still take care of our people. We still manage even during this crisis. But on many farms, the workers can't get themselves the wages that they were getting before—not in terms of how much they are paid for a day's work but in terms of the number of days of work.

Before the crisis, during the dead season the consumption of food was sustained. There was a regular advance of rice that was worked off. Now no longer. Not only that, but emergency loans are not available anymore. The morale of many planters is so bad. A lot of them gave up. They feel that they had an obligation to take care of themselves first and they just forget about their workers. If they felt that there's still some hope for their farms, then they would have taken care of their workers. They have been thinking that eventually they will have to abandon ship anyway so let's cut our losses now, starting with money to take care of the workers.

Land reform?

Our workers do not love farming. They are paid for their work—by the day or by piecework. But there are people who really love farming—they are us landowners. If you give the workers the farm immediately, it is like giving a baby that has been used to spoonfeeding the real food. He will get indigestion; he will not know what to do with it.

Eduardo "Remi" Suatengco
Planter
Bacolod City, Negros

I talked with 40-year-old planter Remi Suatengco twice in early 1987. Both times, we met in the lobby of the only real hotel in downtown Bacolod City, the run-down Sea Breeze Hotel. With his mobile CB radio always at his side, Suatengco has the look—rare for a Filipino planter—of someone actually engaged in farm management.

Boysie Imperial

Eduardo "Remi" Suatengco

I do not own any land yet, although I am an heir to property. My parents are still alive. What I'm doing is, I'm managing the properties of my grandparents, which have not yet been distributed to the five children on my mother's side. My grandmother is a Montilla, one of the older families that first moved into Negros. Agustin Montilla was a Spaniard. The lineage of my father is Chinese. My grandparents would be considered big landowners. The total area is about 800 hectares. As of today, our sugarcane covers only one-half of the total area, because of the difficult financial situation we're in. Several years ago, it was 100 percent—maybe four, five years ago. We also produce rice. Aside from administering the lands of my family, I'm also working my in-laws' farm.

How would you describe the typical relationship between planters and their workers?

Maybe you could describe their relationship as a paternalistic one, wherein the planter is like the father, and the farm and the laborers are like his children. He takes care of them and sees to it that they are provided for; that has always been the system since as far back as you can go. In such a system, you control the community, because everybody is dependent on you and you have a say in everything they do.

I don't think that paternalism is good. I was born into it, but I don't agree with it. But it's something that has to be removed slowly; you cannot just change it overnight. You know, on the farm I embarked on a program that would require their independence. It encountered resistance. They did not like the idea that they will not be able to borrow money from the farm—run to the administration to ask for this or that.

I ask Suatengco about his experience with the NFSW.

I have talked to NFSW people. In fact, I have talked to several of them. Well, I find them reasonable, if you are also reasonable with them. They are human. The experience of many planters is different, because I think their attitude toward the NFSW is that of defensiveness, a negative attitude. The mere mention of the name NFSW threatens them. Because, in their mind, the NFSW is a communist front, a front of the Communist Party. So, it's not really labor issues that are disturbing them; it is the NFSW's political stance. I feel that is the perception of most of the planters regarding the NFSW. My perception of the NFSW is that it has good people in it. They talk about many good things, and I agree with those good things as far as the good things are concerned.

As we are parting, Suatengco says he wants to add one more comment.

The malnourishment problem here is basically a lack of education. The majority of these laborers spend the money they receive on lots of junk food. They buy a lot of Coca-Cola; also they smoke a lot. They don't buy the proper food for their diet—that's why they become malnourished.

Remedios Ortaliz
Doctor
Bacolod City, Negros

I visit the doctora in her large, modern home. A servant lets me in. I sit down with *Dr. Ortaliz in her study. We are surrounded by dozens of opened cartons brimming with medicines. She tells me that these are donations sent from the U.S., for sick children in Negros. I ask Dr. Ortaliz to tell me a little about herself.*

I was born here in Negros. I'm out of a town in the countryside, in the municipality of La Castellana. I guess you can say that I was born in a middle-class family. But with my mother being the businessman in the family, I think we progressed to the top of the social ladder in Negros. I went to school in Negros, I was trained as a doctor in Manila, in the University of Santo Tomas, where I graduated in 1960. And I did post-graduate studies also in Manila. But I have done most of my medical practice here in Negros, starting in 1966.

Three out of five Filipino doctors wind up working overseas. Why have you chosen to work in the Philippines?

I never had an interest in being a doctor in the United States. I was interested in training in the U.S., of course, but I never had the chance. I took the exams and I passed the exams, and I don't know what happened. Somewhere along the way I missed the chance to train in the U.S. But I don't have any regrets. My own family—my mother and three brothers live in the United States. My mother really tries to convince me to go. Very often she calls me and says, Okay, come. You have a place here. I think my heart is here in the Philippines.

What kind of practice do you have?

I started as an anesthesiologist. I trained for that, but during the course of my practice with anesthesia, I also was very involved in community work, usually attached to the church. I observed that about 75 percent of our people live in the rural areas, and they are not getting any kind of health care or social services. With that in mind, I decided, maybe I'm not going to become poor, or even deprived for that matter, if I work for them for a year's time. But after a year, the crisis seemed not to decrease and I said, Okay, another year more. And this month, this being January 1987, I said I was going back to private practice, but I'm not going back to anesthesiology.

This time I'm going back for general practice or family medicine. And I will tie this with a program a group of us medical professionals call *bulig*—a community health program. *Bulig* is an Ilongo word for "reach out" or "help." The top priority is the training of community health workers. We train them for basic and advanced health care. They act now as the first line of defense for referral or attending to very basic health needs.

I have always believed that health is a social phenomenon, that it is a product of the interaction of economic, political, and cultural events that deeply affect the lives of many people wherever they are found. This is true especially here in Negros where most of the lands are owned by very big landowners, and so the workers have become dependent on these landowners, and I think that they have come to accept this dependent life. They thought that they will be taken care of by their *amos* ["masters"] until the time in the 1980s—'83 or '85 or even way back in '80—when it started to really become very bad because sugar collapsed and the big landowners said they could not afford to attend to their workers. Of course, they did not really take care of the workers up until that time. Because of the dependent nature of these people, they thought things would be worked out. So they waited and were patient until such time that all help had been totally taken away from them, and they woke up to a new kind of life and the *amos* don't even visit the plantations anymore. And that is the time when people began to realize and say, This is bad for me and what will I do? I don't have the skills to fend for my family.

One hears so much of hunger in Negros. How bad is it?

Many people would say that Negros cannot be compared to Ethiopia. But for those of us doctors who have known Negros before, I think we are very alarmed. As a physician, I am really very touched by what is happening to the children of Negros. We have here 1985 and 1986 data of malnutrition status in Negros. If you compare, we even have an increase in terms of third-degree malnutrition. Many people would say, You cannot see the malnourished children around. If you are not really keen in observing the status of children, probably you will not know that a seriously malnourished child is malnourished.

If you look at a child, even though he or she is sort of plump and looking well, you can notice the pallor around the nasal and the oral areas and the eyes,

Boysie Imperial

Dr. Remedios Ortaliz

rather big but very lackluster. Because they have "water-logging," you think they're plump. Usually, they start like that until such time that the physiological barriers of the body will collapse, and then they start losing all that water, and then you will have that very skinny old-man look of a child in a kwashiorkor or marasmic stage. In fact, in a recent study of Candoni in the south, I found what you call growth-stunted children, children 11 years old with the height of 5-year-olds. And for these children, the hopes for tomorrow are already gone. Can you imagine if your growth is stunted? That includes the brain, includes intelligence.

The health of the people has become very chaotic. Even the mothers and the men in the community are not anymore interacting; they are so very lacking in energy. Our group visits rural areas. These are the comments that we get: the children are not as boisterous as they should be; even the men, they will approach you slowly and they will just sit there, they're so very weak. So probably you cannot tell who is being lazy and who is lazy because he is sapped of energy, a lack of adequate food.

I think that things were bad enough before. The crisis just made it obvious. The bishop [Monsignor Fortich] is really right when he says that we are going to erupt pretty soon. We are really like a volcano.

Malnutrition Ward
Negros Provincial Hospital
Bacolod City, Negros

*I obtain permission from the hospital administration to visit the "mal ward" with
no questions asked; I simply sign the visitors book. The nurse who shows me the
way to the ward asks if there are nursing jobs for Filipinas in California. She
mentions that many foreigners visit the ward; she seems pleased and proud.*

The ward is on the ground floor of an old, run-down, brick building. My first
impression is that the ward is very crowded and noisy. Small children with big
eyes and blank stares in old-fashioned, white-enameled hospital beds have
overflowed into the hallway outside the propped-open doors. Inside the long
and narrow ward, the beds are close together. Each patient is apparently
accompanied by several visitors, undoubtedly relatives, including little
brothers and sisters. The doctor on duty, a young woman, greets me and
accompanies me through the ward.

You have a lot of children out in the hallways. Is the facility overcrowded?

Yes, it's overcrowded. We have a seventy-five to eighty bed capacity; yet we
get a hundred new patients a day.

Do you have children sharing beds?

Yes. It is supposed to be one child for one bed, but we cannot afford to add more
beds, to expand the hospital; so we just let them share one bed.

*What happens when your facility is overcrowded and a mother comes with her
malnourished child? What do you say to her?*

Well, we usually don't refuse them. If we have to admit, we have to admit. We
just get a bench and let them stay in the hallway, we don't refuse admission as
long as we feel that the child is severely malnourished.

I ask her to tell me about two children in a bed nearby.

This child is Macauili, Corlino. She was 3 years old when she came. She has an acute bronchopneumonia with kwashiorkor. And that is a third-degree malnourished child with a deficiency of vitamin A and with damage to the eye.

She weighs?

She weighed only 7.9 kilograms [17 pounds] today. At admission she weighed 4.5 [9 pounds].

And she should now weigh?

Fourteen kilograms [30 pounds]. You can see that her body weight is less than 40 percent of what is ideal; so she's severely malnourished. Below 60 percent, we consider that already third-degree malnourished.

How often do children die here in this ward?

Usually we have two or three deaths per day.

It must be very upsetting to work here.

Yes, we are very upset, but it does not last so long. You know, we are used to seeing children who are dying. But, yes, sometimes we get very upset, really.

May I ask you about this patient over here? I'm looking at her chart and I'm curious as to what is going on. She was admitted a year ago. How much did she weigh then?

She weighed 7.7 kilograms [17 pounds].

And she should have weighed?

Twenty kilograms [44 pounds], because she is already 6 years old.

What is her current weight, and how does that compare to when she was admitted?

Today she weighs 6.9 kilograms [15 pounds]. She reduced.

What's going on?

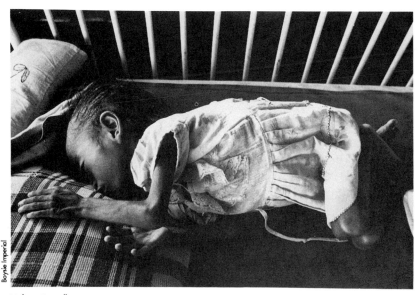

Mylene Arguelles, age 6

I think she got bronchopneumonia. Yes, that's right. Usually it's a complication—bronchopneumonia, gastroenteritis, or, if they did not get measles yet, measles. So when we have a chance, we get the IG gamma or prophylaxis for measles so they will have resistance to measles, but that gamma globulin is very expensive, and sometimes we cannot give it to all the children who need it.

Do you get help from relief agencies?

Yes, sporadically.

And this child here is 6 years old and weighs 15 pounds?

Yes. You see, this child, Mylene, was admitted. But look, she is sharing her food with her sister and brother who are not admitted at all. So her ration of food is divided; she does not get whatever computed diet she is supposed to receive.

Why would their father bring them here?

Usually, one reason. They don't have food at home; here they get food. At least they can eat something here.

If this child does recover, will she be normal or will there be lasting effects?

She will have mostly low IQ, and be very small, but I hope will not be mentally retarded. But usually the IQ level is very low.

Can I ask the father a few questions and perhaps you could translate?

It's okay, he is used to...

Yes, but I would like to ask his permission.

It's all right, he said.

First, I would like to ask his name, how old he is, where he's from.

Wilfredo Arguelles, 31 years old, married, with six children. He works by selling charcoal. He is from Murcia, just a few kilometers from Bacolod.

Where is his wife?

She's right here. Practically the whole family is here. Only two children are left at home. One is left with his mother, and the other with his sister-in-law.

Could you ask him if his work enables him to provide enough food for his children?

Hardly. Not enough, because he sells charcoal. He gets the charcoal at twenty-two pesos, and he is selling it for twenty-six pesos. He is only making four pesos per sack of charcoal. And he's not able to make sales every day. What he does is to go around the city trying to sort of survey who will buy. He is not lucky every day. Sometimes no sale at all.

Does he think there is something wrong being surrounded by sugarcane fields and great wealth and yet he cannot give his children enough food to eat?

He said that it is injustice, because he is looking for work but nobody will accept him to work in the fields. He is more inclined to work in the sugarcane fields, but even more he wants to work in a rice land and he feels that the government should provide something to alleviate people's economic condition.

Would you ask him how does it make him feel as a father to have a child in this condition?

He said he feels disgusted about what happened to his daughter because even though however much he would love to work and has spent most of his time looking for money, he still has no good job to sustain his family.

Who does he blame for that? Does he blame himself or someone else?

He said he is blaming himself. He is blaming himself for what happen to his baby. There are people here in this island calling him and other fathers like him lazy, because he cannot give enough food for the baby.

Does he think he is lazy?

He doesn't look upon himself as a lazy man, because every day he is looking for how to make some money. He cannot understand why other people are calling him and his class lazy.

What hopes does he have for his daughter?

He has high hopes that his baby will be a healthy baby someday. And he said that only what is lacking is enough food to sustain the baby; so he hopes that someday he can earn enough money to give the baby enough food.

Delfin Naperi
Coconut tenant farmer
Parian, Camalig, Albay

I meet Delfin Naperi through the Bikol Coconut Planters Association. Mr. Naperi is a coconut tenant farmer. More than one-fifth of the Filipino people are either coconut tenant farmers or coconut plantation workers.

Mr. Naperi's little farm is the stuff of travel posters: through the sunlit green fronds of the coconut trees, you glimpse a majestic, cone-shaped volcano. A white puff of smoke rises against a brilliantly blue sky.

I'm a tenant farmer. The owner is Felix Camba, who lives in the town of Guinobatan, not far from here. The sharing system here is two coconuts for the owner and one for the tenant. The tenant pays all costs.

Aside from harvesting coconuts, I plant also *camote* ["sweet potatoes"], cassava and other root crops, coffee, bananas, etc. I give part of these other crops to the owner too. The sharing system in the root crops gives 10 percent to the owners and 90 percent to the tenant.

Around here, farm workers on the coconut plantations earn fifteen pesos daily per 1,000 harvested coconuts and twenty pesos per 1,000 coconuts husked. Working hard, you can husk somewhat over 1,000 a day.

You harvest every sixty days or forty-five days. So in a year, you have at least six harvests; you don't get equal harvests. Six months are lean months. We get peak harvests from July to October, and the rest of the year is *gutom*, meaning "hunger."

We tenants are able really to eat only two meals a day. During the lean harvests, especially during the months of February to May, before the onset of the rainy season and when there are droughts, our problem is compounded. I try to make some supplementary income by making charcoal.

Pompeo "Pom" Calleja
Planter and attorney
Legaspi, Albay

Some describe Pom Calleja sympathetically as a wealthy but liberal landlord. Cynics say that he walks the line between supporting the status quo and advocating harmless change.

His home—behind long and high white walls—stands out in the midst of a run-down Legaspi neighborhood. Inside the compound is a big, comfortable house with verandas, a botanical garden with a stunning array of orchids, and a tennis court. Mr. Calleja appears to be well into his 60s. We have our conversation on the shady end of the tennis court.

Pom tells me that his wife has recently "left him" because he is running for office. "She thinks it's crazy to do such a dangerous thing."

I am educated as a lawyer and I practiced law for about twenty years. When martial law came, I decided that as my protest against martial law I should not practice law. I stopped going into the court and accepting clients. I went into a new line of endeavor. I went into agriculture and became a *calamansi* [a small, green, citrus fruit] planter and a coconut grower. I also went into real estate development, and I became a subdivision owner.

What are your sharing arrangements with your tenants?

Sixty percent to me and 40 percent to them. I shoulder all the expenses. The usual practice is 33 1/3 percent to the tenants and 66 2/3 percent to the landowners. I think I should give my tenants more, but I could not go any further. Otherwise my neighbors will hate me, and they would consider me a radical, a communist, because if I give my tenants, let's say, 50/50, in the long run my neighbors would also be forced to do it. So I compromise with 60/40.

I think a good idea would be 40/60 in favor of the tenant—the reverse of what I am able to do. The tenants really work hard and they have more children than the landowner. Of course, they have simple lives, but the landowner simply does not have the right to hold them to that kind of living.

Father Michael "Mickey" Martin
Superior, Columban Fathers
Batang, Negros

*F*ootball, as the Irish call soccer, has shaped Father Mickey Martin. In any conversation he'll find a way of bringing up "football." Despite twenty years of working with the rural poor in southern Negros—during which time I doubt he has often been on the playing field—the Irish-born priest stills lumbers along like a football player. I am curious how Father Mickey's upbringing in Ireland has shaped his perception of twenty years of working with the rural poor.

Growing up on a small family farm, I think that one of the key things I picked up is that we regarded ourselves to be the same as everybody else. Most of us Irish have great difficulty in accepting a society dominated by a few. Gypsies in Ireland would go around, and they were always welcome in our home, and they would eat with us. Our parents would always communicate with us that the gypsies were as good as we were. Looking back on my growing up, I can identify some of the values that I can faithfully and easily give witness to. And one of these is that there should be equal opportunities for everyone. And that people should be allowed to grow.

How did Negros strike you when you first started working here?

I remember one of the older Columbans taking me aside and saying, "God, you're not here six months and you're going around saying that there's slavery on this island. Where did you get these great insights, and you're here only six months?" He was scorning me when he said that. He was reprimanding me. But at least it imprinted in my mind that I thought there was slavery in this society. Some people didn't have access to basic necessities, and other people seemed to do whatever they liked, including going for a trip around the world if they wanted to. And I found myself reacting. I remember sitting down, and I cried, just cried, when I saw the people with no medicine, virtually no food, and, in a sense, no hope.

At that time, or at least shortly after I arrived here, the plight of the *sacadas*—that's the migrant sugar workers—received a good deal of publicity. Their plight was highlighted when a Jesuit seminarian came down from Manila and lived on the hacienda of a relative of his. And with the permission of his relative, he lived with the *sacadas*, and he documented their plight—some of their values, some of their attitudes, and inevitably their hunger. In a place like Kabankalan, where I was assigned, there was a little clinic in the town, and people would come there. We would meet them on the level of: The child is dying—would you baptize the child? The grandfather is dying—would you anoint the grandfather? So our initial point of contact at that time was answering their religious needs. But insofar as I was able to understand what they were saying—and initially I didn't, but little by little, I could understand what people were saying—I would hear terrible stories of hunger and sickness, people dying.

It is difficult for me to remember the cries of just which particular family got to me most. I can recall, for instance, going over to a hacienda to visit a sick person and simply being appalled. I couldn't believe that people would have to live in such subhuman conditions.

For Father Mickey, the sugar and plantation system is at the root of the poverty and hunger of the majority.

Sugar is a fantastic plantation crop. It lends itself to the whole plantation system, and the plantation system lends itself to slavery. The sugar goes from the farm to the mill, and eventually it is sold abroad, and the money comes back into the bank account of the owner. Now, most rice and corn are sharecropped here in the Philippines. But if the landowner gets a part, at least the people get a part of it too. Furthermore, if you aren't even a tenant farmer but you work and harvest the rice of somebody else, then you get a part of your harvest. You get something of the fruit of your labor. You actually have food. So rice, corn, vegetables, and the local crops that are produced here actually help to feed people; they help to feed Filipinos. Sugar goes out to fatten those who are already fat. And the tragedy is that there are already articles written, which I've seen, saying, "There is sugar in your blood and blood in your sugar."

I ask Father Mickey about the sugar industry "crisis" in Negros of the last few years. He responds that it could be a blessing in disguise for the majority of people. He describes the impact of the earlier "sugar boom" on the people in the area of southern Negros where he was working at that time.

The sugar price went up so high in 1974 that people saw sugar as the thing to be in, which meant enormous expansion. Those in the sugar industry tend to be quite shortsighted. The thing was to get more land—rent it, buy it, steal it,

Boysie Imperial

Father Mickey Martin

get it whatever way you can. The rolling hills around the plains of Negros witnessed a scramble for land. Anybody who was anybody went up there looking for more land. Some of these people rented land for a 100 pesos per hectare for fifteen years—terms that they knew were a joke. But because the small farmers who owned those bits of land needed that money, and you gave them some money to feed and clothe their children, send their kids to school, bury their dead, or whatever their emergency was, you got it. The pressure for expansion of sugar land was so great that all money went into acquiring more and more land. The high price of sugar accelerated the pressure on people to lose their land. Areas that traditionally produced subsistence crops—rice and corn, and coconut and native bananas— now became sugar land.

Father Mickey was first "dragged into taking sides" by the grabbing of land from his parishioners.

People came to me from a hilly area and they said, "Our land is being taken from us and made into pastureland. It's not really our land, but it's the land that we've tilled ever since our parents came here and cleared it." It was technically forest land. The government agency that looks after that is the Bureau of Forestry. Only when the Bureau of Forestry declares the land alienable and disposable can it be turned over to the Bureau of Lands for distribution. So these people would keep on applying for this land. That's what the people are taught the process is.

But they got nowhere. How the system actually works is that the Bureau of Lands and the Bureau of Forestry are manned by the friends, families, and the protegés of those with economic and political power—they are the same people. And that way they were the first to know what government land was available. There were many ways by which the rich could acquire more land, and that's what they were doing. In this particular case, a rich person named Casas acquired for pasture lease about 400 hectares that these poor people had been farming.

I went to the Ministry. I saw all the files on how this person had acquired the land. And two weeks later, when I went back, all the files were gone. And they said, "Perhaps somebody borrowed them." What had happened was that the whole evidence that would show that the whole thing was a farce from the word go had all been taken away. You could see the crookery that was going on. Things like that remain in my memory.

Father Mickey says that he has been forced to open his "ears and heart to the cry of the sugar workers" and he has developed a theology of the land.

I'm influenced by the thinking of those—analyzing the social teaching of the church—who pointed out that the church teaching with regard to land ownership from the very beginning was crazy. Nobody can absolutely own a source of life. And land is a source of life just as much as the air is, and the water is. Nobody goes out and claims that they own the water out there, they can't. At least they haven't started it yet here. And I suppose that some people indirectly claim ownership of the air because they pollute it in a big way. How can anybody own what is the source of life of everybody? So the community's needs are way above the needs of an individual—far, far more important.

It is scandalous that a man with, say, 100 hectares of land will send his children to school, they become professionals, meaning the fruit of the land gives them the best schooling, and then at the end of it, they all want part ownership of that land. For me, it's understandable that one son retain something that becomes his source of livelihood. I have no problem about that. I'm not trying to take away all the land from people. But I think that in the past not only did people use the fruits of the land for the benefit of their family, but they paid nothing, very little into the community, except as a sort of palliative and a pay-off. When they pay taxes at all—and these taxes in the Philippines are minimal—they try to get them back again. Because normally they have power over the government, either provincial or local, and they have access to that money. So, in fact, the taxes came back to them twofold and threefold.

The moral bankruptcy of the traditional system here is self-evident. And the resistance that's going to come with any sort of change is also self-evident. I've talked to some planters, including some very good people, and they say, You know, if the government forces us to give over some of our land, well, we can give over the worst 10 percent of our land. If it forces us to give it to the workers, we can give them a piece of land that is so far away from where they now live that they're not going to work it anyway.

Father Mickey speaks at length about how he has benefited from working in the Philippines.

I went to the Philippines thinking that I was to teach people, but I feel I've learned more than I've given. The first time I realized this was when I went home to Ireland on furlough. And I had all these little gifts for my nephews and nieces and what not. I've only one sister, and she telephoned and said, "Michael, I want to help you unpack your things." And I said, "Great, come over later on." It was only later when she came that I opened up my suitcase and took out all my gifts. She earmarked something for everybody, and I was off having a cup of tea with my father. And she said, "Where is your other suitcase?" "What other suitcase? I've only got a bag and a suitcase; I don't have a second suitcase." And then she came over and she was actually shocked, she was pale, and she said, "Where are your own things?" It took me awhile to clearly say I don't have any things, and I realized then that I don't have many things. I did have a tape recorder but I gave it to an old man here—Father Alan, because he loves music—before I went home.

In fact, I really acquired here a different attitude toward accumulation of property, because I saw so many people with nothing. In other words, the poor had evangelized me; they had shown me that I don't need an awful lot of things. God communicates mainly through the poor of the earth, most clearly manifested by Jesus who became one of the poor of the earth. All the time, wherever you look in the intervention of God in history, it was done in this way. If you think God is going to speak through the White House, forget it.

I look at my classmates and friends who became priests in Ireland and I say, God, they have never been evangelized by the poor, and I pity them. I admire them for their fidelity and their kindness, charity and their loyalty. But I pity them because they have not had the opportunity to be converted by the poor. And I say, Thank God I was in Negros, because it was so obvious in Negros who you should be working with. And who your friends should be. So I think it was a fantastic privilege to be so close to so many poor, that they have got through to me, in a way, and that they've changed so many of my attitudes.

Three:
ORGANIZING FOR CHANGE

Serge Cherniguin
Secretary General, National Federation of Sugar Workers, Bacolod City, Negros

S erge Cherniguin is the elected secretary general of the National Federation of Sugar Workers (NFSW). The Federation has more than seventy thousand field and mill workers on Negros, about 15 percent of all sugar workers, counting the children who regularly work in the fields. The Federation has been expanding in other sugar-producing areas in the Visayas, the islands in the center of the Philippine archipelago, where it has an additional twenty thousand members.

Serge is a large, Eastern European-looking man in his early 50s. He speaks softly, and carefully chooses his words. We meet in the evening, in early 1987, after Serge has had a long series of meetings with union organizers and visitors from Europe, Japan, and Australia. The NFSW organizes these "exposures" to present the realities of how the sugar workers live. We talk for several hours.

I wonder about Serge's Russian name.

Yes, my father came from Russia. He was a soldier of the czar. He left Russia after the Bolshevik Revolution. When they surrendered, part of the agreement was that they would be allowed to go to other countries. The soldiers had ships and divided the money from selling their ships. First, he went to China. Then he went to the island of Mindanao in the southern Philippines where he worked in a lumber mill. Then he came to Negros. That's where he met my mother. That was in the 1930s.

At that time, there were several landowners who had Russians as their managers. The Russians proved to be good managers. I was born on the plantation my father managed.

As a child, I worked in the fields. When I was 9 years old, my father got sick and we lost everything that we had. The landowner sent me to Manila to study. My father helped him to get rich and it was his way of expressing gratitude.

Although I didn't finish university, I did take some courses in agriculture. When I came back, the owner said that I will take the place of my father.

Coming back to the plantation, Serge was eager to use what he had learned to help the Filipino people by improving the use of agricultural resources on the farm. He now says he was "idealistic and naive."

We wanted to develop the Philippines. But when I started working on the hacienda, it was different. You cannot develop anything because the situation of the people is so oppressed, and the plantation system is already there and you cannot change it. There was no place to use what you have learned for improvement of the country and the people. It's already a closed structure. The wages are fixed, you have to follow the work pattern, use the same amount of fertilizer. Day in and day out it's the same. In school, we learned how to raise animals, how to raise grains, vegetables, and root crops—everything. On the plantation, nothing but sugar. All around you is sugar. Year in, year out, you deal with sugar and only sugar.

I was frustrated. I thought I was going to help the people on the hacienda. I thought I would run the farm so well that the landowner would give the workers better wages. But in the hacienda system, you are always carrying out the will of the landowner. You obey him or else you will be discharged. So it always ends up with the oppression and exploitation of the workers. You have to deprive them even of their legal rights. You have to control their lives so much. They are not allowed to visit their relatives on other farms without asking permission. If a worker doesn't have permission, he can either lose his job or be suspended. Or he can lose his home. For, you see, the house is given free but it is a means of control.

I even had to lie under oath for the sake of the owner. Before I was transferred to Victorias, the owner of the hacienda in La Carlota, where I worked for some seventeen years, made me swear in court that a notice of sale was posted on the hacienda for three months. But actually it was not. The planter wanted to escape paying the separation wages he owed the workers because he sold the hacienda. The law said that when you sell a farm, you must pay separation wages to the workers unless you post the notice of sale where the workers could see it for three months. There's always a loophole in the laws for the planters! And, mind you, the separation wages would have been only a few thousands compared to the millions in profit he had from the actual sale of the farm.

I really started to question myself. My conscience was bothering me. There is so much suffering around and, as a Christian, you cannot close yourself to the suffering of the workers. It is a real abuse and it makes you angry to see the exploitation of those who work hard. It is very wrong, and wrong is wrong.

Boysie Imperial

Serge Cherniguin

My last recourse when I was transferred to Victorias was to really run the plantation well. In fact, I brought the plantation up to one of the highest yields in the district. I thought that would mean improvement in the workers' wages. But I was so surprised that I was still required to turn down requests for increases in wages.

I realized that the capitalists have nothing but profit in their mind. The landowner I was working for was supposed to be a very good Catholic. One of his very strong instructions when I started to work for him was to respect Sunday, not to let the workers work on Sunday.

I ask Serge if he himself is a Catholic.

Yes, a very active Catholic. In fact, it was really my faith, you know, that changed my life.

The sugar planters of Negros are 85 percent Catholic. Product of the best Catholic schools, sad to say. It was therefore their custom that every two or three years they would have a priest go to the hacienda to preach, to have what's called a mission. Three days of preaching—largely abstract spirituality—and a lot of baptisms, a lot of marriages, a lot of confessions, things like that. On the farm I was managing, the missionaries were the Redemptorists. They were Irish. On one mission in 1972, they were preaching the theology of liberation. I was really thunderstruck, because there were a lot of questions I was asking in my mind, in myself, that got answered. I realized that God does not make people poor. On the other hand, it is people who make other people poor. In fact, God made the world so rich—natural resources and everything— particularly the Philippines, particularly Negros. I even realized that I was acting as an agent of oppression and exploitation, that I was working for the pharaoh.

I remember the particular afternoon when I resigned. It was after we got a very good production. I even expected some praise for what I did. But the owner actually gave me a lecture on profit. More profit, more profit—like that. And right there, I told him that I resign from my job. He wasn't able to speak. He thought I was crazy. And he says, Well, anyway, I will give you some more days to reflect. But I was already feeling so nice, so at peace with myself. Everything was so silent. So I packed my things and left. Later I learned that the brother of the landowner I quit on went to the farm to talk to me, but I was already gone.

I was married, with four children. I had to look for a job. I found work with another planter. He was glad to hire me because he saw my work. At first I thought he was better, but he turned out to be even worse. So I was really disillusioned. I worked for him for three months only.

The final turn of the screw was that the wife of the head supervisor was bleeding. She had a miscarriage, and she was supposed to be brought immediately to the hospital. We have to call to the landowner to ask permission to use the truck. There is a woman there bleeding to death, and you have to ask permission. It's revolting, you know. And then you have to go along with his wishes. He could say yes or he could say no, while that woman lay dying. I even told the man whose wife was bleeding, You'd better talk to the landowner so that you could express the urgency. And what happened was the owner said no, even scolded him. Eventually, I ordered them to use the truck anyway. I said, Go ahead, and I tendered my resignation. They did not believe I'd do it. They even asked me why I was resigning, as if it had been just an ordinary incident. Well, I told them, I've lost the desire to work for you. And again they told me, We'll give you one week, think it over. Again I left right away.

I approached Father Saguinsin, one of the founders of the NFSW. From time to time, we had talks together. When I had worked in Victorias, when the priests were preaching the mission, I think they detected my frustration and disgust with my work. They offered to give me a job. They said, If you ever want, we can give you a job where you will not be in conflict with your conscience.

It was 1975, January, when I joined the union. I told my wife that I wouldn't go home every day at five o'clock, that I must really integrate with the workers. That's how the workers gain their confidence in you. You have to be one with them. It is good that my wife also understands. So that's what we decided, not to be separate but to be really one with them.

What was the impact of such a big change in your life on your family?

When we really decided to integrate with the workers, the hardship we underwent, it was really nothing. Before, when I was on the management side, we really had to live like the Joneses, have what the others have. But when we changed our mentality and took on a worker's mentality, we are not conscious of what we eat, the kind of clothes we wear, the kind of people we associate with. We feel at home associating with workers. We live in the same house.

My wife was immediately very supportive. My wife did not come from the sugar workers' class. Her family was supported by her uncle, who was a policeman within the town. The exploitation, the subservience of the sugar workers, appalled her so much. And she was also behind me, in telling me to quit working for the hacienda—you know, your mind becomes conditioned to the exploitation and subservience.

What were some concrete experiences you had during your initial work with the union?

When I started working with the union, I went with the union's organizers into an area. I helped establish simple economic projects such as garden plots growing cassava and plantains on the river banks. In the place where I went the land is so fertile, and everywhere you go the land is all sugarcane. And along the creek, because it is very deep and the bank very, very steep, that's the only place where the people can plant their bananas, their food. Naturally, there's a lot of erosion on that bank. But the people cannot help it because they have to plant their food there. They could never depend on their earnings from the plantation. Every off-milling season, the people have to depend on bananas they grow, the people have to go everywhere to search for work. And there is so much hunger.

There was a time that a woman worker started helping the union. What the sugar planter did was first notify all the *hacenderos* in the area that the family of the woman must not be given work. The trucks that haul sugarcane to the mills are the only transportation of the people. They have to go in it in order to buy something. And the family of the woman was not allowed to ride any truck. And she was not even allowed coconut leaves with which they could make a roof for their house. And the path leading to their house was even closed by the sugar planters. So those are the sort of things that really strike you. Yes, real persecution.

Then there was another planter. On her hacienda there was a man who was always complaining of low wages. And later on, when she noticed that the other workers started complaining also, she had that man killed. Yes, he was killed by goons. From time to time, yes, you could hear of things like that.

Was union work dangerous?

At that time, organizing was semi-underground. Actually, it was done at night. There were always lookouts so that the farm guards should not learn of anything.

There was solidarity among the workers. But if the union organizing on the hacienda is discovered prematurely, a lot of workers lose their jobs. On the other hand, if it is discovered when the majority of the workers are already organized, then they could resist. If somebody is fired, they could always picket, they could always contribute for the support of those who lost their jobs, they could always pressure, make some strike or work stoppage. So at that time, when we have meetings, when we have seminars, we must make sure that none of the workers who are linked to the management people join the union. Our social investigation has to be really deep and thorough.

On the hacienda where I used to go a lot, secretly, even priests and nuns in their religious garb could not go because they were considered subversive. In fact, because many think I look like a Columban, an Irish missionary priest, I did not pass along the road. When I go with the organizers, I would pass along the creeks, along the sides of the haciendas. All those thorns and bushes!

That's how I learned what are the hardships of the organizers. The organizer I went with impressed me so much, because his allowance from the NFSW was so small and he had five children. There were times when his children were sick and they had no rice. And once in a while, when we were working, he would sit on a stone, put his chin on his palm, and he'd say, I'm worried about the sick children. But then he'd tell me, Know what I do when I feel like this? I think of the sufferings of all the sugar workers, and then I become angry and I start my work again. He had been a sugar worker.

I ask Serge to tell me a little more about the NFSW and its history.

The National Federation of Sugar Workers is the trade union for sugar workers, especially in Negros. It was started by priests and nuns. That was 1971. Before that, many priests worked with the FFF—the Federation of Free Farmers—and the FFF was very active in the 1960s. The FFF came to Negros. They organized the sugar workers, they organized the small farmers, the fishermen. Many priests were involved. But the priests realized that sugar workers were very special, so they should have their own organization.

Actually, what they really saw was the type of leadership the FFF had. The leadership of the FFF was really very bourgeois. The leadership was far from the organizers, very far from the workers, unlike the NFSW, where the leaders really integrate with the workers. With the NFSW, the workers eat with the union leaders. Usually, in the other unions, there is a table reserved for the officers, and they have imported whiskey and some roasted pigs, and the workers just sit there on the other side of the room. When the FFF organizers would go to a plantation, the workers would always kill chicken for them. With the NFSW, we even bring our own rice, our own dried fish. Once there was an organizer in the NFSW who let workers fetch water so that he could take a bath. And that guy was fired, you know. When we work with the people, we must stay with them, work in their houses. And what's happening now is that many of the organizers are supported by the people they organize, just like in the Bible, like St. Paul.

The NFSW educates, mobilizes, organizes, so that the workers demand their rights. It's the workers, not the organizers, who go to the *hacenderos*, the administrators, the overseers, to demand better wages or whatever.

Under Marcos, the NFSW was able to organize in spite of so many organizers being killed. More or less twenty NFSW organizers were killed, and hundreds were imprisoned. Because of that, the NFSW's credibility with the workers never diminished.

How is the NFSW attempting to deal with the "crisis?"

When the crisis deepened in 1984, the NFSW started the farmlot program where workers, through dialogues with planters, are able to borrow land and plant it with food. Now we have 4,000 hectares, that was the last count. In addition, we have nearly 1,000 hectares the union was able to acquire, which is worked cooperatively.

It doesn't seem like much land.

It's really very little—only about 1 percent of the land owned by the sugar planters in Negros. We're hoping that we can convince planters to lend more because, according to the sugar workers, they have gained some experience in raising their rice and corn. They say that they could do better this year than they did last year.

How does a farmlot get started?

First we give our members seminars: these are your rights, you are supposed to receive this much. So the workers go to the planters and tell them, "Give us what we are supposed to be getting or give us farmlots." All the plantations have idle lands because of the crisis. There's less planting. Actually, they're milling only one-third as much as they used to.

It's really only the medium planters and the small ones who will talk with us. The big planters, they won't dialogue. They just arm themselves. That is why, even right after Aquino came into power, we have four union members killed in the north. Three of them were organizers and another one a union member. They were killed because of the land question, because of the farmlot question.

Now the collective bargaining agreements we negotiate include that a certain part of the land must be set aside for the workers to plant. The sugar planters decide which part of the land is lent for a farmlot. Therefore, the worst part is always given. The planters are teaching us how to cope with bad lands, how to maximize bad lands. If they give us only the space in between the rows of cane, we always take the opportunity. The workers plant even that. They have to eat, you know.

I have heard reports that some planters have plowed under the food crops of workers. I wonder if that is still happening.

Yes. There are some farmlots in the north that were plowed under by the sugar

Union-organized unemployed sugar workers have petitioned hacienda owners to lend them "farmlots," small amounts of unused land on which to plant rice for their hungry families. Many owners have refused. On some haciendas, desperate sugar workers have nevertheless gone ahead and planted.

Robert Gumpert

planters, and even in one place the landowner's goons harvested the plants of the workers. In Hacienda San Isidro, the goons were able to get three big truckloads of fresh corn from the workers' farmlot. The police always look the other way. Recently, goons even attempted to murder the parish priest of Escalante, who has helped workers plant food crops. But luckily, providentially, the priest took a different car so that when he passed by the ambush site, he was riding in another car, and the goons were not able to fire on him.

The planters are so greedy, they're just too greedy. In fact, they're only forced by the circumstances to share their land. What they're afraid of is that the workers will claim the land they plant on in spite of our promises that we're going to sign letters, guarantees. Then too they are afraid that there's going to be a land reform and that this land-lending is the first step. And some are afraid that if the workers will have already other means of work, they will not work on the sugar plantation. And there's another thing happening here. Some sugar planters have started already to diversify to rice. But it really makes you think, because they're paying less than what they used to pay to the sugar workers.

But this is the first time, in the sugar planters' mentality, that they ever shared their land. For the worker, this is the first time he has planted anything and got the whole of it for himself, not giving any share to a landlord. So for both, there are changes. This is a historic event for them. This farmlot program is really a breakthrough.

Robert Gumpert

What happens when a planter refuses the workers' pleas that he lend some of his idle land?

There are instances that the workers go ahead anyway and plant idle lands out of desperation—in order to survive. The union also has a hand in that because we help the workers to understand that it is their duty to ask for land if they see their families hungry—not really ask, but insist. So it creates a mentality among the workers. When they grab idle land and plant it, that is a good sign, because land reform should really be pushed by the people from under.

What do the workers grow on the farmlots?

Last year what they grew was rice, corn, and sweet potatoes. We are trying to introduce animal raising, and vegetable raising and other sources of carbohydrates, but it's a slow process of education. Even the gardening we teach the workers is called nutri-gardening. They are taught what vegetables to plant with particular vitamins and nutrients for particular diseases. We help them get *carabaos*. We teach them the value of milk and how to milk the *carabaos*. In these programs we get financial help from some friendly organizations overseas.

We even help the sugar workers learn how to maximize their time, because actually what developed among the sugar workers with such very low wages— you are supposed to work the whole day from sunrise to sundown for a few pesos—is that slowdown attitude. We are trying to change that attitude, because once they work for themselves, everything will go to them.

I ask Serge about Governor Lacson's plan for granting debt relief to planters defaulting on their loans in exchange for ceding 10 percent of their lands to the government. This plan would transfer the lands to the workers as "livelihood plots."

We're not opposed to it, even though it's only 10 percent of the land, land on which the workers also have to put up their houses. We need at least 40 percent. We're not opposed to the plan, even though the workers would have to pay for the land and, most of all, even though it's voluntary for the planters. And we're not opposed, even though the planters are the ones to pick the land, and we know from the farmlot program that the worst lands will be picked. Why do we go along despite these serious objections? Because we feel that the sugar workers are hungry, and that they must have food right away. Right now! And if they have food, they could strengthen their organizations.

Yes, we are desperate. We really need land. One morning we might wake up and find the World Bank, IMF are bankrolling the sugar planters. Then what will happened to our borrowed lands in our farmlot program? So out of desperation—we accept the governor's proposal, confident that our farmlots would fall under the scheme.

That is why now, under the Aquino administration, the people's organizations must go on, must really be strengthened. And that's why we are really critical of President Aquino, because rather than helping people's organizations strengthen she's really moving to the right and toward violent repression of people's organizations.

Serge pauses. His final reflection on the land issues is somber.

This problem of inequitable land ownership has to be solved. It could be solved in a violent way or it could be solved peacefully, but definitely it's a problem that has to be solved. On the one side are sugar planters who want to maintain their status and are quite willing to use violence to do so. On the other side are sugar workers who see their children dying of hunger and who cannot stand it anymore.

I'd like to say that I hope it can be solved peacefully. But, you know, it looks very dim. I have to say that it *could* be solved peacefully, but I doubt it will.

❖ ❖ ❖

In Bacolod in January 1988, I speak with a worried-looking Serge at NFSW headquarters. Union organizing, he says, is "paralyzed." The military, together with armed vigilante groups supported by the planters, are conducting a "reign of terror." Many milling associations now levy a tax on members for each picul of sugarcane milled to finance vigilante groups organized by the military. A week or two before an election for union representation, the military sets up a unit on the hacienda or near the sugar mill. They show the movie "The Killing Fields" followed by a lecture on the threat of "another Cambodia" in the Philippines, and go door to door, warning people of "the communist union." As a result, reports Serge, workers are afraid to vote for the NFSW; instead they vote either not to be represented at all or for a pro-management union.

Serge hands me copies of documentation compiled for human rights organizations on 24 "salvagings," or summary executions, of union members and organizers (a number of them are also activists in the Basic Christian Communities, according to the documentation) since Aquino came to office. "When you were here before, our main concern was hunger. Now, I am sad to say, it is political repression. The human rights situation is absolutely worse now than under Marcos."

Eliseo Silva
NFSW Farmlot worker
Negros

I n February 1987, I visit a farmlot on one of the several haciendas belonging to Jose Montelibano. The hacienda has 368 hectares; the farmlot, operated by a cooperative of seventy-eight workers and their families, has a little over 11 hectares. Part of the farmlot is worked by groups with five families each, and part is divided up and worked by individual families. The farmlot chairman is Eliseo Silva. An agronomist working with the National Federation of Sugar Workers (NFSW) farmlot program acts as translator, and we are surrounded by other farmlot members and children during the interview.

Our wages were very low—no daily wages, only piece rate. We made at best only about eighteen pesos per day. We organized a dialogue with the landowner to borrow a little piece of land, but he refused. He said he was afraid that once we borrowed the land we would never return it if he wanted it back. We had a second dialogue, and the landowner again refused. But we were all united. We went ahead and planted some of the back land anyway. We planted rice. When the landowner found out, he decided not to fight us.

Yes, we were afraid when we planted his land. We thought that maybe we would be charged with land-grabbing and be arrested. But our hunger united us. We were forced to cultivate this piece of land because of our hunger and our children's hunger. Since the sugar crisis struck two years ago, they have left almost half the land on the hacienda idle. We've lacked work and been hungrier than ever. So we were afraid to cultivate this land, but our hunger forced us.

Many planters have told me that sugar workers don't know how to grow rice and other food crops.

Almost all of us living in this hacienda know how to plant rice, but the problem is that we lack enough fertilizer and insecticides.

Robert Gumpert

With 80 percent of the country's land in the hands of fewer than 20 percent of the landowners, the country's rice is grown principally by farmers who do not own the land they till. Rents for tenant farmers are so high that they have little incentive and are too impoverished to buy fertilizer and make other investments to increase production. Average rice yields in the Philippines remain among the very lowest in Asia.

Has the farmlot program improved their situation?

A little. But we still earn very little from the hacienda and the farmlot is not yet sufficient for our needs. With more land we could grow more food and we could afford to send our children to school. We could buy medicines and clothes and other things we need. But most important of all is schooling for our children. Knowledge is very important.

Is the farmlot land reform?

No, it's not land reform. With genuine land reform, we would get title to the land. And we would get more land. Cory Aquino promised genuine land reform, but so far nothing has happened.

Would genuine land reform mean dividing up the hacienda among the workers?

This land was once planted with lowland rice, but when the sugar boom came it was transferred to sugarcane. With genuine land reform it would be put back to rice and the farm would be managed by us workers. It would not have to be broken up.

When do you have time to work on the farmlot?

No problem. Sugarcane does not provide enough regular work. During the dead season there is no work. Even when we are working we have only three days a week. So we have time for our farmlot.

How does the union help?

Well, we are still in the process of negotiating with the owner. We need additional farmlots, especially during the dead season. The union also helps us cultivate this farmlot. The NFSW helps finance fertilizers and other things we need or else we could not cultivate this farmlot. Recently, the union sent me to Manila for training about integrated farming, which we will start next year. That means multiple cropping because we need to plant things that don't require as much water as rice, like mongo beans. We will be able to better maximize land use.

In negotiating for more land, how much are you asking for?

We plan to negotiate 30 more hectares. But I don't think Mr. Montelibano will allow that.

So will you just take it again?

I'm afraid we cannot do otherwise.

Is that land reform?

[Eliseo and the others laugh.] Maybe that's how it's done.

Elma Alcala
Sugar worker, Hacienda Consuelo
La Carlota, Negros

The first time I talk with Elma Alcala is in January 1987. Mrs. Alcala is a wiry, weathered, but feisty mother of three in her late 40s. She is a sugarcane farm worker and a union organizer. Night has fallen and we speak by a kerosene lamp in her small bamboo house, which her family shares with two other families. Looking down on me from the wall behind her is a black-and-white portrait of Jesus. He looks angry. Later Elma tells me that her elder son painted it and that this angry, silent Christ is "observing what is happening in the Philippines."

I was born in this hacienda in 1940. My parents were born in Panay, but their age is 15 years when they came here. Both my father and my mother worked in this hacienda. I started working when I was only 7 years old.

When I was very young, my father is earning three pesos. Because my father is a tractor driver, he is earning more than we are in the sugarcane field. But, even with my father, my mother, and me and my five brothers working, our income is not enough for the whole family.

The most sacrifice I make is from 1975 up to now. Because we are working through piecework, the more we work the more income we get. But, even if we work twelve hours a day the most we can receive is only twenty pesos— when the rural minimum wage is thirty-two pesos. The only persons who are receiving thirty-two pesos are those who are close to the management like the watchman, the foreman, the private armies, the relatives of the overseer, the drivers.

In 1982, Roberto S. Benedicto, the crony of Marcos, bought this hacienda. All the workers were locked out. Benedicto says that he can change the workers because he is the new owner of the land. And even if we are begging that we want to work, that we know how to work, that we are qualified workers of this

Boysie Imperial

Elma Alcala

hacienda, they never listen to us. Benedicto hired migrant workers from neighboring districts and Panay. They are *sacadas*.

This is one reason that we are now organized, that we now have the union. Before we had a union we were without the knowledge of our legal rights. What the management says we believe. We only work, work, work and we know that our life is not getting better but going worse. But through the education of the union, we now know our rights, we know what is happening. But up to now, we do not feel justice, we do not feel justice. That is why we file cases in the labor court.

Benedicto fled to Hawaii with the Marcoses. I ask if Elma and the other workers have been reinstated on the hacienda payroll.

No, we still have not been allowed to go back to work. And we have already sent a demand to Malacañang to President Cory to reinstate us in our work. But we receive no response.

How have you survived, if you have been locked out by the hacienda's management since 1982?

At first, we do not know what to do, because we never before experienced being locked out. But determined that we do not surrender to the management, so that we sugar workers should achieve a base of freedom, we planted vegetables and banana trees on a very small portion of land by the river bank. We have to do it by force, because they will never lend us any land. Every time we plant we are harassed by the military. They send a tractor to plow up our plants. But through the determination that we have to eat—and our children know it—the children barricade the plants. The children are in front. They are ready to die if need be. They know that our vegetables are the only source of our living; we cannot buy rice. And we mothers and fathers are convincing the tractor driver, we are organizing him, telling him the situation, so we get the sympathy of the driver so that he would not plow up our plants.

Management trying to destroy the workers' crops did not go out with the fall of Marcos. While crony Benedicto fled and the Aquino government "sequestered" Hacienda Consuelo, Benedicto nonetheless continues to run the hacienda through his administrator and encargado. The last time management bulldozed the crops was just two days before our interview.

Elma lets me in on a "secret." Because the administration won't let them plant food crops for their families, they go into the center of the sugarcane field and clear an area and plant vegetables, like eggplant. The overseer hasn't caught on yet.

Elma tells me she has been imprisoned twice.

On one hacienda there were 12 hectares of land that the management did not plant. The workers there were very hungry. In June, they asked permission to plant rice. The land will be vacant five months. They asked the overseer for permission to plant the rice for three months, and after that they would return the land. At first the overseer permitted them to, and so the workers started planting rice. After the landlord knew, he called in the military to stop the work. There were so many military, hundreds. Then through the NFSW I helped them appeal to Bishop Fortich and he made an arrangement with the landlord that we will have a dialogue in the Bago City Hall. We were invited to attend the dialogue. So we went there—we were 126 workers in all. And the bishop and Father Saguinsin and our lawyer were there. We were begging the landlord that we just wanted to borrow the land for three months. And Bishop Fortich is also telling the management that he is guaranteeing that after three months the workers will return the land.

At noon, they said, We are going to rest because the soft drinks are coming. The conversation is getting hot, they said. But then the military get inside the conference room and they surround us and arrest all of us right in front of Bishop Fortich. And then we are all shouting, Monsignor, what happened? Why is it that they arrest us and we are just doing the negotiation? They never listened to Bishop Fortich telling them to stop. They get the microphone from Bishop Fortich and then arrest first Father Saguinsin and then our lawyer. They bring Father Saguinsin and the president of the union to Bacolod City and the rest of the 126 workers they put us in prison in Bago City.

We women are so very, very noisy. We're asking everything—we were thirty-six and in the morning we were demanding to get all our children and put them inside the jail because nobody will feed our children at home. And we are asking them for what we need as women. We are shouting, we are asking them, we wanted them to give us what we need immediately. So because we are so noisy and they cannot give what we want, they let us go out at nine o'clock the next day. But the men remained nine days in prison.

What did they say you had done wrong? What was your crime?

They say we are subversives. I don't know what is the meaning of that. I'm not inciting to rebellion. We just wanted to plant. We wanted to eat because we are hungry. And before the bishop, the workers are promising to pay for the land and they sign that they are going to return the land after three months after they harvest. But they do not want to give up the land, and destroy what was planted.

And the second imprisonment?

At another hacienda we had an action of 150 workers. We were asking for payment to the workers for weeding. They called in the military, and we were all brought to the police. But because we are so very many—the children are with us, the children are very noisy, they are spitting, they are urinating in the office of the chief of police—they let us go home. That's why we brought the children.

Elma talks about the management's "private army."

It's an army that is paid by the management. There is no legal registration. They are appointed by the management. You are in my private army, this is your weapon, you guard me and my property. They're really a goon squad.

A .38 and a shotgun were pointed four times at me here on this hacienda by the private army of the management. The last time was only this August 25. They stopped me and threatened me with a .38 and a shotgun in front of that big house over there of Benedicto, because on August 24, I joined an action in the neighboring hacienda. The workers there are very hungry and they asked three times for a rice advance from the management's 2 hectare rice plantation that was ripe already. The manager answered that he cannot give what the workers ask because the sugar production now has collapsed, so he cannot do anything for his workers. So what the workers did was the next day, six o'clock in the morning, without the knowledge of the manager, they harvested the rice. I was out there with them and then at seven o'clock the military already is there. They said, Do not go out because you are robbing the manager's property. The workers answered that they are asking already three times, that they are very hungry, and he never listened, and that's why they do this thing. They are going to pay for the part of the rice that they get, they are going to pay for it later when there is work.

We were very lucky because there is a visitor from, I think, the French television—two persons. They went there because they heard there was an action there. And when they saw the military, the military were drunk already because the manager is giving them liquor. As I said, it's very lucky. They cannot harass the workers because the television people were out there and besides, the workers are very well organized—so much that even if they will point M-16 Armalites, they will not go. So there in front of the military they dried the rice they have harvested in the heat of the fire and then pounded it, and then cooked it, and then let their children eat in front of the military because they are very hungry. That is the reason they said to the manager and the military, What are you going to do with us, for we are determined to harvest the rice because our children are already very hungry. So the manager cannot do anything but to accept what the workers wanted.

Because Benedicto is the owner of that hacienda as well as of this hacienda, the manager recognized me. So the next day two private army people were here. They stood in front of me and pointed at me a .38 and a shotgun. But it's very lucky because I have plenty of friends—even the tricycle drivers are my friends. It happened that the two tricycle drivers were there; so they cannot shoot me, because the people are looking at them and they are very much embarrassed by this time that they have their weapons out. So they get inside the compound.

You know, I pity them, because I know the background of those people. They are very illiterate. They came to the town. They only stay here as private army people because their land was grabbed. That's why I pity them—they are very poor people also.

Once the management offered me a job—6,000 pesos. I was picked up in the city. The administrator wants to talk to me alone. They brought me there. It was dark already and there were military men inside. The manager said, Elma, I want to help you and I want you to help me. I want you to convince the remaining families to stop suing and to accept the 3,000 pesos each family we are offering. I am going to give you 6,000 pesos and I am going to give you some land and I'm going to make a house for you and I'm going to make your son finish his studies. Because he did not want to let me go, I said to him, Let me talk to my husband and tomorrow I'm going to tell you what happened. And I never came back to him up to now.

I ask her about the "crisis" everyone in Negros speaks of.

Especially now, the only hope of the sugar workers is to get land, even if only 10 percent of the land. In Negros it should be given to the sugar workers as a cooperative farm. Ten percent only we are asking. It is not really enough, but even that portion the management will not give us, will never give us. Ten percent will never affect the landlords' livelihood. Take this hacienda here, for example. Three hundred hectares. We were asking for only 30 hectares for all the workers here, but still they will not give us. Three hundred hectares in sugar land is big property and it's only one of their haciendas. They have invested in big businesses through the money from this land. That's why we will never believe that they do not have money.

We continue asking for land, because we know that we are the ones working for very long hours while the landlord is just waiting for the profit. That's why we say that we have the right to own the land. It's a moral argument. We are all Catholics.

What is your biggest problem these days in organizing?

The government is calling our union communist. But we do not know what communist means. What we want only is that we could live. There is propaganda from the government that the communists do not believe in God, that the communists are the ones who let the people work and all the property goes to the government. But if all our properties are in the hands of the Communist government and we can eat our whole life, our children can go to school, maybe it's not so bad.

I have talked with one of the government officials. I told him, maybe the time will come that all of us will be communists. I tell him that you have to help us get land right now, not in the next ten years yet, because we are very impatient already with what we experience in the Marcos regime. We love Cory. We put Cory in office because we believe that Cory is very honest. We believed that Cory will help us. But nearly one year already, we never yet feel justice. We believed that there would be at least a little change, a little help from Cory. But so far nothing.

We are growing very impatient. We are human beings, we want to live. We want to live! How can we live if we do not have work? If we do not have land? That's why we cannot wait so much, especially the locked-out sugar workers. If the people who are working cannot live, how much worse is it with we who do not have work, we who do not have land? What do they think of us? That we are animals? We are human beings! We want to eat! That's why we are asking the government, When? But until now there is no response.

In August 1987 the military picked up Elma and took her to the stockade. She was interrogated about the union. During interrogation her head was repeatedly banged against the iron bars of the stockade window. (I was told this when I was in Negros in January 1988, by someone who saw Elma shortly after she was released.) She was accused of being an NPA member and was forced to sign a "surrender" document so confessing. (NFSW officials told me that the military claim that in the latter part of 1987, more than three thousand union members and organizers "surrendered as NPAs.") Elma was also forced to go on the radio and denounce the union. (She did so, a Catholic priest told me, in such a way that anyone would know it was a forced statement.) Every Saturday she must report to the stockade. For reasons of her safety she has not openly met with anyone from the media or from abroad since her arrest and torture.

Worker occupation
Jose Montelibano estate
Silay, Negros

Three hundred farm workers from the haciendas of Jose Montelibano, patriarch of one of the wealthiest planter families in the Philippines, have broken through the wrought-iron gate of his residence in Silay, a half hour north of Bacolod City. The workers and their families are in their tenth day of encampment on the grounds of Mr. Montelibano's Victorian estate when I arrive. Under coconut palms and amid carefully nurtured orchids, rosebushes, and potted plants, they have erected hand-painted banners and placards with their denunciations and demands. Gutom, "hunger" in Ilongo as well as Tagalog, is a word one learns quickly in the Philippines. It appears on many of the signs. Most of the demonstrators stand in clusters talking, some are singing. A few of the women are preparing food over small campfires and the children are playing. These workers are members of the National Federation of Sugar Workers (NFSW).

Mr. Julieto Barrios, a middle-aged worker, is the NFSW spokesperson. We speak through an interpreter. He is wearing a "We are the World" T-shirt, a fairly common sight in the Philippines. He is from Hacienda Gretchen, one of Mr. Montelibano's five haciendas. Altogether, more than a thousand workers and their families live on Mr. Montelibano's haciendas.

We are demanding several things. First, we want our salaries increased, including payment of the minimum wage. We want our houses repaired. We want to be advanced rice rations during the off-season. We want a farmlot to grow food for our families. And we want to have hospitalization and other legally mandated benefits.

We were forced to stage this mass action and picketing because of hunger and because of the other conditions on the haciendas. Otherwise we and our children will suffer terrible hunger. So we decided on this bold move of coming here to town and picketing Mr. Montelibano's residence.

We are surrounded by a dozen other workers and some children. Several intersperse comments supporting what Mr. Barrios is saying. One woman holding a crying baby says, "Sir, no rice. The problem is no rice. No rice for baby. No milk."

I ask how much more pay they want.

If we work on a daily basis we are paid twenty pesos a day. But only a few people get this amount because most of us can't get daily work. Instead we work on a piecework basis and, because there are so many of us working on a piecework, we earn only five to ten pesos a day. We want to be able to work every day, to have daily work rather than piecework, and to be paid the minimum wage which is thirty-two and a half pesos.

According to Mr. Barrios, Mr. Montelibano does not provide his workers with any health benefits. I ask him to explain the picketers demand for rice.

Right now we are not being given a rice ration because the landowner says he can no longer afford to give us rice. No, the rice we want is not a gift. We want rice rations, but we agree to pay for them when we earn some money.

What size farmlots are they demanding?

It all depends on the landowner, how many hectares he is going to give.

Do they see possibilities that Mr. Montelibano will lend them some land?

None.

Has Mr. Montelibano come here to talk with you? Has he agreed to any of your demands?

No, he is staying in another one of his residences. It's in Bacolod. His lawyer has been here, but so far no offer has been made.

One worker in his 20s tells me that he was born and raised on a Montelibano hacienda but hasn't seen the planter since his childhood.

Judge Reynaldo Alon is also here. He has come because he has been asked to issue an arrest order for the workers occupying the estate. He tells me he is trying to convince them to leave, so that he won't have to call in the police or the military.

Mr. Montelibano wanted to talk to them, but not today. He set a date, Monday. He said, I can give probably all their demands. But the way it was done, using people power, that would be a bad precedent, no? Now every time they would want something, they would just come to my residence and picket with all those placards and everything denouncing me. Right now, he said, I'm not feeling well because of what happens here and it is of no use to talk when I'm not feeling well. Probably by Monday I could have a bit of rest. You just tell the people I have the rice and I will give them rice then. They can start working again, and probably on Monday we can arrange an increase in salary. That is what Mr. Montelibano says.

They have five demands. If they get three of them, that's okay, no? Mr. Montelibano promised me that he might even give them all their demands but not the way they have picketed this place and taken over his residence. Imagine a prominent citizen of Silay being denounced for nonpayment of the minimum wage! And people do not know whether that is true or not. But these people, after meeting among themselves, they have decided to stay. So I'm placed in a predicament. I have to comply with my duty as a judge because there is an injunction case filed on which I have to act. If Mr. Montelibano promises to meet them on Monday what is the use of their staying here? That's what I'm telling these people.

I ask the judge if from his years of experience is it conceivable that there are wealthy hacenderos who do not pay the minimum wage?

[*He laughs.*] I think so.

But isn't that tantamount to slavery?

Well, slavery is if you are commanded to do work, but these people are not forced to work; they labor of their own free will.

Father Romeo Empestan
Director, Basic Christian Communities
Diocese of Bacolod, Negros

*I*n some areas of the Philippines, and notably in Negros, Basic Christian Communities, or BCCs, have sprung up. On the morning of my visit with Father Romeo Empestan, the director of the Basic Christian Communities of the Bacolod Diocese, the Manila newspapers are carrying wire service reports on the Pope's "concern" about the popular influence of "liberation theology" in Brazil, where there are now thousands of similar comunidades de base.

Father Empestan's office is in a modest building on the grounds of the diocesan seminary, close to Bishop Fortich's office and residence. Father Empestan is in his late 40s. He tells me he's been a priest for "more than twenty years." Balding from the top of his forehead, he looks educated and serene. He is in lay dress. His office is decorated with a crucifix and several posters in English, Tagalog, and Ilongo about Jesus and hunger, poverty and justice.

I ask Father Empestan if he grew up in the countryside and if as a priest he has worked there much.

I was born on the island of Panay, in Iloilo. My family is a rural family. We live in a barrio. The land in Iloilo is distributed relatively equally, so that at least everybody there has enough to live. My father used to plow our land with his *carabao*. We had about 5 hectares of land, but parts of it were hilly and covered with plenty of coconut trees. We planted our own vegetables. That is why when I came here after high school and entered the seminary, it was a big shock for me. I saw big houses, mansions. I saw big cars, Mercedes Benzes. There are also squatters and poor people in Iloilo, but not like here, where there are such big lifestyle differences.

In 1974, I got my first rural parish, in Pulupandan, about thirty kilometers from Bacolod. It is only about ten square kilometers, but it was thickly populated, and on three-quarters of it were several haciendas. I counted the landowners in the area, and I could name only about six big landowners. In fact, they had even branched out from one family, Spanish colonizers. In the *poblacion* itself, I counted only about sixty families who were not squatters; all the rest were squatting on the land of the Montilla family. As squatters, they had to pay a small cash rent and they were used as political backup during elections. The landlord would say, "Vote or *gabot*." *Gabot* means to uproot. "You vote for my candidate or else I will uproot your house."

The parish then was owned and being maintained by this *hacendero* who used to give me four *cavans* [97 pounds] of rice every month, and I was supposed to be obedient to whatever he wished. But I broke away from that tradition. During the first six months, I used to say mass in the haciendas. I gave sermons about human rights, the rights of the people, about human dignity. At first the owner told me that they could no longer give me rice, giving the excuse that the crop was not good. So I said okay. After six months, they picked me up in their big car and took me to their big house, a traditional Spanish hacienda house. They served me chocolate and all these things. Then the *hacendero* told me, "Father, we have no more car to fetch you; so we cannot have you for mass anymore." I said, "Never mind, I'll just ride a tricycle," which I actually did. But after four or five months, they told me, "Frankly, Father, we do not want you to say mass anymore in our haciendas."

I got really worried. So what I did was I asked some contacts I had in all the haciendas to recruit about five to eight people, workers who I was sure were not connected with the hacienda administration or the government, and who were willing to work with their people. I asked them to come to the church that is in one of the barrios independent of the haciendas, where every night, or at least three times a week, I held a seminar, which started at seven o'clock in the evening up to four o'clock in the morning. We talked about human dignity, Philippine history, the church's teachings on social justice. At four o'clock in the morning they go out silently to their haciendas. They recruit others to be sent to these seminars in the parish. I think in six months I was able to hold these seminars affecting almost all of the haciendas.

What went on in one of these secret "seminars"?

We always started from the Bible. It is inherent in the Filipino people to be very religious. We started with the creation story—God created all things for all people—from which we reflected on human dignity. Our reflections on the Exodus experience had a big impact on the people. They saw that God was with his people when they fled from slavery in Egypt and went to Canaan. They said, "Ah, land reform is right there in the Bible! That's good news!" I referred to the land reform in Canaan and showed them that it could also be done at present. Then we took up Philippine history together with a social and

Boysie Imperial

Father Romeo Empestan

structural analysis. Then we talked about the mission of the church. What should the church be doing now? It should be organizing the poor. So we talk about the BCCs and whether we should put a BCC in their area and how they would do it among themselves.

We had a core group of activist members of the BCCs who studied all about the socio-economic-political situation. We had to have a careful investigation before we let anyone into the core group, to make sure that they were not an informant for the landowners or the military.

Were you harassed by the landowners?

Because initially the BCC work was so secret, harassment by landowners and the military and the police didn't come until much later—after my third year. It was then that the mayor was surprised when we had a big celebration of the BCC Day. The mayor was surprised that thousands of people were flocking to the church. There were some harassments. They threw stones at the church and the convent.

Who?

The landowners had plenty of hired people. I'm sure they were carrying short guns. When I was not there, they harassed and terrorized six or so lay helpers there. "Where is the priest?" they asked. But when I was there, they wouldn't do anything.

Another time, I was driving a Volkswagen "Bug" with some catechists. We went inside one of their haciendas, their territory. I was on a sick call. Then this pickup suddenly overtook me and the landowner got out, approached me, and said with his eyes burning,

"Father, I want to talk with you!"
"Okay, let's talk," I said.
"Don't you know that I'm prohibiting you to come inside my hacienda?"
"I did not know that."
"You are teaching my people to fight against me. You are teaching them to be communists!"

"You might be misinformed. I tell them about their rights as Filipinos and as children of God."

"I do not want to see you here anymore. Next time I see you, something will happen to you!"

"Anytime my people will need me, I will enter any part of your hacienda, because it is my obligation!"

He softened. Then he embraced me!

He embraced you?

Yes. He said, "Father, I want to be friends with you. I have many friends who are priests. You go up to my house and let's have a drink." I said, "Maybe sometime."

Did you ever take up his invitation?

No.

Did you go back into the hacienda again?

Yes. But no more mass. I still go inside there.

The repression and the economic and political control were direct in Pulupandan. Once the landowners tell you to stop doing your bible services and you don't, they will cut your ration of rice and they won't give you your monthly salary. The barrio captain, who was usually part of the hacienda administration, will make accusations to the police that you are subversive. The military had my name on a list of subversives and they circulated the list, but they did not pick me up.

Were the workers at that time in Pulupandan being organized by the NFSW?

That came later. The church was ahead in organizing in Pulupandan. I organized the hacienda workers, the dock workers, the mothers, the youth, the fishermen, and some professionals. During those times, the NFSW had very limited personnel. Later on, in 1977, the organizers of NFSW arrived. I turned over the leaders that I had helped develop to them. They were weaned from the church, but they were still members of the BCC.

I stayed in Pulupandan up to 1978. Then I was reassigned to Kabankalan in the far south. If you have heard of the highly militarized area in the south, that's Kabankalan.

I was one of the first three Filipino priests who were integrated with the Columban Fathers. I continued with our BCC program, but in a different setting. Much of the area was mountainous and could not be reached by car; you had to walk ten to twenty kilometers. All the plain, good land—about a third of the area—belongs to the big haciendas. The rest is farmed by what we call "settlers." Settlers are people who have cleared government land. They receive a piece of paper that says they have permission to stay on that land, but they never get a title. They farm there, but with little security.

Many of these settlers joined BCCs. It was very easy to organize settlers because they did not have an *amo*, a direct master or landlord who controls them.

These poor settlers feel the situation of injustice very concretely. First of all, most of them had the experience of being ejected from the plains in other areas of Negros in the 1950s, when big landowners and capitalists were land grabbing. They were forced to vacate.

I was there from 1978 to 1982. That was the time of the height of militarization in the south.

What does militarization mean?

During those years, a batallion of military men, called the Long Range Patrol, was assigned to the place. The landowners, led by the mayor who was also a landlord, made a petition to the provincial commander to send troops there, because the people were already protesting and because there were organized areas influenced by the NPA. Sympathy for the NPA was growing. If you ask people what they think of the NPA, they don't react negatively. They say that what they do is good, that they are protecting the poor. Better than the police! If you lose your *carabao* and go to the NPA, they will get it back to you the next day. But if you ask the police, he will get it and keep it.

So the military came into the Kabankalan area. They took over the local police. They patrolled the hinterlands and the mountains. They picked up anybody they suspected of being NPAs or NPA sympathizers. Some of those salvaged were only sympathizers.

One learns quickly in the Philippines that "salvage" is the brutally ironic military jargon for summary execution.

Among their first victims were two that I could never forget. They were our leaders in the BCC in Kabankalan. In 1980, we had a Holy Week celebration in one of the big barrios. We were four priests in the parish in town. I thought there were many people in the mountains who cannot benefit from the Holy

Week celebrations because they were too far. So we went there and had our celebrations. Two officers of the BCC participated in the passion play where the scene at Calvary was depicted. These two played the roles of Jesus and the apostle. Right after Holy Week, they were picked up by the military. We went looking for them all around the place; we checked all the headquarters and the provincial commanders. They all denied knowing anything, but we had witnesses who saw them picked up by uniformed men who were riding in a weapons carrier. The NPAs don't have weapons carriers, so it must be the military. After one month, while some people were plowing their fields, they discovered a hole, where they found their hogtied bodies. They had been buried alive.

But why did the military murder them? Certainly not for being in a passion play.

They were leaders of the BCC. I suppose that what threatened the powers-that-be was that, when a Basic Christian Community is organized in an area, people begin to stand up and speak out.

The big problem of Negros is the passivity of the people. The people here are used to being dictated to by the *hacenderos*. This is very sad. This is the fruit of colonization and the result of the problem of landlessness. People have been deprived of their right to decide because they are poor. For an *amo* to be answered back by his worker is a blasphemy. But this is what happens when the workers are being organized. Usually, the *hacenderos* would comment, "Now, you know how to answer us back, huh!" Then they would blame the priest because they say it's the priest or the church that taught them how to answer back.

To me, the military is just a blind instrument of the *hacenderos*. They have been brainwashed that these people in the BCCs are being used as fronts by the NPA and the Communists; so better eliminate them.

Whatever the repression, the BCCs grew rapidly. Father Empestan says that by 1986, there were more than 1,000 BCCs in about 700 different areas in the diocese, which has only 78 parishes. His work is to help establish and nurture these communities. I ask if the bishop has been supportive.

We saw Monsignor Fortich growing, thanks to the people. What helped him was also the issue in the south. We had here a Church-Military Liaison Committee that was created by Marcos. Any complaint against the military was brought to this CMLC, which was composed of the bishop and the provincial military commander, among others. They would go to the areas where there were charges of injustice. For our part, we mobilized thousands of people to be present there, including the victims. The victims families spoke in front of the bishop and the military, with thousands of people at the back. It was a hearing—like a people's court. People would ask, Commander, I want to ask you what happened to my husband who was picked up, etc. These concrete experiences had an impact on the bishop.

We also rearranged his pastoral visits. Before, his visits were very traditional: he goes somewhere only to confirm people and give a sermon. We went to the barrio and arranged so that before he spoke the people engaged in a dialogue with him: Monsignor, these are our problems here, we lack roads, we are hungry, our barrio captain is this and that. After that, we started the mass. So the bishop had to respond to their problems. It really changed him. His former colleagues were big *hacenderos* who would bring him wine and good food. He comes from the landowner class, but because of his exposure, little by little, he understood the people.

Are you and other BCC activists labeled communists?

The landowners use everything to discredit people who are pushing for land reform. They call us communist, subversives. They organized the anti-communist crusade, all these things. Some are even working hand in hand with the military. For example, here in Bacolod, you now have this new BAC-UP. It's said to be an association of homeowners in the big housing subdivisions, and that they work with the military and the police, and that it's antidrug and for peace and order. Actually, it's a monitoring system of who they think are the people who are subverting them. This BAC-UP gets good support. I mean, they have a good police car, radios, meaning to say that they have a big source of funding coming from outside. I don't know yet which is the source, but they must be supported from outside. Now if you go to a subdivision—even a priest—they check the car, they get your license; then, when you go out, they return your I.D. They're very strict, if you go inside subdivisions now. But as of now, it's more intimidation than anything.

And now we have this Anti-Communist League. Your General Singlaub, you know, has been here. Briefly, the ACL is a group of women who believe that they are very good Christians and to be a Christian is to be anti-communist. Meaning to say, that communism is evil per se, that you cannot derive anything good from communism, and that anything is justified in stopping communism. So anybody who talks about land reform, who talks about social transformation, who talks about a preferential option for the poor, they are all communist fronts. That really hits the church, because the church's stand here is a preferential option for the poor.

These members of the Anti-Communist League are always having meetings with the colonel now in charge of the military here. They are friends; it is very obvious. And these people go around giving seminars, often accompanied by military men. They gather people and they show the movie "Killing Fields"—they get it from the U.S. Information Service, I think. Then they say, "Do you want that to happen to your country?" That if the NPA come, they are ruthless people and they will kill you for the sake of killing. So the people are scared. They also say that if there is communism, your family will be separated—your wife will be in the home, your son in the army, your husband in the factory. Families here are very close and it is a big threat to them that family relationships will be broken, especially when the old will be separated from them. They worry about who will take care of the old. Beware of the priests, the military tell them. The priests are trying to organize you so that you will become communists and you know communists do not believe in God, they are atheists. That is their main political line: that the communists are atheists, do not believe in God.

They have a big impact on the people who have not come in contact with our church seminars. Many believe those things. But where they are in contact with the church it is a big help because then they are able to differentiate between faith and different ideologies. We tell them that Christianity is faith and it can be planted in any ideology, even communism, and anyway, at least here the communists are not like they are told.

We have recent reports that even in BCC areas, a half hour before people have their own Sunday Bible services, some of these Anti-Communist League people arrive with the military, a sergeant or a lieutenant, and they give a lecture about the communist threat before they worship.

Recently all of these attacks have been intensifying. Some of the Basic Christian Communities have been disrupted.

In fact, aren't some colleagues of yours, priests, in the New People's Army?

Yes. It was a good option for them. For the Philippine church, it was a breakthrough to go out of the system and try something else and work it out. I think of them as pioneers who maybe paved the way for a new Philippines.

Are ordinary people scandalized by priests being in a communist guerrilla army?

In my experience, I could not find any instance in which the common people reacted against these priests. I don't think they were scandalized.

Have you yourself ever considered joining the NPA?

I have thought of that. I have thought that if the military would pick me up, I cannot serve the people through education and through their organizations. It would be better to work underground and continue my work with the people than stay in prison.

The priests who have joined became so hot with the military that they could not work within the normal parameters of the church, and they believed that what the NPA are doing is also partly what the church is doing. We in the church still recognize them as our priests, but they are not now working within the program of the church.

We hear so much of the "communist threat" in the Philippines. Is it a threat?

I would have to say first of all that the communists here are also human beings. They smile, they laugh, they sing. But they have made a commitment that in order to free the Philippines and to develop the Filipino people in general, there has to be a change in social structures. Because of this direction, they have decided to work for the restructuring of our society. In their analysis, they have concluded that the government, the big businessmen, and the foreign interests here will not smilingly give in to the demands of the majority of the people, especially to the absolutely essential demand for land reform. They believe that they have to arm themselves both to protect the people and whatever modest gains the people have made through their organizations, and to create a system that will bring more freedom and progress for the majority of the people.

And what would communism here mean for religious beliefs and practices?

For me, the communists are even good for the church, because the church has been so identified with the colonial religion where initiatives must always come from the top and never from the base. The church has always been so identified with the status quo that it has sometimes been insensitive to the experience of the people below. But communism has served as an eye opener for the church. I think many communists are now living the Bible more in their lives than many priests. When they go underground, they make many sacrifices for the people. So I think it's a lesson to the church that it is not those who only say "Lord, Lord" who can enter the kingdom of heaven, but those who do the will of the Father, those who concretely work for the liberation of the people. I think these people here who have taken the NDF or Communist position are teaching us a lesson of selflessness. It is up to the Filipino people to adapt this kind of ideology to the Philippine situation.

As for any real threat from communism, I'd say that the landowners are just using all this anti-communist propaganda. What the *hacenderos* actually fear is not communism but that they will lose their land. If the NPA tomorrow would say, "No land reform; we will respect all your properties" then I think the *hacenderos* would not sing the same song. They would applaud the NPA. What the *hacenderos*, the landlords, are against is not the "godlessness" of communism but that their land will be subjected to land reform. I don't think it has anything to do with God.

During the time before Vatican II, the landowners made chapels and they gave donations to the church. But when the church tried to speak about the rights of workers, little by little they questioned us, and they were asking for dialogues. So a series of dialogues was held. The content was a talk about the social encyclicals, the right of laborers to organize unions. These are church documents, but when we discussed them, it quickly ended up that we're subverting, that we are subversives. The landowners were defensive and they attacked the church.

It is very clear now that dialogue cannot really change the situation. So we shifted to why not organize the people so that they can talk for themselves, and themselves go to the landowners so that they can have their own bargaining. So then the landowners hated us all the more, because they said we're causing trouble. So now they're trying to propagate counter religious movements. For example, the charismatic movement. A kind of religion that only touches on personal piety not social issues: "Praise the Lord" and such.

Is this charismatic movement imported or it is indigenous?

It is an imported movement. There's a Catholic version, then some are Protestant; but all of them sing the same tune—that these things that are happening, even our hunger, are the will of God; so we have to pray more without touching the social roots.

[The American evangelist] Jimmy Swaggart is very active here, along with others whose names I do not know. They pick up Filipino lay leaders—giving them good maintenance, of course—and they go around recruiting. And last week our catechist told us that there is some kind of foundation, this Jonathan Foundation, Inc., which is recruiting people, because if they get enrolled they will receive money from people who will write to them from abroad. And they say that this is approved by the cardinal and by the diocese, but we know that it is not. Meaning to say, they're using all means to reinforce the kind of vertical religion, which is trying to cover up the main problem in the Philippines and in Negros. Vertical religion is myself and God, without touching any social realities. It is very passive, very fatalistic.

During all these years as a priest here and against such obstacles, what motivates you to keep going?

What attracts me personally as a priest, what inspires me, is that once the people understand their rights, their dignity as persons, it makes them very cohesive and very strong in their commitment. I've seen them arrested many times, some leaders up to five times, and once a whole barrio was arrested, all the members of the Christian Community in the jail, one day and one night, all the children, all the wives and the old men. And they left the jail even more convinced of their cause. So it's very inspiring for a priest to see that ordinary people with a little help of their faith can become so committed to the cause of liberating themselves.

Zacharias Nota
Chair, Bikol Coconut Planters Association
Albay province

*Z*acharias Nota is a 50-year-old coconut tenant farmer near Legaspi, the
provincial capital of Albay in the Bikol region. He is chair of the Bikol Coconut
Planters Association, Inc. (BICPAI). He is also active in the Peasant Alliance
of Bikol (KMB) which is the Bikol affiliate of the KMP.

*We meet at the KMB office just outside Legaspi. From there we ride a crowded jeepney
(a jeep converted for passenger transport) to a coconut plantation. Here and there
among the coconut trees, we pass pretty bamboo and straw-thatched houses, each
with a few pigs and chickens roaming around, and with flowering plants on the wooden
window sills. "These are all tenant farmers," Mr. Nota says. He greets men, women,
and children, many of them by name. We stop at one house. The farmer uses a long
bamboo pole with a knife at the end to cut down a few ripe coconuts for us. He splits
each coconut open on a spear fixed into the ground. We sit on wooden stools and
speak to one another through an interpreter.*

Because of poverty I finished only elementary school. My children have done
no better. So when the peasant movement started organizing, I joined.

About 60 percent of the coconut tenant farmers and farm workers in the region
are organized in the KMB. Some areas, such as this one, are almost 100 percent
organized. We have some small landowners—say, with 1 hectare or so—but we
do not have any members who are landlords.

We are working for a reduction of rents for tenants and better wages for workers.
Also, KMB wants to reverse the sharing system. Because the landlord does not
contribute labor to the process, the greater part of the harvests should go to
the tenants.

In Bikol, we are currently working for a 50/50 arrangement and for the tenant
to be able to plant food crops between the trees. There are some cases where

we have gotten landlords to agree to 40/60, winning 10 percent more for the tenants. In a few advanced cases, there are now arrangements where only one-third goes to the landlord and the bigger part to the tenant.

Why does the KMB not go all the way and advocate no rent?

Actually, in its long-term program, the KMB wants free land distribution. But in the meantime, we are working for the minimum program of rent reduction.

Another of KMB's goals is genuine land reform. This, of course, is a nationwide demand. But in coconut areas it has special meaning. When Marcos launched his program of land reform on September 21, 1972, that land reform was for rice and corn lands only. There was discrimination against tenants in non-rice and non-corn areas.

Genuine land reform should cover all agricultural lands. The Number 1 target should be land owned by absentee landlords. Smaller lands being tilled by the owners themselves will not be distributed.

Renato Tilanas
Coordinator, Small Farmers Association of Negros
Barangay Batuan, Negros

*R*enato Tilanas is the program coordinator of the Small Farmers Association of *Negros (SFAN). A small rice farmer himself, he appears to be in his early 30s, and lives an hour south of Bacolod. His is a typical peasant house—floor of bamboo lattice, walls of bamboo matting, and the roof thatched with the fronds of the nipa palm. The house has pretty planted flowers here and there. Some neighbors, also members of SFAN, come to listen to us talk—through an interpreter. The surrounding rice fields glisten in the hot sun.*

I was born here in Negros Occidental, right in this area. My father was also a rice farmer, and I grew up as a farmer.

We pay rent to the owner who lives in Valladolid. He has 60 hectares. We pay about fifteen *cavans* (1,455 pounds) per crop, per hectare. Even if our crop fails, we have to pay the fifteen *cavans*. It is very difficult. Since this is an irrigated area, we have two crops a year, and so we pay thirty *cavans* per year to the landlord. We pay for all inputs, land preparation, and irrigation costs. In a good harvest we make fifty *cavans*, sometimes less.

I rent one-half hectare, which is part of the land my father rented. We subdivided my father's land among all of us brothers and sisters.

Can you support your family with one-half hectare of land?

No, but I have some sidelines. I am a tricycle driver. We have a backyard garden. And we have some chickens and pigs. My wife manages the garden and the chickens and pigs. And she also takes care of the house and the children.

What are the origins of the SFAN?

In the late 1970s, the government introduced an organization, called the

Samahang Nayon, to help farmers unite to improve our livelihoods. In the SN, we were required to pay ten pesos annual dues, five pesos membership fee, plus one *cavan* per crop, per hectare. That was the Barrio Guaranty Fund, in case of crop failure. But when we actually experienced a crop failure, we received no assistance. We figured out that the total SN monies, from the BGF membership fees and the annual dues, was 98.4 million pesos, which the *Samahang Nayon* had deposited in banks. For example, in Negros Occidental, they established the CORBAN [Cooperative Rural Bank]. Then the farmers had to borrow the money back from the CORBAN. And the interest was first 16 percent and then up to 36 percent on the farmers' own money that was deposited in the CORBAN.

That was our sad experience of what we got out of the government program of the past regime. So we started organizing the farm people. We used to say, "Why not have an organization that will serve us?" And most farmers said, "We like that idea."

We started an organization to help with the farmers' perennial problems. For example, during the dry season, the irrigation system could not supply water to all the fields. The SN would not help us regulate the use of the water. Our organization did.

We had been demanding higher prices for our products and lower prices for our farm inputs. Nothing happened. That is another reason we started our organization. We first organized the SFAN in this area—that was 1979. Four farmers got together to organize the farmers in this area. I was one of the four. Then we went to nearby places to organize more farmers who saw the contradiction of *Samahang Nayon*.

In this area now I think we have some 80 to 85 percent of the farmers involved in the organization. We are now province-wide and we have twenty-three thousand-plus members out of forty-three thousand small farmers. The majority of our members rent their land; some own the land. You can have 2 hectares maximum, either rented or owned, and be a small farmer. If you own more than 2 hectares, we call you a rich farmer. We have some rich farmers who are members but, according to our constitution, they cannot be officers.

When we established our organization, it was supported by church people. In our area, the Catholic Church has Basic Christian Communities. We first organized the Basic Christian Community farmers. Most of our members are church members also.

Joseph Collins

Renato Tilanas

And what are the farmers' most common problems?

Land monopoly. In this area and others there are landlords who have land-grabbed the small farmers. High land rents, high irrigation fees, low price of produce and high price of farm inputs, usury—with moneylenders charging up to 200 percent, militarization, and no government program for small farmers. Those are the general problems of the small farmers. And in each area there are particular details.

What can SFAN do to help a farmer who has the problem of high rent?

We have some experience in this. We negotiate with the landowners that the maximum the farmers will pay is fifteen *cavans* per hectare. We get the farmers to talk to the landowners and make an arrangement to lower the land rent.

What if I'm a landlord and I refuse? Will you threaten me in some way?

No, we will just let you understand the situation of the farmers—their expenses, their yields, the prices they get, etc.

What if I still refuse to lower the rent?

Most of the landlords are convinced. They offer us their suggestion of a lower rent.

Because they feel guilty? Or they feel that you are nice people? Or they feel scared?

No, no, actually we try to talk to them honestly. Honest to goodness, we just show them the situation of the farmers—their income, what remains to the farmers after his harvest, and so forth. What the farmers find is that it is all the more effective if you stand as a group rather than as individuals. That's where the Small Farmers Association of Negros plays a role that the SN never did or would.

Here's an example of how we work. Let's say we have one landlord and sixty farmers. First, the organization unites the sixty farmers. Secondly, we help them plan the method and process to negotiate with the landlord. Thirdly, we establish the negotiating panel selected by the sixty farmers. Fourth, they negotiate with the landlord and we counsel them.

How can SFAN help with the problem of usury?

Let me share with you some actual experience with a usury case. The usurer lent 100 pesos to the farmers. After two to three months in cropping, the farmers must pay three *cavans* of *palay*. So, when the price of one *cavan* is 100 pesos, it is 300 pesos for 100 pesos borrowed—200 to 300 percent interest in just one season. This is typical. Our organization collected data on that usury, and we introduced the data to our legal aid department. The legal maximum interest is 12 to 15 percent only. We united our members involved in that usury and then we fought the usurer with our lawyers. Yes, we took the usurer to court and we won.

Does the Small Farmers Association work only to lower rents or does it also agitate for land reform?

Actually, the main goal of the Association is to achieve land reform. But it must be genuine land reform, because during the Marcos regime there was a land reform—in fact, many tenant farmers in this area were in the program— but the amortization and SN costs were so great it was not profitable to the farmers.

What is the genuine land reform you are demanding from the Aquino government?

Genuine land reform is the giving of land free to all who would work the land without any amortization. If there must be such amortization, it should be much lower than that declared by Marcos.

Mr. Tilanas informs me that there is also a human rights committee within the SFAN.

Because, you know, we, the farmers and the farm workers, are the ones most affected by the atrocities committed by the military and the goons. That's why the Association monitors the abuses of the military and the abuses of the landlords. Just last September, the military salvaged a member in Reposo.

As I told you, we small farmers have quite a problem with being land-grabbed. Right here, the landowners tried to get back their land from the farmers by using the military. But we sent in members of the Association so the landowners could not get onto the farms. Yes, they were locked out. We made a barricade. We succeeded, and we have succeeded in some other areas here in Negros Occidental.

Four:
WORKING AGAINST CHANGE

Cardinal Sin, Manila's archbishop, pronounced the June 1988 land reform law "another miracle." Far from miraculous, this law, land reform in name only, is the predictable product of the elite democracy that has been restored to the Philippines since the ouster of Ferdinand Marcos. Adept in the trappings of formal democracy, the landed elites have succeeded—for the time being, at least—in frustrating the aspirations of the majority of Filipinos. Tracking the blocking of these aspirations reveals much about the state of democracy in the Philippines.

In June 1986, four months after the overthrow of Marcos, the KMP, the National Peasant Movement, presented the government with a "Program for Genuine Land Reform," which emphasized free redistribution of land and the abolishment of absentee landlordism. Minister of Agrarian Reform Heherson Alvarez initially pronounced the KMP program "reasonable," but the matter went no further.

During this crucial period, the American Embassy showed no enthusiasm for agrarian reform, recommending instead job-creation programs in the country-side and siding with those like Defense Minister Juan Ponce Enrile (Marcos's Defense Minister and co-architect of martial law), who complained that the military was not being given free rein to wage all-out war on the NPA.

Corazon Cojuangco Aquino, once in the presidency, backed away from her campaign commitment to land reform, arguing that it was more urgent to set up the constitutional framework for the "new democracy." On occasion, she let slip deep misgivings about land reform. "By sharing out land, you only create more problems," she said barely two weeks into her presidency, "because sugar cultivation, for instance, is definitely uneconomic if carried out in small plots." This argument, so dear to the hearts of export-crop producers, has been debunked in numerous studies by respected Filipino agricultural economists. Perhaps Aquino also has been proven susceptible to pressure from her family (her brother Jose is the leader of the antiland reform bloc in the Senate) and from the elite landlord circles in which her family moves. She also has had to contend with a military who tend to view land reform as "communist."

Aquino hand-picked the Constitutional Commission, thereby rejecting calls for a popularly elected body. The commission drafted a Constitution that stated that "the State shall encourage and undertake the just distribution of all agricultural lands." But it failed to include specific land reform provisions—which would have been approved in the plebiscite on the overall Constitution—given the sheer weight of Aquino's popularity at that time.

Not only was this momentous opportunity for land reform passed up, but Aquino's commission dismissed qualifications for any future reform legislation that, among other things, would invite endless court wrangles by anti-reform landowners. Particularly crucial, the Constitution enshrined the right of land-owners to "just compensation," which most commissioners said meant market value for their land. This would raise the cost of land reform so high that the government would have no hope of financing it, and therefore could never undertake it. Peasant organizations and other reform advocates argue that market-value compensation is not only too costly but deeply unfair since tenants have already paid many times over for the land through the exorbitant rents paid to landlords. More fundamentally, genuine agrarian reform seeks to redress social inequities, especially inequalities in the control over wealth and therefore power; fully compensating elite owners would do nothing to redis-tribute wealth.

Disappointed with the Constitution, some reform advocates began pressuring President Aquino to launch an agrarian reform by exercising her extraordinary lawmaking powers during the six months before a Congress would be elected and then convened on July 27, 1987. Most advocates and opponents of reform agreed that, as with every elected legislature in the nation's history, the new Congress would be dominated by landowners and therefore land reform would be precluded. Indeed, no parliament in Asia has ever carried out a successful land reform. Every successful land reform in Asia—in Japan, North Korea, South Korea, Taiwan—has involved coercive expropriation of landlord properties.

The minister of agrarian reform and the president repeatedly rejected the KMP's requests to meet with them during the second half of 1986 and into 1987. For months, Aquino was silent on the issue. She did not even seek to enforce the existing minimum wage in agriculture. Nor did she decree lower rents. Many landlord practices that violate longstanding laws are not enforced in a country where judges invariably are beholden to landlords.

There was also no presidential action on the first demand of reform advocates: that the government distribute to landless peasants those lands confiscated from Marcos and his cronies (especially those they had stolen from peasants), as well as abandoned farms and the considerable amounts of land foreclosed or eligible for foreclosure by government banks. In the closing months of 1986, the KMP launched a campaign to occupy such "sequestered" and often idle lands. More than 50,000 hectares (125,000 acres) were seized by land-poor families and almost half of those hectares planted with rice and other food crops. At least eight peasants were killed in clashes with law enforcement officers.

The Ministry of Agrarian Reform held its first public consultation in Septem-ber 1986. The venue was an air-conditioned meeting room in a government

Task Force Detainees

The body of Amado Cayao, National Federation of Sugar Workers chapter president in Silay, Negros, murdered on July 4, 1987 by eight masked men. Under President Corazon Aquino, the NFSW has experienced an alarming increase in repression by the military and landowner-financed "vigilantes." By her third year in office, 34 union members were killed and some 2,000 more illegally detained and interrogated.

building in Manila's trendy Makati district. All the padded chairs around a horseshoe-shaped table were occupied by about fifty landowners, all men in country-club attire. Standing at the back of the room were about forty men and a few women, caps in hand, looking like they had come straight from rice paddies. Among them I recognized two farmer-organizers of the KMP and spotted the logo for another farmer organization on a T-shirt.

Copies of the Ministry's draft report on the status of land reform were handed out for discussion. Flipping through one, I was struck that it was entirely in English. Landowner after landowner took the microphone, each lambasting in English the pro-reform implications of the report. After about forty minutes, a weather-beaten farmer came up to a microphone and in Tagalog said that if the discussion were in Tagalog then the farmers would be able to participate. The department deputy responded saying that "of course" anyone should feel encouraged to intervene in the "national language." The farmer then spoke briefly. A landowner retorted initially in Tagalog but then slipped back into English, charging that "President Marcos took our money and now President Aquino wants to take our land." Then electrical power failed. Without the air conditioning, the windowless room quickly became insufferable. The consultation was indefinitely adjourned.

Frustration mounted among those working for reform. From January 15 to 22, 1987, hundreds of KMP-affiliated peasants camped for a week in front of the Ministry of Agrarian Reform, but the minister refused to meet with them. On the final day, over five thousand peasants marched on Malacañang Palace. On the Mendiola Bridge leading to the palace, police and marines fired repeatedly into the crowd, killing as many as nineteen unarmed demonstrators and wounding many others. No warning was given or nonlethal devices such as water cannons used, as so often happened during the Marcos years.

Only in the wake of the massacre did President Aquino sit down with the KMP and some smaller farmer organizations. She established an Inter-Agency Task Force on Agrarian Reform to draft a presidential decree to be signed before Congress convened. The committee's first drafts drew heavily on the work done by the few pro-reform officials in the government's agrarian reform agency. As decrees, they would have affected all agricultural lands, including coconut and sugar plantations, the traditional heart of power in the Philippines.

During this critical period, the government's "big talk" about land reform galvanized opposition by landowners. They inundated newspapers with articles and full-page advertisements, arguing that land reform would be disastrous for the economy. Some vowed to resist with private armies. Most significantly, landowners rallied to go all-out to capture the new Congress. At least 90 percent of the members of the new House of Representatives are landowners, many at the upper end of the social ladder.

In late May, dozens of farmer and other "pro-people" organizations united around a common program of agrarian reform, based on the principle of owner cultivation. By joining this broad coalition, the militant KMP compromised on several longstanding demands in the faint hope that a modest but meaningful reform might yet be saved. The KMP leadership agreed, for example, that landowners should receive compensation on a sliding scale, with the higher payments per hectare going to the smaller landlords, many of whom are not wealthy.

Aquino's task force went through no fewer than fourteen drafts, each more watered down than the one previous. Obviously, irate landowners, including members of the president's own family, were being heard at the palace. With less than a week before her decree-making power elapsed, Aquino issued the "Comprehensive Agrarian Reform Program (CARP)." On the one hand, CARP declared that land reform should happen. On the other hand, it doomed real land reform by leaving the when, where, and how up to the Congress.

Congress convened in late July 1987. In the House of Representatives, the common program of the farmer organizations became the basis of a Comprehensive Agrarian Reform Bill sponsored by the handful of reform-minded representatives. After initially launching a pro-landlord bill, the anti-reform majority in the House cunningly switched tactics: over a period of months, they attached an incredible array of limitations, exemptions, and loopholes to the reformers' bill, while keeping its original title and number. Just before the bill passed, its exhausted original sponsors all withdrew their names in disgust and despair.

Rep. Hortensia Starke
Planter and member of Congress
Negros

Negros planters typically keep at least three homes: one on the hacienda (where they are least likely to be found), another in the suburbs of Bacolod, and a third in a fashionable district of Metro Manila. Not a few also have another home in the United States. Mrs. Hortensia Starke is typical. Mrs. Starke is more than a planter. She is known for airing her views on the issues of the day on her radio program. She is also running for Congress. Her house in the Capitolville subdivision of Bacolod is an attractive, split level complete with a tropical Japanese garden. It is February 1987.

I'm married to Mr. Raymundo Starke. That is how I got my American name. My business is sugar. I have also a rubber plantation in Mindanao and some extra hectares which I've acquired, but they're just a reserve for something later on. And I have diversified into rice, and now we have started a nursery for ramie and are looking to develop a prawn pond. I want to go into prawn culture, because it's supposed to bring very good returns, the highest returns in aquaculture that you could possibly imagine. Prawn culture is the latest investment craze in Negros.

My sugar plantation is in Kabankalan. It is a big, beautiful plantation. On one side it has a hill and on the other side a river. So it's sometimes called "God's Little Acre."

I am a Lopez. The Lopez family has always believed that you must always hold on to your land. It is good to buy land as an investment, but it is not good to sell land. My mother followed that philosophy. So when she died she had quite a bit of land and we divided it among six heirs.

I will tell you the story of the Lopez family. It's very interesting. Negros was once just a jungle. All of this was jungle, jungle, and nothing but jungle. It was inhabited just by the little Negritos. This was during the Spanish era—let's say the 1850s—when my grandfather heard about the island of Negros as a promising place for sugarcane. So he came over and developed and planted and pioneered. He started with as much as 4,000 hectares. But when he died, he had sold 1,000 and his thirteen heirs inherited the remaining 3,000 hectares. They all went into the sugar business and made money from sugar. I'm a third sugar planter generation already.

What about those Negritos, the people in Negros before your grandfather came on the scene. What ever became of them?

The Negritos were never many. They sold their lands and then they moved backwards into the mountains. And then they moved backwards and more backwards and more backwards. And right now, there are very few left. I think, the Negritos, who were never civilized, maybe they died from childbirth. In the old days, you know, if you have ten kids you would lose four and you would have six left. So maybe the Negritos had five, they would lose three. They would have two left. And eventually, even these two died out. The race just simply died out. You see them once in a while going around. They look so poor and primitive. But the race died out.

Looking at a copy of Mrs. Starke's formidable family tree, I ask her to point out the famous people.

One of them is me!

Others?

Well, this cousin of mine, Eugenio, was what we call a kingmaker. He created a monster. He backed Marcos for president. He was also a super entrepreneur. He took over sugar mills, then he bought Meralco, the Manila Electric Company, and the *Chronicle*, and the Chronicle building, and T.V. and radio, and transportation, and lots of other things. And here is his brother Fernando, the revered politician. He was vice-president of the Republic. They both started with sugar. Eugenio got his basic capital from sugar here in Negros. We're all in sugar. Just like President Cory Aquino.

And, you know, when Marcos took over and declared martial law, they lost their *Chronicle*, they lost their Meralco. But with Aquino they got it back. Marcos is gone. They got it all back now.

Mrs. Starke directs my attention higher up her painted tree.

This is Captain Eugenio Lopez, celebrated as the avid land acquisitor, son of Basilio Lopez. And all these descendants of Basilio and Eugenio made their mark with the alliances of their sons and daughters to other prominent families. There are all big names of the Lopez family tree—Jalandoni, Ledesma, Benedicto, Gamboa, Justiniani, Montinola. These are all sugar families who made a fortune. They all came from Jaro and Iloilo. Their fortune and prestige have been closely related with the sugar industry. All the big names in Negros now are found on our tree. Like Governor Benito Lopez—here he is. His son was Eugenio the kingmaker and super entrepreneur. And here's Dolores Lopez, the cultured lady with thirteen children and thirteen haciendas—a great Filipina. And here's Rosario, the "amazon," the great sugar industrialist. She owned two sugar mills. She was on horseback. She was a great Filipina. She was my aunt.

Discussing the workers on her plantations, Mrs. Starke refers to them as "partners." Is this how she really looks at them?

Well, that is the philosophy, I should say. But how could you be my partner and you do not know anything about the business? So you cannot really be my partner. You're my partner only in a philosophical sense, because without you, I cannot go on and without me, you cannot go on. So we are partners, but not in the sense that you are an investor. You are simply a laborer, an employee, and I'm the employer. To think that the employer-employee relationship is a partnership is only philosophical—it's all theory.

The NFSW has recently been organizing on Mrs. Starke's hacienda in Kabankalan. What does she think of the union?

The problem with the labor unions—and here we are talking about the NFSW—is they are never satisfied. They will ask for some today, and more tomorrow, and more and more and more. For no reasons at all, people are striking. And my people have education and they have housing and they have security. Why, they would have to give up so much just to be a member of the union! To unionize means that they want more money, they want more pay, they want more benefits. There's a limit, you know, to what you can do. To hell with sugar if the workers ask that much! I'll go into prawn culture and I'll only need three men to run my prawn farm. And I'll make ten times more money. So they better be careful, they better watch out. Because, you see, an investor, like anybody else, uses his head. He thinks how much money goes in and how much money can he get out. And if he says there is no security in this investment, then he might just pack off and leave. To hell with that! he'll say.

As a political candidate, what is Mrs. Starke's position on agrarian reform? Does she support the governor's idea of putting 10 percent of hacienda land in default into the hands of the workers?

Boysie Imperial

Hortensia Starke

There's nothing wrong with it. That's not much land. It's not going to kill me or impoverish me. And if it will make some people happy, that's okay. They've been working here for many, many years—give them something extra. Give them a little reward.

But, you know, they cannot choose the land. And some of my hectares are hills. It's not all prime land, you know.

The only thing that I'm in doubt about is whether they'll do anything with the land. You'd really have to work hard to make it profitable. They're not inclined to it. After working all day in the fields, they want to go home and just take it easy. So you have to start them on a new philosophy, a new orientation to work harder—to work like a Japanese, like a Korean, like a Taiwanese. Tell them, they could do this, they could do that. Some people only work twice a week. When they get enough money, they want to go back to the hills and rest. It's very Filipino, you know.

My own people are too spoiled. They only want easy jobs. What's an easy job? Well, dropping the fertilizer. Putting all the trash in the field on one side. Weeding. And being a guard—they just sit there and guard—now, that's easy!

Perhaps my eyes show disbelief that any plantation workers in the Philippines have been spoiled.

Yes, I've spoiled them. And I'm not the only one. All the sugar planters have, you just ask them. That's the way it is. That's the truth. I don't think we sugar planters are exploiting our people. I think we spoil them. Anyway, cutting cane is the hardest work, and I want to eliminate it. We really should mechanize that.

Would most planters be willing to part with 10 percent of their land?

Not all of them. I have surveyed. Maybe half of them, and half of them not. They'll fight it. They said they cannot be mandated—it should just be voluntary. They are resisting. You cannot blame them, because these plantations are probably inherited—lands which have been handed down from generation to generation. It hurts a lot when you know that your parents or grandparents worked very hard to develop it, to acquire it, and to care for it. And then suddenly, somebody says, "You have to give it up now."

You have a land reform, and you will be surrounded by beggars. They will just simply come to you, looking for work. They'd have the land, but they wouldn't know what to do with it. It had better be accompanied by a complete package of technology, management, financing, marketing, infrastructure, and housing for new settlements. Because if it is not accompanied by all that, these people will end up just looking up in the air—jobless people and still knocking at your door asking for your help, "Ma'am I used to work for you, why can't you give me work now?"

I, on the other hand, am working very hard, using technology we learn from school and the IRRI [International Rice Research Institute]. We're using a lot of irrigation equipment. If my land goes to the workers, they will get only half the yields I get, because they don't have the tools, they don't have the fertilizers. You see, the government expects you to assist and manage them and to provide them with the technical know-how and wherewithal. This is very unfair. First of all, to rob you of half of your plantation and then to oblige you to teach them how to run it because they don't know how to run it. Otherwise, they will come back to you and beg again for loans, you see. And you have to teach them everything. I mean you have to start all over again, sixty-five times—sixty-five families we're talking. Do you want me to carry on a class sixty-five times? I wouldn't have the time nor the inclination anymore to provide a school for rice farming. Think of it! To expect me to teach them—I'm not a rice teacher. I can teach you singing and piano because I'm a musician, but I cannot teach you rice farming because I didn't even take it up myself. It was my son who took rice farming up in IRRI, you see.

The reform we need is not land reform but for the government to help us landowners and then we will help our people.

Mrs. Starke admits to me that she, like the vast majority of the planters, is way in arrears in paying off her loans from the government banks.

I think it is foolish to pay our loans until we really sit down and get a new policy in which the bank, which is the Philippine National Bank, a government institution, and the Republic Planters Bank, another government bank, will realize that banking per se, for the sake of banking, is no good, that banks have to help the people, that's why they are banking. They should change their orientation. They're banking for the people, not to help themselves as bankers. So I have a position paper that says that the bank must not try to make money from the people. It must only help. That's what they're here for. Once they see that, maybe we will really be on the road to recovery.

If she isn't making payments to the bank, how can she keep on operating her sugarcane plantation?

Oh my God! I'll tell you. We pole-vault. Before, we were against pole-vaulting, because it is dishonest. You know, you have a contract with a particular mill and you're supposed to mill there, because that's your agreement with the bank. You have a chattel mortgage, which means if it's in your name, you've mortgaged your farm. The chattel, which is your sugar, will be sold, and the bank will retain all the proceeds. So I told my son, let's not pay. Now, they're talking of land reform! Let's pole-vault everything, like everyone else. So we're now pole-vaulting, milling it somewhere else and in my son's name so the bank cannot keep any of the money. But I am getting all the money. And I'm saving this money to invest in prawn farms.

The planter here is a victim of Marcos who stole billions from us through setting up a government monopoly in sugar sales. And he is a victim of the banking policies. Third, he is victimized by the poverty of the people who have no jobs and nowhere else to go except to plow a bit of land and plant some corn so they can survive. So, this is what is happening now: we sugar planters are victims of Marcos, the banks, and the poor.

How is it that Mrs. Starke could teach singing and piano? Does she also have a career as a musician?

Yes, but that was a long time ago while I was in school. I went to Georgia, I went to Julliard and to Hunter College in New York City, and I majored in music. I got a certificate as a piano teacher. And I've studied guitar. I was singing many years in New York. Well, that was when I was single. When you get married and you get involved in the family and all that, you have to have priorities. What is your priority? Do you want to be an entertainer? Do you want to be a mother? Who will provide for your family? Do you mean to enlarge your business so as to have security? The Philippines is not like the States. In the States, entertainers make millions. Here we don't.

My mother always told me that you must take care of your farm because you must have security. If there is anything in life to fear, she said, it's being out in the streets. So enjoy the fruits of your capital, but never sell your own capital which is your land. Just enjoy. Make it provide, make it yield as much as possible—which I'm doing. This way I can provide for my children who have lived in the States, who have studied abroad. They're now grown up and married with foreigners. They've gone in different directions. One is in the movies, one is a clinical psychologist in Vienna, and one is well-married and invested in Malaga. The only one left in the Philippines is my son.

❖ ❖ ❖

Three months later, in May 1987, Mrs. Starke is elected to Congress, representing Kabankalan, the district that includes her sugarcane hacienda. In Congress, she is appointed the vice-chair of the Committee on Agrarian Reform.

On January 20, 1988, at eleven o'clock at night, two hundred NPAs entered "God's Little Acre." They burned her house (Mrs. Starke was in Manila), ransacked the office, and carried off forty sacks of rice and seventeen carabaos. The rebels were careful not to damage the workers' homes and returned one of the carabaos when they were told it belonged to one of the workers, Mrs. Starke tells me in a phone interview four days later. An NPA person familiar with the case informs me that Mrs. Starke is considered a "despotic" planter by the NPA for her activities against land reform in Congress, and for firing a number of her workers in Negros and Mindanao involved in labor union efforts.

On March 20, 1988, Congresswoman Starke addresses a convention of 600 planters and calls for the "taking up of arms," if Congress enacts a land reform bill. She is loudly applauded, according to the wire services.

Antonio "Tony" de Leon
Planter
Bacolod City, Negros

The sugar "central" in Bacolod City mills the cane from the surrounding areas. *The planters who mill there belong to the Bacolod-Murcia Sugarcane Planters Association. Antonio "Tony" de Leon is vice-president of the Association. He is also an officer of the National Federation of Sugarcane Planters.*

Wiry and bald, Tony de Leon chain smokes. He sits with his legs crossed, shaking his one leg incessantly as we talk. He appears to be well into his 60s. His Spanish-descent father was the U.S.–appointed governor of Jolo in the southernmost part of the Philippine archipelago. As with many planters, some of his children have moved to the United States.

I have been in this business for twenty-five years now. I came here to Negros with a bank. Then I acquired some land. I plant sugar and rice. I used to have cattle, but there were so many robberies I sold my herd. It's a pretty good business—you got the ups and downs of the sugar industry—but overall a very good business.

How bad is the hunger situation in Negros?

I've not come across hunger here in Negros yet. There is no such thing as hunger here, because you go down to the market, there are many things for sale, foodstuffs especially, vegetables, rice—everything. So I don't think there's much hunger in Negros. Anyway, you can always plant.

How are relations nowadays between planters and workers in Negros?

The planters have changed for the better. There's a new breed of planters now. Because they are more socially oriented, social consciousness has become in. They realized that it is a two-way street, not a one-way street, that labor is also your partner in this business. Without labor, you cannot survive.

What do you think of the demands many are making for land reform?

No, that is not the solution either. It's unworkable, because if we turn over our land we also have to be given the due compensation. It must be a fair market price. They can't simply get your land and tell you they want to pay 1,000 pesos when the government has evaluated your land at pretty high figures. If they just get your land and don't pay you the price that is the fair market value, it would be unfair, undemocratic.

The problem is, the government doesn't have enough money for land reform. The government already owes us more compensation for all that Marcos took from us planters. On top of that, land reform means first you have to buy the land, and then you have to subsidize the new owners with all sorts of programs. That's too much money.

If Aquino wants land reform, what about Hacienda Luisita? Many have talked about that, but not openly. But they are whispering, "Why touch us first when that thing is the biggest single plantation? Give it up. Show the way and we will follow. But don't push us first." Everything should be divided. If you divide ours, divide hers also.

In your view what is the relationship, if any, between the church and the communists?

That is a beautiful question. There are so many leftist leanings in the church, I would say, because of the theology of liberation that began in South America. They want to adopt that here in the Philippines.

Many leading elements in the Catholic Church were in the forefront of the ceasefire movement—calling for a ceasefire and to accept the communists into normal society here in the Philippines. I include Monsignor Fortich—Commander Tony.

I do not know what has made so many Catholic priests lean to communism. I don't understand it because they cannot reconcile the idea of a godless society with the Catholic Church. When communism preaches a godless society, there is no God, and the Catholic priests are taking that line hook, line, and sinker. I don't know. I cannot reconcile that even now. I was brought up in the Catholic school, but I cannot reconcile how they will do it.

Most of the planters are God-fearing Christians. But for some time now, we are feeling alienated from the bishop and most of the priests. In fact, many of the planters now are joining other religious denominations like the Baptists. And you will notice that very active nowadays here in the Philippines are these American missionaries from Utah, the Mormons, they are very active here.

They are building churches all over the place. Some planters are becoming Mormons.

Bishop Fortich should have retired already. He is overstaying. He can contemplate and meditate up there in the mountains. Maybe the NPA can put up a monastery for him up there. There are four or five priests up there already.

You know, the church has not made a very definite stand on land reform. But they have been agitating for landholdings for the poor, according to the sermon that we have been hearing lately. That everybody must have their just due and to enjoy the fruits of the earth. But not everybody wants to become a farmer. So how will you reconcile that statement—that everybody wants to have a piece of land to farm—but not everybody wants to become a farmer? Like my kids, only one or two want to become a farmer like me. The rest have their own career or profession. They do not want to be farmers. So how you can reconcile human choice with land reform?

Another thing is that those that agitate for land reform forget that Christ told us that there will always be poor people. You cannot eliminate the poor and make everybody rich. That is an impossible dream. Christ did not say that all of us will be rich. The poor will always be with us. That means that we cannot eliminate poverty from society. We always have the rich and poor, the haves and the have-nots. Even among nations, there are small nations, big nations, rich nations, poor nations. Even with people, there are tall, short, stout, thin. There are Negros and there are Whites, brown people and Japanese people. We cannot all be equal.

But Christ also said that it would be easier for a camel to pass through the eye of a needle than for a rich man to enter the kingdom of heaven.

Well, I don't think there are so many rich people in Negros now. There are still many richer people in the city, especially in Manila. You do not see flashy cars anymore in Negros. A lot of the wealth made in the Philippines has been made here, but it has been taken out and diverted, some of it is even abroad.

❖ ❖ ❖

In January 1988, Tony de Leon and Enrique Rojas, president of Bacolod-Murcia Sugarcane Planters Association, tell me that the situation is much "cooler" now than when I visited them the year before. The NPA is less of a problem. Is this because the military is being more "professional," no longer indulging in random salvagings? Tony de Leon corrects me: "But you need salvagings."

The next day, according to a newspaper account, the NPA raids Mr. Rojas's hacienda in Murcia and executes three Alsa Masa members working in his security force.

Tadeo Villarosa
Spokesperson, National Federation of Sugarcane Planters
Bacolod, Negros

adeo Villarosa is the 35-year-old son of Joaquin Villarosa. I have been directed to him through Romeo Guanzon, president of the politically powerful National Federation of Sugarcane Planters. Mr. Villarosa helps formulate the policies and positions of the NFSP, Guanzon tells me, and would be a good spokesperson for the Federation.

My family has always been in agriculture. On my father's side, I am the fourth generation in agriculture. On my mother's side, I am the third generation. So we've been here in Negros for a long time, before the coming of the Americans.

I studied in Manila. I graduated with a B.A. in economics from La Salle University there, and in 1974 I graduated from the Asian Institute of Management with an M.B.A. Ever since I've graduated, I've been here in Negros. I passed through all the years when the Marcos government monopoly on sugar marketing was in place. Now with the Aquino government, we have the start of the free enterprise era in sugar.

We have three plantations—actually they are what you can call family farms; they're incorporated and all the shareholders are the members of the family. And I'm in charge of these three plantations. They've been in the family for four generations.

What has been the impact of the sugar "crisis" on your workers?

You distinguish between us and our workers. That is a mistake. We look at our workers as part of the corporation. When you talk about—let's say, IBM—you don't talk about the stockholders of IBM as a separate entity from the executives and the workers of IBM, do you? We're one, we all belong to one company. It just so happens that I own all the shares and my workers don't own any, but it's one company, no? So when you help the firm you help not only the stockholders, you help also the laborers.

Our company was hard hit by the crisis. We almost lived hand-to-mouth, you know, just rolling over our cash flow to get the work going on the farms. And that, of course, affects our workers, because how can we pay them and how can we give them any labor benefits when we don't even have enough to pay the interest on our bank loans?

The National Federation of Sugarcane Planters is on record as opposed to land reform. Would you comment on the Federation's position?

We are more concerned about upgrading the living standard of our workers than with giving them our land. How the planters would upgrade the living standard of their workers should be left up to the planters. The Federation feels that the Sugar Industry Foundation is the vehicle to deliver livelihood projects to farm workers and also to teach them, because, you know, you have to make the workers more responsible with such projects.

For instance, a planter could establish a garment factory that would employ his farm laborers for the delivery portion of the operation. So you can come up with factories where a piece of the work you can contract out to your farm laborers. Another project would be pig raising in a backyard thing the worker builds—a pig pen. A worker in this way could easily make 200 to 400 pesos margin on a pig in three months. Setting up a cattle operation, you can get the workers into the fattening thing.

So we are not looking to land-based ways of helping our laborers. If Aquino wants land reform, let her start with her own immense sugar farm, it's far bigger than anything any of us have here.

You got to keep in mind that the propaganda of the insurgency here in the Philippines is land reform. And that they would give 100 percent of the plantations to the workers and with zero compensation to us planters. You take the land because it's yours—that is their propaganda. This estranges us from our laborers, our people.

Now, if you start playing around with any notion of land reform, then I think you are lost and you are as good as dead. Land reform is what the enemy promises, and if you start talking about land reform you play into the enemy's hands. But if you can prove to the workers that you can uplift their living standards by engaging in activities which are not based on distributing any land but through supplementing their main form of livelihood, which is working for you on your farm, then there is hope.

How do you feel personally about land reform?

I am opposed to land reform. Why? Simply that this is my property, and I want to give it to my children. I should not be forced to give it to anybody else, other than to those I want to give it to.

Later, Mr. Villarosa contradicts this.

Personally, I am not against land reform. As long as there is full market value compensation. In fact, personally, I feel that within the next five years I should be moving my investment in farm lands into other things and other places.

Have you had any problems with the NPA on your farms?

When there is an armed presence on your farm, you do either of two things: either you fight them or you pay them and give up.

On one of my farms, I was told that they were going to do a "teach-in." And I told the owner of the house where the teach-in was to be conducted—I gave him my own "teach-in" right there and then—about what dangers will arise when you have communism. I told him, in Ilongo: *"Bahala ka!"* *"Basta,* I have warned you." I have told you that those are the dangers and once an armed incident happens here, I know you'll be the first guy whom I will point to, to be investigated by the military."

I have three people whom I have entrusted to get reports on anything that happens on the farms. These three guys don't know that each of them is reporting to me, and when the stories of the three do not coincide, I right away dismiss them because somebody is making intrigues, you know. I always also get wives to tell me what is going on, because wives get stories that are not otherwise available.

Are these workers or overseers that provide you information?

Well one is an overseer, and aside from him I got two more: one ordinary worker and then an ordinary worker's wife. I talk to them only on a one-to-one basis.

Are they paid extra money for keeping you informed?

No, but you know, these are people that our family has helped in some major ways in the past. Like a child got sick in their family and they asked our help. A loan was given to them for medicine. Now they feel they are in debt to our family, and I choose them because of that.

Boysie Imperial

Tadeo Villarosa

Let's clarify. Are you talking about NPA, underground armed insurgents, or labor union organizers on your plantations?

According to my people who attended the teach-ins, those who conducted them are carrying NFSW I.D. cards. I think what they are doing is that whenever a teach-in is raided by the military, they identify themselves as union organizers; but the topics they are talking about are not in any way related to the formation of a labor union.

And what topics are these?

Well, their main topic is the disparity between the landowners and the workers. They try to find out and analyze why the disparity is occurring. And they are always talking about the control of our land.

According to Mr. Villarosa, the NPA can "take your farm right from under you."

They are very polite. They meet with you and present their analysis and what they suggest you should do because of the prevailing crisis situation, like make some concessions to the workers. They make some suggestions like, Why don't you lend some portions of your vacant land to the workers? Or, Why don't you raise the wages for some types of work? And then they go away. And once you have implemented any of their suggestions then they have gained credibility with the workers. And the next step is they will be approaching you for some support: "Maybe you would like to donate something for the improvement of our movement because as long as you do, people here on your farm will be happy. Not one of your workers will go against you as long as you follow us; there'll be no trouble on your farm." That's the assurance they make. And before you know it, *they* control your farm, and not you as owner of the land, because the workers now respond to them, not to you as owner of the land.

Which is a bigger threat to the planters in Negros—the Catholic Church or the communist insurgency?

You know, yesterday I was in Cebu [important island immediately to the east of Negros], and I heard mass there. What a contrast! Because there, the priest's sermon was in line with his vocation, with what he is an expert at. You go to mass here in Bacolod, especially at the Cathedral, and they are talking about things that are not in their line of calling. I mean they were trained as priests, not as politicians, political analysts, scientists, or whatever. But they are talking like experts on social conditions, land reform, etc. And they are always creating in the people's heads the idea of *Pigado versus Manggaranon*, meaning the poor versus the rich. That's always the line of their sermons.

The problem is that the priests are very credible with the people. But I think that credibility is being lost. Most of the workers on my farm go to Baptist, Iglesia ni Kristo, and Protestant churches. Well, I'm not stopping them, because if the parish priest is teaching them communism, couched in a Catholic lingo, they are better off with a Protestant pastor. At least he is talking about spiritualities. In the Catholic Church, here at least, 40 percent of the priests are allied to the communist movement.

Bonifacio "Boni" Peña
Planter and "war lord"
near Bago City, Negros

In the Philippines, you will hear from time to time about "war lords"—landowners who, like many in prerevolutionary China, maintain their own "private armies." Perhaps the most notorious Philippine war lord of recent time was Armand Gustilo, a hacendero with a private army in northern Negros. He was also the president of the National Federation of Sugarcane Planters, a congressman, and the governor of the province of northern Negros. (The province was carved out of Negros Occidental by Marcos for his friend Gustilo; the Aquino administration rejoined it to Negros Occidental.) Gustilo died in a hospital in Houston, where he had flown for a heart operation, shortly before I arrived in Negros.

Bonifacio "Boni" Peña is described by his cousin Remi Suatengco as a "small war lord now, but he's building his army. He'd like to be the new Gustilo." Peña is not an easy person to meet. People declined to introduce me to him, because when the book comes out they "don't want to be gunned down."

One Sunday morning in September 1987, I travel (along with a German freelance magazine photographer) to the hacienda, some fifteen miles south of Bacolod, where I'm told Peña keeps his principal residence. We talk our way past the armed guards in military fatigues at the gate and they radio ahead that some foreigners are on their way. We drive up to the tall wrought-iron gates of a two-story mansion. There are more guards with machine guns, along with barking German shepherds. A man in his mid-30s, dressed in olive-colored pants and a white T-shirt, and wearing a holster, appears on the porch and gives a signal to let us in. This is the small war lord.

Mr. Peña ushers us into a high-ceiling, mahogany-beamed living room. We sit on an L-shaped couch in the center of the room. On the cushion to Mr. Peña's left is a revolver and a walkie-talkie. Four of his "men," each with an Armalite and an ammunition belt slung around his hips, stand watching.

Mr. Peña turns to me and says, "Shoot!" A somewhat unhappy choice of a word *under the circumstances. How big is your operation? I ask.*

I'm working something like 1,000 plus hectares that have always belonged to the family. And I'm leasing something like 400 to 500 hectares from other persons. So I'm actually cultivating some 1,500 hectares on a total of fourteen farms. But not all are planted in sugar; some are cattle. We're planting something like 700 hectares of sugarcane. I have six, seven hundred workers. I am supporting over four thousand people.

Sugar must be profitable?

Yes, especially now that the price of sugar on the domestic market went up. One thing nice about this government—there's a free market now in everything.

But I owe a lot of money to the banks. So I pole-vault, of course. That way, rather than pay the banks, I can plow back what I get from the mill into the farms and acquire more lands.

Is there a labor union on any of your farms?

None. There's none, zero. My people have never wanted a union. Why would they? When they get sick, they have free medicine. When they die, we bury them. They're happy.

Do you think that the Philippines is moving more and more toward a civil war?

No, no. It's not true. In fact, with this Alsa Masa thing, like south of here now, it's very peaceful. The Left is losing support in the south. Because of the military and their Alsa Masa.

How does the Alsa Masa work?

It started in Negros late last year. It was put up by members of the Armed Forces. They train them. They arm them with these homemade guns. And then they put a detachment of Alsa Masa in a red barrio, one that is infiltrated, controlled by the Communists, by the NPAs. How do we know a barrio is Red? Well, we look at whom they voted for in the elections. If they voted for Left candidates, for *Partido ng Bayan*, then we know. Anyway, if you put up an Alsa Masa in a barrio, two things will happen. Either the communist sympathizers will surrender or they will just leave.

And if they surrender?

Bonifacio Peña

Then they should join the Alsa Masa.

Do most surrender?

I think 90 percent surrender.

And what happens if someone doesn't surrender and doesn't run away?

He is captured and, you know, he's killed, if he has a case against him. But if there's no case, you just monitor him. He will be neutralized, in other words. He just stays there, he can work, but he is neutralized.

Does the Alsa Masa have economic projects for the people?

That's the problem with Alsa Masa. They don't have the financial support. The people here, they don't have the money. We planters support them, but we need to give more. Then Alsa Masa could plant corn, rice, bringing in seeds and fertilizers. Show the people that you don't need the NPA to have economic projects.

What about any of the foreign development agencies? Do they help Alsa Masa?

Yes, some of them do, I think. Governor Lacson is helping the Alsa Masa, and he's getting the assistance of these agencies.

While this Alsa Masa thing is supported by the military, the military gets its support from the civilians who are the big landowners. And right now the NPA are liquidating us, the big landowners who are helping the military. One example is Mr. Gatuslao. He was a very close friend of mine. He was the president of the BIBAN Association, that is, Binabanan Isabela Sugar Planters Association. I'm also in that area; I'm one of the directors there. I was talking with him last week. He was telling me, you know, Boni, you are right all this time. Before I was laughing at you, all your bodyguards and everything, but you are right. And he told me, I doubt that I can last until the end of the year.

I read that Mr. Gatuslao was killed only two days ago. He didn't have bodyguards?

He did, but he was only riding in one car. He should have had a back up car.

How many people are in your security force?

Not many. Twenty or so. But I am expanding.

Why do you have a security force?

I want to protect myself. I want to live to the age of at least 50, 60. I don't want to die early. And my security force secures the farms, so that they won't be infiltrated by leftists, by communists.

What can someone like you do to save Negros, save the nation, from the communists? How can a big planter like yourself take the offensive against communism?

Yeah, that's good. I like that. I'd say we are something like one hundred planters who are willing to do this. We're all the big landowners. Maybe many won't support us physically, but they will support us morally and, of course, they support us with money, through the various associations.

So what do you do?

Well, after the new army commander arrived I asked him what he can do to help us get weapons. He told me to form this PCFC, Philippine Constabulary Forward Command. It's a civilian anti-communist militia. And we formed it. In fact, the trainer is here now, Lieutenant Celino.

He gestures toward a uniformed officer who has just walked into the room. He explains that in addition to his security force on the farms, he's now busy working with Lt. Celino training farm workers to be in the PCFC.

They're still my farm workers. But they carry firearms, like Armalites. They'll get an incentive of maybe 200 pesos a month. But they'll still get paid for their work.

The PCFC, they go out not only on the farms, they go out into other areas. What for? To prevent infiltration, union organizing. Because in our view the union—yes, the NFSW, of course—is a front organization for the communists. It's their legal front. The PCFC is to prevent NFSW organizers from moving about. They do this together with the control team of PC [Philippine Constabulary] and military.

So, say I'm a planter. I think there's someone from the union talking with the workers on my hacienda, holding seminars, etc. Then I should contact the PCFC?

No, you contact the control team, who's usually the army or the PC.

And what will they do for me?

They will go there and try to stop these organizers. Actually, this is not organizing we're stopping; it is brainwashing. They are brainwashing the people. It is a brainwash of class struggle, the fight between the rich and the poor. And usually these people, these organizers, are armed. That's why the people there have to go to the meetings. If the landowner has no security force, they will have to join the meeting or else after the meeting they will just go up to your house and say you are not joining the meeting, you are against us, you have to be eliminated. That's how they form a union.

But the Philippines is said to be a democratic country and, according to the Constitution, doesn't a union have the right to go on to a hacienda and try to organize?

But there's such a thing as private property. That gives me the right to stop them. Definitely. Don't tell me an organizer on my property is legal. Anyway, we're in a war here.

Do you do anything to educate your workers about what you would call the threat of communism?

There's a training for the PCFC. They teach the people how the communists infiltrate, etc. The army has a special team, and the PC also has one, who gives these lectures to the people. The landowners of the barrio will ask for the setting up of a PCFC.

But what about ordinary workers who are not in the PCFC?

Actually, right now there is this religious group that is anti-communist. Philippine Independent something or other—I can't remember the name. They are anti-communist. They go up into the mountains and then they lecture. And they're very effective; they're getting people out of the Catholic Church. Because definitely there are communists in the Catholic Church.

Are you Catholic?

Certainly.

Do you still consider yourself Catholic?

Yes.

Would you join this religious group you just referred to?

Of course not. I do pray every night.

Now this anti-communist religious group you were referring to, do the planters support it?

Yes, from the planters associations.

You're not happy with the Catholic Church?

I am not. I am disappointed.

Why?

Because they're asking our people to fight us. You just go to the ceremonies of the priests here. They will just say that it is a class struggle, a fight between the rich and the poor. Seven or eight years ago, I got so angry with this priest who was talking with my people that I almost hit him. His name was Father Empestan.

We move to the question of land reform.

If there is land reform, we might as well pack up and leave the country. Because definitely, the communists will take over.

But many tell me the opposite: if there is no meaningful land reform, then the communists will take over.

Look. In Bago City, the tenanted lands that Marcos with his land reform gave to the tenants during his time are right now organized by the Left, by the communists. Rice-producing lands. The same in Valladolid. They are organized by the Left, by SFAN. The same in San Enrique. They are organized by SFAN.

Is it fair to say that the Small Farmers Association of Negros is communist?

Yes, you can ask all the policemen here in Bago, San Enrique, Valladolid: Where do these communists come from? Where do they get their mass support? They'll tell you, from the small landowners organized in SFAN. You know if you are a small farmer, you cannot fight. Let's say you own 2 to 5 hectares, you cannot resist the infiltration of the Left, because definitely they will just kill you. They will kill you like a dog. You cannot even buy firearms. You cannot fight. You cannot hire people to protect your properties. It's as simple as that, and these communists, they know that. These small farmers don't want to join this group SFAN, but they don't have any choice. I think you will agree with me.

What about Japan, a rich nation now? They had a thoroughgoing land reform. Millions of small farmers were created.

Okay. Land reform is good, if there is no insurgency problem. You know the communists are asking for land reform since the time of Marcos. Now, if the government will say, we'll give you lands, who will be the heroes? The government of President Aquino? Definitely no. It will be the communists who will be the heroes. And we lose. Instead of the communists taking over three years from now, they take over one year from now.

What should be the relationship between planters and workers?

You know the mentality of the Negrenses is that they want someone to take care of them, some sort of godfather who can take care of their basic needs. Like food, if they don't have any, you can give them some. Maybe not 100 percent, but 30, 50 percent. Or if the husband will get another wife and if the first wife will complain to me, I will tell the husband, now you stop that. And he will stop it. You are their dictator.

Aren't you saying that you think of your workers as children?

Well, you should treat them like part of the family.

But they're children. Not brothers, not sisters. They never really grow up to be independent adults.

That's the way it should be. Right now at this stage it's got to be that way. Or else we will lose this war. Of course, I know what's best for my people. I know because I have lived with them, I have talked with them, I have eaten with them. I know what they want. If I ask them if they want my land, then they will tell me, Why would we want to get your land? To whom are we going to go if one of my children will get sick and I have to spend ten thousand for the hospital? Or from whom do I get money if I need to bury one of my children? To whom do I go if one of the military soldiers will abuse in our area? Which does not happen often—these abuses of the military are very seldom right now.

So these people want protection. And what is happening? It is the enemy who is giving them protection. It's the communists. Like when, say, this guy there in the mountains will complain, My landlord slapped me or whatever. Maybe it's true, because the landlord was a drunkard. Or that he tried to rape one of his daughters there. So what happens? The communists say, Let's go to the landlord and discipline him right here and now. Maybe we will make him apologize to the people. Then we have a chance to show the people that we are the authority in that area, not the landowner, not the military. So this is a psych war, a propaganda and psychological war we're in with these communists.

Edgardo Cordero
Major, Armed Forces of the Philippines
Hinigaran, Negros

With the Marcoses flight into exile, the military changed its name to the "New Armed Forces of the Philippines." The military command on the island of Negros (comprising both western and eastern provinces) was consolidated and officially dubbed "Task Force Sugarland." Given the strength of the insurgency in Negros, Task Force Sugarland is considered an important command. In 1987, its batallion strength was more than seven thousand.

Senior officers in the government's "New Armed Forces" have orders to "cooperate" with journalists. Camp Aguinaldo, the national command center, issues letters of introduction for journalists to the top brass in those regions journalists request to visit. The three times I went, with the appropriate letter from Manila, to Task Force Sugarland headquarters in Hinigaran in southern Negros, the commander, Colonel Coronel, was "out." Finally I decided to interview his assistant, Major Edgardo Cordero. The major rose to the occasion, but every few minutes would lament, "It's too bad the colonel isn't here to respond to you."

According to the major, the threat in Negros is not the armed NPA (he estimates their number at only seven hundred fifty on the entire island) but the mass or popular base, who he thinks are "many, many more."

There is a rapid expansion of their mass base. This is an unarmed group. This is the real blood of the existence of this armed group. It is these very elements that give them protection as far as their needs are concerned. They give intelligence information—for the armed group lacks some communication equipment. The moment the people see our soldiers coming, it is this mass base who pass this information from one house to another, until it reaches the armed group. Above all, they are the water for fish, which is the armed group.

This communist ideology expands so much here because of the mass base. We do not deal anymore on the armed group—this is minor. What is important here is the political fight against the CPP [Communist Party of the Philippines]—their black propaganda, their expansion units convincing the people to accept this ideology by creating black propaganda, feeding them wrong information, giving them wrong assumptions as to our activities, and leading the people not in the correct way. This is all black propaganda.

And, you know, people in the hinterlands sometimes are easily swayed. That is why we need more troops here. Not as combatants but as people who could check in regularly on every area so that we should have counter actions on their propaganda and inform the people of the right way. Because, as of now, the troops cannot cover the whole area of Negros Island to conduct a dialogue and a *pulong-pulong* to tell the people the difference between the foreign ideology and our very own ideology, which is the democratic ideology. We need another batallion of 7,000 troops to disband all the mass base organizations.

The major is concerned that the new Constitution is interpreted by many to require the disbanding of the Citizen Home Defense Force (CHDF), a civilian paramilitary organization set up under Marcos, notorious for human rights abuses.

Our desire is to maintain the CHDF, because this is our magic eye as far as the identification of the communists among the people. It is the people who know the communists; so only an organization set up among the people can do the job. That is why CHDF must not be locked up because a certain few members commit atrocities. It should be valued because of its purpose and usefulness, in the conduct of the fight against the expansion of this foreign ideology, which is communism. It is a counter propaganda against the black propaganda of the communists, against the priests.

Against the priests?

Yes. Our problem here is that there are some churches, but not all churches, that are helping the activities of these communist terrorists. As a matter of fact, our intelligence tells us that out of 137 Catholic priests here in Negros Occidental, 130 are already incriminated by this ideology. Meaning to say we have only 7 priests on our side.

Why do you think, if the military intelligence estimate is accurate, that almost all the priests are communist and NPA sympathizers?

Well, one of the factors that leads them to side with the NPA is their feeling of not being given much importance. Because formerly, the priests were not coordinated by our military organization when it comes into their areas to do operations. You know how people are, the moment you neglect them, they feel hurt. And the other group—the NPA—gives them so much importance. That

Jeanne Hallacy

Philippine Constabulary, the national police force, patrolling an area where there is suspected peasant support for NPA guerrillas. According to the International Red Cross, in 1988 more than 30,000 families were uprooted from their homes due to military operations.

makes them into supporters of that organization. Secondly, it is inevitable that lots of our brothers in uniform have done some things during the time of deposed Marcos, some things against the dogmas and the policies of the church. These are two factors that lead to the dissatisfaction of the clergy with the military.

Are you referring to salvaging by the military?

Yes.

Is that a serious problem in Negros?

Before, yes. Even in a family, you cannot always assure that everybody is good. There are some of our brothers in uniform that have not been that good and this has been exploited by the other organization, especially by the Communist Party of the Philippines.

But lately all soldiers have been rehabilitated. All soldiers and officers have been indoctrinated not to abuse civilians, not to kill them. We indoctrinate them that this is now the policy of our government. The soldiers on Negros Island now report to us that they are liked by the people because of this new trend.

How does this pulong-pulong work?

Well, we go to an area and have a dialogue with these people we know are in mass base organizations supporting the communists. So far, many have already signified their return to the folds of the government. As a matter of fact, we have already conducted seminars to rehabilitate these people. Like for instance, in La Castellana, which is one of the areas of the 11th IB [Infantry Batallion], almost two thousand of these people have surrendered and returned to the folds of the law, and allowed themselves to be rehabilitated by attending our seminars conducted in the area.

Is the NFSW one of the mass organizations you are thinking of?

We are very much sure that the National Federation of Sugar Workers is already infiltrated by the communists.

I understand that the NFSW is an organization recognized as legal by the government.

It is a legal organization. But this legal organization has already been infiltrated. There are some people who have become members of that organization, but they have another objective and that is to make that organization as their front, in line with their activities.

Do some military personnel work with the landowners as security guards or in training guards?

Never. We are not giving any security to these landlords. Now, by accident, a military detachment can be established on a hacienda. But that is just because we believe in its tactical importance. If we live on the landowner's property, that is purely a coincidence.

Would the military help the president of the Republic enforce an executive order for some type of land reform?

But you know an executive order sometimes hurts so many people. The commander-in-chief of the Armed Forces could not have the military implement such an executive order. No, the president could not possibly do such an executive order like that—sharing the land with other people. There would also be some opposition in the legislative body, because some of the members of the legislative body would be affected. Whether you like it or not, some of them are owners of some big areas of land.

As far as Task Force Sugarland is concerned, the most important thing is that land reform should mean individual land titling. It should not put land under cooperative titling, or it will wind up just like a commune.

What is the danger there?

The moment they title any land to a cooperative, as the NFSW wants, it's just like a commune where all people have to work together and only a few will benefit. That's communism. If part of a *hacendero's* land is going to be titled as a cooperative, then he should lay down his life to fight against that. Whenever we see a cooperative farmlot, we know that there the communists are at work.

I thank Major Cordero for his time.

It's always a pleasure to meet with foreigners.

Five:
GOING
UNDERGROUND

Policymakers in the U.S. have always viewed land reform as a way to undermine insurgency. This strategy was behind the land reform measures during the U.S.–Philippines war of 1899–1914. It was also true in the period following World War II.

The Hukbalahap (a shortened version of the Tagalog for The People's Army to Fight Japan) was formed during the Japanese occupation of the Philippines during the war. The "Huks" were a hybrid army of members of the old Communist Party (PKP) and non-Communist peasants and peasant leaders who came out of the decades of organizing around grievances with landlords, especially in the fertile plains of central Luzon. Many landed elites in central Luzon collaborated with the Japanese reign of terror in order to rid themselves of "bad elements" among their tenants. But the Huks proved to be a guerrilla force of legendary effectiveness against such opportunistic landlords, as well as against the Japanese and their Filipino intermediaries.

While collaborationist landlords fled to Manila, tenants in some areas spontaneously took over farms, implementing dreams of land reform. The Huk nationalist fight against the Japanese, combined with elements of agrarian revolt, made the Huks heroes to most peasants in central Luzon. Many Huks were farmers by day and guerrillas by night. By the end of the occupation, the Huks constituted a shadow government in major parts of central Luzon; in some areas, the Japanese-installed authorities were secretly Huks.

With the defeat of the Japanese, General Douglas MacArthur readily pardoned the Filipino elites who had collaborated with the Japanese. At the same time, the U.S. armed forces officially viewed the Huks as "communistic." Far from being rewarded as resistance fighters, the Huks were to be hunted down as subversives. American troops escorted landlords back to their farms where these elites attempted to pick up where their rule had left off in 1942. Their tenants and peasants were demanding reforms in tenant treatment and farm worker wages, mainly agitating for a 60 percent share of the net harvest, rather than the customary 50 percent.

The landlords fought back against the "communist threat" with considerable help from American military and intelligence agencies. (Most influential was Edward Lansdale, the CIA officer who was the inspiration for the novel *The Ugly American*.) The U.S.–organized and armed Philippine Military Police broke up tenant meetings, arrested striking farm workers, and hunted down Huk leaders. Peasant leaders were evicted from tenant plots their families had worked for generations. Homes of Huks and suspected Huks and their sympathizers were raided, and dozens of men, women, and children were killed with machine guns.

The Huks returned to their wartime guerrilla formations, ignoring the Communist Party's directive to avoid armed conflict and wage only "parliamentary" struggle. The landed elites and Washington nonetheless charged that the Huk rebellion was a Moscow-directed ploy to "Sovietize the Philippines."

The CIA and other U.S. agencies launched a multipronged counterinsurgency program, and prepared for the direct use of U.S. troops if the program faltered. The program called for "professionalizing" the Philippine armed forces; aggressive and well-equipped military strikes; psychological warfare, including "black propaganda" against the Huks (and the "horrors" these "godless Communists" would wreck); "community development," which turned out to be government publicity about future reforms; offering land through a resettlement program to those who surrendered; and, eventually, a CIA/Madison Avenue–orchestrated presidential campaign for reform-mouthing Congressman Ramon Magsaysay who was of peasant origin.

At the same time, the U.S. Mutual Security Agency (as the Agency for International Development was known at that time) brought in Robert Hardie to study land tenure and make recommendations for reform. Hardie had been part of the U.S. team in Japan that developed the model of sweeping land reform carried out during the U.S. military occupation, also later applied in Taiwan. At the end of 1952, much to the consternation of the Filipino elite, Hardie's report called for a comprehensive and rapid redistribution of land to landless tenants.

As soon as the Huk rebellion faltered in the face of the counterinsurgency program, however, Washington recalled Hardie for being "overzealous." Instead, the United States promoted President Magsaysay's program—resettling tenant farmers from areas where high rates of tenancy seemed to breed strong peasant unrest to Mindanao's frontier areas (often claimed by indigenous peoples). The basic agrarian structures of the country were left intact; and, despite the propagandist fanfare of the program, fewer than one thousand families were resettled, only 246 of them being surrendered Huks.

Author's Note

In Negros, I make contact with the NPA underground through an intermediary. I want to see for myself an area under the control of the New People's Army of the National Democratic Front. On earlier visits to Negros, I had been told that whether I would be able to visit one of the guerrilla fronts would depend on how "hot" the military situation was at the time.

At the appointed hour, two young men in a jeep pick up both me and a local person trusted by the NPA, who will be my interpreter. We head northward up the main road from Bacolod and, after a half hour, turn east on a dirt road leading to the mountains.

On both sides of the road we drive by green walls of sugarcane. This is one of Mr. Montelibano's haciendas, I'm told. We travel, gradually climbing several kilometers, as far as the road is passable by jeep. From there, one of the two young fellows who came in the jeep guides my companion and me on a half-hour hike to a two-room hut apparently belonging to the NPA.

Two hours later, about four o'clock that afternoon, two young NPAs show up. They are from the secret "base camp" farther back in the mountains. They will be our guides to where the commander of the northern front awaits us. One guide, with an M-16 slung over his right shoulder, is Ka Danny. (Ka is short for *kasama*, or comrade.) The younger one, Ka Jo-Jo, is unarmed. The hike is single file up and down the hills at a good clip, ever farther up into the mountains. Soon we have excellent views of the northwestern quarter of Negros Island, the major towns, sugar mills, and the sea stretched out below us.

After almost five hours of nonstop hiking, we stop for the night at a peasant house. The family seems to know Ka Danny. Obviously, it's no surprise to them that some NPAs march by. After a little conversation with the family, we all settle down on the hard bamboo slats, my clothes still damp with sweat. The last thing I recall is Jo-Jo, who has heard I have worked with the land reform in Nicaragua, asking how far it is from Negros to Nicaragua.

The next morning, we rise a good two hours before dawn. We hike for more than three hours, up and down hills, fording several creeks. The trail gets a little easier to negotiate as the sky lightens. I can now see quite a few small, abandoned fields. Our first stop is at a peasant house in view of a beautiful terraced rice field. Here we have some rice and a little fish for breakfast. Our

NPA family in a "safe house" in northeast Mindanao.

Jeanne Hallacy

host, a middle-aged farmer, tells us that the *kasamas* helped him terrace the field.

Shortly before noon we join up with the commander, Ka Diego, and a small company of about forty or so troops. We move expeditiously through the countryside, in and out of tiny villages and past isolated peasant houses rousing countless dogs from their slumbers. We go past *carabaos* bathing in a stream; men with a two-man saw making rough-hewn boards from hardwood logs; two men carrying a basket hanging from a long pole, the basket full of small fish that shine like silver dollars; two women sitting on the ground winnowing rice in big disk-shaped straw baskets. The impressive irrigated rice terraces were once owned by landlords in the cities we are told, and now are in the hands of peasants, courtesy of the NPA.

The peasants we pass invariably greet us and are greeted in return. Everyone is obviously accustomed to the sight of passing rebel troops, a few seem enthusiastic, most pleasantly indifferent. At a few houses, some of the soldiers stop and gulp down offered water.

Three or four hours into the march, darkness abruptly surrounds us. Rain has begun to fall, and it begins to seem cold. We come into a little village of wood and tin huts. Ka Diego has decided that we are going to stop for the night. The troops break up into small units to stay in various houses. I go with the commander and several others into an ample four-room wooden house on stilts, with a dirt-floor cooking area off the back.

Our host is Rogelio, a 57-year-old farmer. Rogelio tells me that NPAs are frequent visitors to his home. Indeed, he calls them "close friends." He says that the *kasamas* provided him with land and helped him terrace his farm. When they stay in his home they bring their own food.

In the course of three days with the NPA in northern Negros, I conducted the first four interviews of this chapter. All the interviews were done through the interpreter.

Ka Danny
NPA soldier
Northern Negros

Danny is wearing a faded red T-shirt. On the front it says CAPAS, which, he says, stands for the Cassava Planters Association, an association of small farmers in the hills of northern Negros. On the back of the T-shirt it reads "Fight for Freedom, Justice and Democracy" and "JAJA" (Justice for Aquino, Justice for All), referring to an organization formed in the aftermath of the assassination of Benigno "Ninoy" Aquino.

I am 28 years old. I've been in the movement one year and three months. I joined because I encountered a lot of problems like hunger, poverty, and oppression where I lived. I think that by joining the NPA I can eliminate the bad elements in the society. Also, we render service to the people, like helping them build irrigation systems, helping them with transporting some of their seeds and other things related to production.

Speaking of agricultural production, does the NPA have a policy of growing the food it consumes?

We produce 45 to 60 percent of the rice we consume. When it comes to doing the work of producing the rice, we have a rotating schedule. Sometimes you will be assigned twice a week to till the land on the rice farm.

We are tilling an abandoned land, once privately owned by a large landowner. We put in irrigation—the dams and the terraces and everything needed for rice farming.

Do you have any relatives in the NPA or are you the first in your family to join?

I joined the NPA with my three brothers, all at the same time. We joined the NPA because we thought that only through joining could we be free. It is the only way out of bondage.

How do your parents feel about so many in the family being in the NPA?

Our family accepts our option openly. Our parents look forward to our struggle benefiting the vast majority.

What were you doing before you joined the NPA?

We were working on a sugarcane hacienda and at the same time working on a rice plantation.

How did you join up?

There are no application forms for the NPA. But before I joined the movement I was a member of the NFSW and that's where it all started—I joined that legal organization and later I went underground.

When you were working on the hacienda, were there any things that really made you and the other workers angry—that led you to say enough is enough?

The overseer used to treat us like dogs. Whenever we were resting, he used to look at his watch and time the length of our rest. Never more than five minutes. All day long we work in the fields and the management makes us work harder and harder, without compensating us fairly. And because of our poor income we were short of rice. We would go to the *amo* and ask for rice as a loan, and he would slam his door in our faces. That makes us very angry with the hacienda.

Alan Berlow

Ka Danny

We were earning seven pesos a day, when in fact the Ministry of Labor said that the sugar worker ought to receive twenty-eight pesos, which still wasn't enough. With seven pesos you could not even sustain yourself. A kilo of rice then cost five pesos and you could not buy fish for two pesos.

Were there any ways you and the other workers could revenge yourselves?

Revenge was not in our minds. But what we did think about was reform, a good reform based on the legitimate demands of the sugar workers. We did have a strike on the hacienda. We also joined the other mass actions, like rallies, pickets, and street demonstrations in other haciendas in order to air our grievances with the management, and also in order to exchange ideas with hacienda workers from other places.

Have you ever gone to school?

I have not been to school even once. I have not experienced what school is all about.

Has the NPA taught you how to read and write?

Yes! (*Smiles broadly.*) We have a buddy system in learning, where one who knows how to read and write teaches another comrade who has had no schooling and how to apply what they read to a situation now. There are some programs of the NPA that teach us how to understand comprehensively the problems, issues, and other things that face the Filipino people.

Are you married?

Yes. My wife is becoming an NPA.

Do you have any children?

Yes, we have two kids—two boys.

Are your brothers also married, and do they have children?

Yes, all of them are already married and have families.

Who takes care of the children while all of you are in the NPA? You don't even have any income, do you?

I'm not worried. I have no income because I am in the NPA and cannot give financial help to my children. I'm not worried because the people take care of the children of the real soldiers of the people. There is a legal organization that helps the children, but I cannot disclose its name.

What is the hardest thing about being an NPA, Danny?

The problems I am encountering right now are the same as those I was encountering before joining the NPA. The only difference is that a brighter future lies ahead. If I die of hunger not joining the NPA—I'm better off dying with a bullet fighting for that future. I live now for the cause of the people and for the freedom of everybody.

Ka Diego
NPA commander
Northern Negros

K *a Diego is 37 years old and the commanding officer for the northern front in Negros. He joined the NPA four years ago. Marching for a long stretch behind the commander, I notice that he is wearing only one rubber thong. He deals with the problem by switching the thong from one foot to the other every ten minutes or so. He seems mild-mannered and pensive. While his troops lie down to rest, he often stands off to one side and stares in the distance, thinking.*

Before joining the NPA, I worked as a laborer in a certain small factory in Bacolod City. I cannot tell its exact name nor the nature of its business.

Before I joined the New People's Army, I was already deeply involved with the revolutionary movement, especially in organizing sugar-mill workers. I was working both with legal and underground movements in the city.

I finished high school only. My wife and I were married ten years ago. She is actively involved in the movement too—the NPA. Our children are left in the care of our parents.

How successful would you say the NPA has been in northern Negros?

By and large, the movement here in northern Negros is very successful. We started an organizing unit here in 1983, and we were able to educate almost all the sugar workers and other peasants in the countryside about the revolutionary struggle. Then we opened a guerrilla front in the area, particularly in 1985, when we confiscated a large volume of firearms and were able to conduct a tactical offensive against the enemies, the military and the landlords we consider to be fascists.

Have your tactics changed since the 60-day ceasefire?

No, it is still guerrilla warfare. The only difference is that now we attack more often and with greater force because we have a greater number of fighters.

I notice that some of the weapons your soldiers carry are very old.

We find it hard to acquire firearms. We have only confiscated arms—from the military and landowners.

Does the NPA have a policy of not hitting economic targets such as the sugar mills?

Sugar mills are not our target because if we hit the sugar industry and paralyze it we will be harming the sugar workers. The main targets of the NPA are the military units and the fascist private armed troops of the landowners.

How good are the government soldiers?

The soldiers of the government are not well disciplined. They have detached themselves from the feelings of the people. The only thing they have is good military training and firearms, but it comes to nothing because they lack this discipline of being close to the people.

I view the government's armed forces now and those of the Marcos regime before as the same. They do not do anything different or new.

Are there any circumstances under which you would be interested in negotiating with the government?

When it comes to negotiations or to another ceasefire, we are still willing to negotiate. Our line of communication is still open as long as the government is sincere in granting our demands and in implementing what is agreed upon.

Has the NPA accomplished anything here in terms of agrarian reform?

When it comes to land reform, we are still on the minimum level because some of the landlords are not yet ready to cooperate with us. So right now, our demands are the lowering of the rents and also the distribution of abandoned lands to those who will actually till them. In northern Negros, there are many abandoned lands, especially those owned by the Gustillos and Villasins, now being occupied by the peasants.

We hope to introduce further land reform, but first we have to engage in intensive nationalistic education about the main target of genuine land reform,

The New People's Army implements "minimum" land reform in areas under its control. Landowners lower rents to tenant farmers and raise farm worker wages. Lands abandoned by owners are put into production, sometimes by NPA soldiers.

which is to give lands free to the tillers. Also, one of our goals is to establish a department of agrarian reform.

What do you mean by "nationalistic education"?

By "nationalistic education" I mean that while the farmers are here on the farm, tilling the land, they are not limited to their farms. They are to be conscious and aware of what is happening in the whole picture. For instance, they must be conscious of what is being done in the country's economy. They must be conscious of the intervention of the multinationals. So when we say nationalistic education we mean that the people must be aware of the whole problems of the Philippines.

I've been told that many of the beautifully terraced rice fields are cooperatively owned. What is the role of cooperatives in your land reform?

Cooperatives solidify the farmers' movement into a powerful voice for their demands. It also eliminates the middleman.

Typically now, families are members of cooperatives for some land and have individual responsibility for some other land. In most cases, they are engaged more in the cooperative movement. They continue as individual farmers only where they are not yet ready to accept cooperatives. We need to educate them that there is a need for cooperative farming.

With the cooperatives, distribution is according to the work done by the member. Right now we are studying other approaches in terms of the work process and the distribution of produce. We want to know more of what is being done in other countries.

In these areas of substantial NPA control, what do farmers do with their surplus production?

They sell their surplus in the market, which is not under NPA control.

Is the NPA engaged directly in the production of food?

There are isolated cases. But it is seldom that the NPAs till the land because the main function of the NPA is to fight and defend the interests of the people.

Do you impose taxes in the areas controlled by your movement?

There are cases where we impose taxation on the landlords. We choose only landlords who are capable of paying. Right now taxation is not being implemented with the small farmers, but the small farmers give to the NPA, to the movement—whatever they have to give. But we have no fixed tax.

Have you participated in some ambushes or attacks?

I have participated in ambushes and other attacks on military detachments in northern Negros.

Have you personally killed any people?

Sure, I have killed soldiers.

How many?

I cannot count them anymore.

Why? Were there too many?

I cannot count them because I do not particularly think of that, sir. I'm not particular on the number of soldiers I have killed.

What do you feel in your own experience when you have killed someone?

Our reaction in killing the enemy is more anger than compassion, because we regard the military as oppressors and extortionists of the poor.

Ka Kim
NPA soldier, medical unit
Northern Negros

K *a Kim sits on the floor at Rogelio's, leaning on the knee of another woman NPA who is softly playing a guitar. Ka Kim is thin and wears a "Ghostbusters" T-shirt. A hammer-and-sickle pendant hangs from her neck.*

I am 26 years old. I've been with the NPA for a year and two months.

I want to have a socialist form of government. By a socialist government, I mean the kind of government which does not enrich itself at the expense of the sweat of the toiling masses. And a kind of government which does not suppress the vast majority.

I belong to the lower class. My father works in the sugar industry and I worked on a rice farm. We are four in the family, two boys and two girls. I'm the youngest. I am the only NPA in the family. My two elder brothers are involved in legal work, in organizing the sugar workers.

Inside the armed struggle there is no sex discrimination. Everybody is treated alike. There are a lot of women fighters in the movement.

In the NPA, I am a medical officer and at the same time a fighter. When comrades suffer common illness, like fever and headache, I give them the necessary medicine. When someone is wounded in battle, I sometimes do the first stage on the bullet wounds. If the comrade needs an operation and it is beyond my knowledge, I will take the necessary steps to take the patient to the hospital.

Have you been in battle?

I was in on an ambush on the military. I felt very nervous during the battle, but

Alan Berlow

Ka Kim

I tried to overcome it. I killed an enemy solider. No NPA was killed, thank God.

Are you religious?

Yes. Before I was religious and even now I remain religious. I also consider myself a communist.

Supposedly, Filipinos must love each other; they should not kill each other. But there are some Filipinos who take advantage of poor people—especially those in the upper bracket oppress those they can easily oppress. And atrocities by the military are very rampant. What they do to the people is too much, and they must be eliminated from society.

The rebel soldiers have left their guns leaning against the outside of the house. Some children sit by them listening to two women NPAs, one tapping out a beat on her leg, as they sing songs of the revolution. I ask someone to help me understand the words. "Let us crush the enemy. Let us ambush the fascist troops as they wade through the river and roam the mountains."

Ka Belen
NPA organizer
Northern Negros

I talk with Ka Belen, NPA. She is 25 years old. Unlike Ka Kim, she is unarmed. In the NPA, she works as an organizer in what they call the POT, the Propaganda Organizing Team. The day-to-day work here in the countryside is to organize or to increase the mass base for the NPA. Ka Belen would like to become a regular fighter, but doesn't feel she is ready for that responsibility.

I go to four or five areas in the course of a year. I talk with the peasants. I investigate how they live, their social condition, their economic condition, and other things that affect their daily lives. We tell them that they have social rights, like the right to send their children to school, the right of the government to protect the lives and property of civilians.

I have never met the military here in the countryside. If I ever did, I could go to any house in a community wherein I have already organized. The peasants would protect us.

I've been with the New People's Army for two years. Before that, for eight years I was with a legal organization, the NFSW, the National Federation of Sugar Workers. Before I worked as a union organizer, I was a sugar worker. From the time I was 12 until I was 15, I weeded the sugarcane fields.

My father is a tricycle driver and my mother is a housewife. We are seven in the family. I'm the only one working in the NPA or a mass organization. In fact, no one in the family even knows I'm with the NPA. They think that since I got married, my husband and I have been working on the hacienda. Some of my relatives work in government offices; so I don't know what their reaction would be if they knew me and my husband were NPAs.

Father Vicente Pelobello
NPA commander
Negros

It is January 1987, the time of the 60-day ceasefire between the government's armed forces and the New People's Army. Father Vicente Pelobello has "surfaced" as one of those representing the NPA and the National Democratic Front (NDF) in negotiations with government representatives in Negros. Bishop Fortich has invited him, together with other NPA/NDF "panelists," to stay at the Sacred Heart Seminary in Bacolod, where Father Pelobello was once the prefect of discipline.

In the "priest's dormitory," men and women are cooking over a gas burner and a half-dozen M-16s have been set casually on top of nearby tables. The middle-aged man who opens the door turns out to be Father Pelobello. The years as a guerrilla fighter in the hills have not taken away from his soft-spoken, thoughtful, seminary-professor demeanor.

I have been a Catholic priest for twenty-five years. I was born in Negros, in Bacolod City proper. My family is middle class. My father is a cashier in the city; my mother, a public school teacher. They came from poor class origin, from Panay.

Even now, my parents are deeply religious. They understand the revolutionary cause and they wholly support the movement, although there are members of the family who are still overcome by the anti-communist hysteria propagated here by the Anti-Communist League and some reactionary classes.

Actually, my evolution as a revolutionary started in the early 1960s with the trend in the church of humanism, personalism, and involvement in people's lives and struggles, and then with the Vatican Council in 1965.

I was involved with the Young Christian Workers movement here in Negros. The sugar workers, commercial service workers, hacienda workers, and also fishermen lived in my Bacolod parish and my Villamonte parish—that's a barrio here in Bacolod. During our YCW convention in Davao, we had a confrontation with a manager who used armed goons to break up a picket, and some of our friends were wounded during the shooting. We joined the picket as part of our practicum: our integration with people's struggles and demands. That's only one of my experiences that led me to integrate more with the worker's struggles and deepen my commitment.

Later, I was assigned to the parish in Sarabia. It was a depressed area. Most of my parishioners were sugar workers, plus a few landlords and middle-class professionals. It was during that time that the worker's movement started. That was around 1971 to 1972, just prior to the declaration of martial law. So I got involved. It was the church's commitment to uplift the livelihood of the workers and was part of our mission—our preferential option for the poor, the deprived, and the oppressed. The local mayor and I had a confrontation. In the parish, we were only supporting the workers for higher wages, better living conditions, and human dignity. But we were met with stiff resistance, threats against our person, and curtailment of our activities. We were maligned as subversives and communists. Nonetheless, we continued to say mass and give seminars, both openly and secretly. We had several education sessions and carried out organizing work through the church programs. A few planters were progressive, and they allowed their workers to be given political education.

But the majority of the planters in the northern part of Negros were against people being organized and enlightened as to their rights and duties. The mayor, himself a planter, was able to convince the municipal council to pass a resolution considering me persona non grata. They wanted to oust me from the parish. After martial law was declared, there was a threat, although not big, to my person and perhaps of my arrest. The people rallied behind me, especially the sugar workers, and the lay leaders in the parish, and there were some clergy who supported my cause. So I did not leave. The bishop was also behind me.

Then I was brought closer to the revolutionary movement. There is an underground popular organization, the Christian Nationalist Liberation. It was gaining ground and taking roots among church people. So little by little, through sharing ideas with Father Jalandoni and Father de la Torre, we came up with an option for revolutionary armed struggle as the only road to solving the fundamental problems whose manifestation is hunger and poverty, especially among the sugar workers.

But how do you, especially as a religious person, justify the use of violence?

While the official church, as an institution, opted for nonviolence, we in the underground mass organizations of church people had to conclude that non-violence was ineffective, because even the minimum demands that we were

Father Pelobello

asking for the sugar workers were met with stiff resistance and with violence. So for us it was logical and just to take up more drastic methods of working for change. There is a prior violence from the institution, the establishment. We have here, for instance, the private armies of the big landlords, like the private armies of the late Gustillo. The violence we waged was to defend the people's interests, the people's rights. It was not violence for the sake of violence or to create anarchy, to destabilize, but violence with a purpose. It was not indiscriminate killing. We value life, that's why we take up arms: to defend the life of the majority of the deprived, oppressed, poor people. We have to recognize that there is a prior violence.

Father Pelobello continues the story of his evolution.

I was now supporting the underground through the giving, the lending, of facilities and communications for the revolutionary movement. I was still the parish priest in Sarabia, but from 1972 to 1979, I was already secretly supporting the national democratic revolution and the underground revolutionary movement. In 1979, I went underground fulltime. It was during the time that the Marcos dictatorship launched intense militarization here in Negros, and there was a series of arrests against church workers. Besides that, the revolutionary movement needed fulltime cadres for more intensified political work, for base building and then broadening our alliances, building up the mass base, both in the countryside and in the urban areas. So, I felt the need to go underground as a fulltime worker. One of the comrades was arrested in a UG house, which I facilitated; so my name was implicated. According to reports, the military was building up a dossier against me and it was only a matter of time before I would be apprehended.

How does the bishop view you?

The bishop considers me a priest on leave. In fact, I have proposed to him the idea that I celebrate mass and he is open to that. But I think I would rather reserve that for the future in case, perhaps, we would be victorious and I can return to active ministry. Yes, the people consider me a priest. They still accept me. Actually, priests are given high regard in a Catholic country like ours; even if they are married they still revere the priest.

What does the NPA do?

Let me tell you what I did when I went underground. During that time the NPA was in the defensive stage. It was a matter of building up guerrilla bases in the countrysides, building up people's organizations, improving their economic livelihood. In the first year of my work underground, I was assigned in Panay Island, on the border of Aklan, Antique. We helped in forming cooperatives among the peasants. At one time, we planned a dam to irrigate several hectares of rice fields. So, it's a matter of us leading, then the people's organizations doing the manual work. We also helped in our own small way in manual work. We were able to cut through a hill so that the water would flow down toward areas of rice farms. That's one example of how we promoted economic well-being.

Here in Negros, there are also economic projects lately (although I cannot reveal the places because the NPA/NDF is an underground organization). However, we were able to collate reports from the south. The economic projects that were launched there consisted of cooperatives—consumer cooperatives, meaning they pool their resources and then buy consumer goods (cooking oil, soap, etc.) in gross. They were also able to branch out into marketing. The peasant guerrillas in the zones would pool their products and then find good buyers from the city here and bring the products down here. In exchange, they're given cash. So, with the cash money, they would be able to get a supply of their basic needs—food, clothing, etc. There are also other farming projects, like fishponds, poultry, piggeries, and vegetable farming.

Within the guerrilla zones, criminality is already minimal. Cattle rustling, robbery, and other criminal acts are almost totally eliminated, so that people may devote themselves to economic development.

But in the absence of criminality, militarization took over. So you have also a hindrance to the full economic development—like evacuation, harassment, *tong* [extortion] at the military checkpoints. Actually, the militarization outweighs the work that we have done in the economic sphere. Once the military pinpoint cooperatives already functioning, they mark them as subversive, and they would try to dismantle them. So these cooperatives had to go underground and that limited their activity and full-blown functioning.

Most generally, the NPA defends the gains of the people's struggles from the landlords. There are areas here in the south in which land-grabbing was rampant in the early years of martial law. Martial law facilitated land-grabbing. There are many peasants whose lands were grabbed. These lands were virgin forests they cleared. Once they cleared them, they were able to plant bananas and other food crops. Then these big landlords came with papers declaring that these are pasture lands. They brought in a few head of cattle and fenced this area with barbed wires. These landlords used their armed goons, and even the military, to drive away these small farmers.

There were clashes between the military and the NPA and the armed goons in the area. Several landlords who were collaborating with the military were punished by us. It was a blow against the political power of the landlords in the area, and in the process many of them left the area and no longer attended to these pasture lands. So the people came back and claimed that land for their own, and did their best to cultivate and produce on that land.

You speak of the military extorting money from the people at checkpoints. But what about the charges I have heard from some that the NPA has lost a lot of support because of its own taxations?

Actually, the NPA was supported from the beginning by the people through voluntary donations and contributions. It was only later that taxation as a policy was experimented with in a limited area and in a limited period. But the target was against big planters, big businessmen, and multinationals operating within the guerrilla zone. In the process of implementation, there were weaknesses and excesses; so we decided to review and revise the policy, and right now taxation has been stopped. Still, there is the system of voluntary contributions through persuasion and political education. We try to follow a policy of voluntary contributions from big landlords and businessmen. The thing that complicated the taxation was that other armed groups pretending to be NPA, with or without the support and encouragement perhaps of the military, also taxed the same people whom we were dealing with. Some were deceived. So it was a matter of black propaganda launched by the military against us.

What is the program of the National Democratic Front?

The National Democratic Front desires peace and progress for all the Negrenses. But peace and progress demand not only palliatives—the temporary alleviation of poverty and hunger—but radical changes in the system. Otherwise, the same cycle of poverty, hunger, and militarization would continue. So that's why the Cory Aquino government and the NDF should unite on how to approach—on how to see these problems—and approach these problems in a thorough and whole-sided way.

On the national level, the NDF has already drafted general programs and policies in the economic, military, political, cultural, education, and even foreign relations fields. But they have to be given flesh and to be particularized in the different regions in the country. Here in Negros, we are attempting to draft a program on economic recovery, medium-term and even long-term, but to do so we have to collect more information. Right now, during the ceasefire period, we are holding democratic consultations with several sectors in different areas. For example, we go around and talk with planters—not only progressive planters but even reactionary ones. What are their specific plans regarding the future economy of Negros? We also hold consultations with church people. In fact, tomorrow a people's congress will be held and that brings together several sectors. It's not sponsored by the NDF; it's in the open and the NDF is interested in the congress. It's organized by an alliance organization consisting of several sectors. Anyway, the point is that we don't have a monopoly of good ideas as to the future of Negros economy, although we have analyzed the basic fundamental problems of Negros as part of a semi-colonial, semi-feudal system and found that we need a genuine land reform program and a national industrialization. But these still need specific implementation guidelines.

We are flexible. We are willing to undergo phases of implementation; for instance, step-by-step implementation of a land reform, not outright confiscation of all haciendas. We have to consider the different classifications of land, the different classifications of planters, and also the attempts of the civilian government, if any, to break up land monopoly. They see the problem. Feudalism has been recognized by the church and even by the civilian government as a fundamental problem; that's where hunger and poverty come from. That's why we consider the governor's scheme—while it falls short of a genuine land reform—a positive step. That's the official stand of the NDF. [Governor Lacson had proposed that sugarcane farms subject to foreclosure by the government bank instead be allowed to transfer 10 percent of their land to the workers for garden plots. After months of a brouhaha, the proposal went nowhere.] It has gained the support, according to some estimates, of 75 planters—out of the 9,000 landowners. But anyway, these planters have influence on the others and perhaps the scheme would be a start of a momentum toward genuine land reform.

We are open to the idea that some individual planters would turn into Filipino industrialists by converting their capital toward industrial capital.

What are the NDF's sources of inspiration?

Even church people can use Marxist tools of analysis without necessarily being Marxist. There is kind of an eclecticism. We can get good ideas from other countries and even from the U.S.—for instance, from the Americans' struggle against the British and their constitutional debates. And we can study, let's say, the vast progress of America toward economic development. So we can learn from the western countries, from communist countries, and from socialist countries.

But what we must keep coming back to is this: Why is Negros so rich in natural resources and yet its people so poor? There must be something wrong with the system. Even the priests and the bishops recognize this need for genuine land reform. So there is such a vast interplay of ideas in the world today that you cannot really pinpoint what ideology does land reform come from. Anyway, ideas can be accepted by us from whatever source.

But while collaboration now might occur, don't Christians ultimately have to fear Marxists, fear communists?

I think we have to erase from our minds the fear of Marxists as violent or ruthless people—heartless or no feeling for humanity. Many of the NDF/NPA come from a Catholic background. In my long years of association with Marxists, they are not the way they are painted by the Marcos regime and by Reagan. And I think we Christians have nothing to fear in the event of the victory of the national democratic revolution. Religion would not be eradicated and the communists will not turn out to be anti-religion. We believe that the Christians who compose the majority of the Filipinos can find a reservoir of motivation in their faith to work for genuine democracy and national freedom from foreign domination.

Rocky Segovia
Tenant farmer
Albay province, Bikol

*A*n hour from the provincial capital of Legaspi, in the gentle hills at the base of Mount Mayon, is a "twilight zone"—a buffer region between a government-controlled area and an NPA-controlled area. Over the past few years, with the substantial NPA/NDF influence, "revolutionary land reform" has gotten underway here: Three years ago, farmers "seized" the hacienda on which they were sharecropping.

From the jeepney stop in Maura, a little village straddling the highway, I walk a half-hour on a dirt road toward the volcano. The path here was an entrance onto the hacienda. The first farmer I come upon stands shirtless in the ankle-deep mud as he bends over to transplant tender green shoots of rice. He is middle-aged. His exceptionally muscled torso, I later learn, comes from his youth when he was one of the province's top boxers. When he learns that I would like to record an interview about his life and his farm, he hesitates. Polite discussion convinces him I will change his and everyone else's name and the name of the place. He smiles and asks me to give his name as Rocky, Rocky Segovia.

Hacienda Heredero used to be a coconut plantation. It was 150 hectares and was only coconut trees, all tended by waged farm workers. The owner was Sr. Buenaventura. He also had other land, altogether totaling more than 300 hectares. His family was Spanish. Shortly after liberation from the Japanese occupation, he went off for Spain, leaving his administrator in charge.

In the early 1970s, Sr. Buenaventura changed the administrator to Sr. Sergio Rodriguez, also Spanish. He started to have tenants. A tenant had to give seven out of ten coconuts to the owner. Long-term farm workers were the ones likely to become tenants. In 1974, I became a tenant, having been a worker on the hacienda for several years. Before that I lived where you got off the jeepney, trying to make a living by repairing sewing machines.

Sr. Rodriguez was very strict. Let me give you just one example. If a tenant picked up a coconut that had fallen on the ground without permission, he was expelled. This is the way it was up until 1979.

In 1979, Sr. Rodriguez died. Then a lawyer by the name of Mariano Muñoz became the administrator. He switched to more tenants. All tenants had to sign a six-month contract. It was renewed only if he and his brother, the *encargado*, were pleased with you.

We were not allowed to plant for ourselves, between the coconut trees, bananas or other permanent crops like guayabo, mango, or papaya. For if we did that, it would be more difficult for the administration to expel us—maybe they'd have to pay for the crop. We didn't like this.

In 1982–83, Attorney Muñoz imposed even more policies that we didn't like. For instance, for every seven vegetables that we worked to raise in the creek beds, like gabi leaves, camote, cassava, we had to give one to the administration. Security guards were always inspecting us, every basket you were carrying. This really made us angry with Attorney Muñoz.

Even to use a single coconut, which had fallen, in a meal for our families, we had to first go to the *encargado's* house to ask for permission. Depending on where in the hacienda your house was, that could be a kilometer's walk or so. Security guards roamed around keeping an eye on us. If you found a coconut fallen from a tree, you'd have to quickly split it open and take out the coconut meat and then shred up the husk and spread it around so that no one would see it. Those security guards were told to be on the lookout for scattered husks.

About this time, seven NPAs began to secretly come on to the hacienda. We didn't know at first that they were NPAs. They carried no guns. They would say they were hired to cut grass with a bolo. But they talked with some of us and learned about our situation. They came many times. They learned that we were very angry with the Muñozes.

The NPAs then began to give instructions to a group of us they had selected.

Were you one of the ones they selected?

No, I was not included. The NPAs said that we should unite together and make a petition and send it to the *encargado*. We should tell him that we are claiming the land. You have to give the land, we should tell him. We've been here a long time. The owner hasn't been here or even in the country for forty years. This land now is ours.

We didn't hear anything back from Attorney Muñoz. So we went ahead and took over the land. Of the fifty-five families here all but three joined in on the seizure. I decided not to. I said that I just wanted to work and not to force Mr. Muñoz. I didn't say so, but I was suspicious of the NPAs who were working with us, suspicious of their honesty. But once the others seized the land it was done and I joined in. We formed a cooperative and began to collectively harvest the coconuts.

Then the younger Muñoz, the *encargado*, came here with the military. They told us that we had to stop what we were doing and that we would have to report to the PC [Philippine Constabulary] headquarters in town and that they would do an investigation. We were charged as robbers—with stealing coconuts from the owner, Sr. Buenaventura. We were a little frightened and not sure what we would do next. But when we got back here, the NPAs told us not to worry. The NPAs sent a message to Attorney Muñoz asking if he has proof that he has the right from Sr. Buenaventura to administer the hacienda. Attorney Muñoz never replied. Then the NPAs told us to take over the hacienda. The *kasamas* sent a message to the Muñozes telling them never to enter Hacienda Heredero again.

We were happy like we've never been before. No one would prohibit us from planting bananas and rice—food for our families. After a while we decided to divide up the land among all the families. The problem with the cooperative was a lack of enough trust. For instance, on the cooperative's bank account there was only the name of one of the members. We thought it better to divide up the land.

In addition to harvesting the coconuts, we have planted rice and other food crops like tomatoes, pechay, and other vegetables. Altogether I'd say that there are now about 30 percent fewer coconut trees. But since we have planted so much rice and vegetables overall, more is being produced than before. We find we are better off having our food secure. What's the sense in raising and processing coconuts to sell to the merchants to get some money to buy rice when we can grow our own rice? Still, with the coconuts, we have money for other things that we need. We could buy fertilizers to produce more rice, for instance. And we could improve our lives. We could buy carts, ready-made pants, T-shirts, salt, dried fish, and even galvanized steel for roofs, a few beers. It's nice to have both coconuts and rice—and no landlord.

Those NPAs I told you about did turn out to be corrupt. Part of what we had given to the landlord we now gave to the NPAs as a contribution to the movement. It amounted to one-third of the harvest. But they were keeping it. Other NPAs found out about this and they took care of them. Those corrupt

NPAs fled. Some were executed. Two of those who fled are today in the Alsa Masa here that we're having so much trouble with.

Rocky tells me that they all are members of the Peasant Alliance of Bikol.

The KMB is our voice. The KMB does what we cannot do because we are busy planting on the farm, doing much work. They can gather up what the people need, what the people say. They can pressure public opinion and the government officials.

❖ ❖ ❖

In January 1988, I talk again with Rocky Segovia. We meet in town. He is deeply troubled.

All of our hopes and dreams are for a peaceful life and peace of mind. But it is no longer peaceful here, and in the past months we have grown afraid. You know, we have no land titles and the NPA recently has lost control in the area. The Alsa Masa is a big threat. Anytime, Muñoz could come back and claim the land again for Buenaventura. This land would go into trouble again. We have stopped improving our land and our houses. And, since we seized Hacienda Heredero, President Cory's executive order outlaws us from ever getting titles to our lands through any land reform.

You can tell those who read your book that this is a very hard time for us peasants now. We're walking in the middle of two swords—but one sword we can trust.

I ask Rocky to tell me more about the Alsa Masa.

The military introduced the Alsa Masa. Members get two weeks training from the military. They get rifles from them too. They levy a 5 percent tax on the farmers.

The godfather of the Alsa Masa here is the ex-mayor, the Marcos mayor, of this town. He is a rich landowner.

They tell us that the Alsa Masa is to protect the people from the NPA. But so many complaints are now rising up. What the members of Alsa Masa do in practice is the opposite of what they say. They are worse. They are the most feared now. Even if not every farmer always agreed with the NPA, we never feared them. Because of the Alsa Masa's way of arresting suspects. They arrest at night.

They came to my house. But I was not there. I was here in town. Now they are telling people that I ran away from them and that I have done bad things. They charge that I am an NPA commander, that whatever I say the NPA will do. But I am only a farmer.

Even when the NPAs stop at our house, they bring their own food. But the Alsa Masa say that we are supporting the NPAs.

If Mr. Segovia is in his house—he's dead, that's what they tell people. Since that time I don't go to my house, but stay here in town. I hire laborers to work my land, but they're afraid too.

The Alsa Masa members are farmers too, but many of them are the type that hang out, don't work. Many of them are teenagers. Their fathers work, but these youths are lazy. Some have committed crimes. Two are ex-NPAs—I told you about them—driven out of the NPA because they stole from us farmers.

One of the Alsa Masa leaders wants my land. There's a story behind this. In 1984, my wife was going on the train to visit our daughter who works in Manila. Someone tried to hold her up. She struggled and the robber pushed her out of the train near Manila. She was hospitalized in Manila for over a month. I went to Manila to be with her. No one worked the farm except for this guy Rolando, but he didn't have my permission to do so. So when I returned from Manila I was surprised to find him working my farm. He tried to claim that my brother-in-law had given him permission, and to get him off the land he demanded 15,000 pesos for the work he had done. I refused, of course. Anyway, I don't have that sort of money. I am an ordinary farmer. So this guy would not get off my farm.

I took my case to the *kasamas* [the NPA]. The *kasamas* told me to enter my farm: "We will handle this—there's no reason to pay that fellow 15,000 pesos." Rolando and my father talked to each other in the presence of the *kasamas*. The NPAs told Rolando that he had to give back the land. Rolando lowered his money demand to 1,200 pesos. I told him I had no money. This was 1986.

Now Rolando is a member of the vigilantes, of the Alsa Masa. It is he who accuses me of being a communist. It is he who wants to take my land from me. He already has his own farm. He is just greedy. But I complained to the OIC [Officer in Charge, the Aquino-appointed mayor], and the OIC sent a letter to the man telling him to come into the municipality office to talk the matter over. But he has not come.

The sympathy of ordinary farmers and farm workers here is with the NPA. They are well disciplined. If they make an accusation, it is based on much study of the accused. The Alsa Masa simply accuse and then they kill you. The *kasamas* really observe; they get proof before they act. And they are our best hope of having our land.

Some barrios are forced by the Alsa Masa to organize Alsa Masa units. People are afraid of them. They torture. They use electric wires. But I know one barrio where the people are very united. The Alsa Masa said you have to organize an Alsa Masa here, but they said no.

The Alsa Masa tells the people to report anything suspicious to the ex-mayor, the Marcos mayor.

My wife's cousin is one of the Alsa Masa's victims. He is a tricycle driver. He was mauled with the butt of a gun. They charged him with giving a ride on his tricycle to an NPA commander. But he has no idea of whom he gave a ride to. And anyway, as I told you, they call me an NPA commander.

The Alsa Masa cannot bring us peace. Many people cry out, Why does President Aquino permit the Alsa Masa?

You know, my religion [Seventh Day Adventist] is against killing. Even the Bible has the commandment Thou shalt not kill. But you may have to kill to defend yourself and others. Maybe you will have to join the NPA.

Lorenzo Nunala
Tenant farmer
Candoning, southern Negros

I am with a rebel army in an area of southern Negros where, only months before, government armed forces brought in heavy mortar. My teenaged NPA companions, armed with M-16s, seem happy-go-lucky. They speak little English. The older youth wears a cap emblazoned with "Rambo." We keep a vigorous pace, marching single file, and we take turns singing. I recognize a Chilean song from the Allende years in their Ilongo and Tagalog repertoire. We call out afternoon greetings to peasants in their fields.

We stop at a typical bamboo-and-thatch peasant house in a little barrio. Lorenzo and Edith Nunala, a farm couple in their 40s, live here. Ka Sam translates for me with Lorenzo, with whom I first speak. Edith listens intently and interjects clarifications and additional comments in English. Many years ago, she says, she went to grade school; the instruction in those colonial days was in English.

I'm 40 years old. In 1971, we came here. My parents worked in La Castellana Hacienda. I escaped from that hacienda because I didn't like the low salary— it's not enough to live on. When I came here, we cleared the land and worked as tenants under the *tertiano* system—one-third of our produce went to the landowner and two-thirds to us—but we shouldered all the expenses. We planted about 3 hectares with *palay* and corn. We live here in the barrio.

It's much better here than in the hacienda because here we can plant several kinds of crops—rice, corn, cassava, vegetables—and the family has more to eat.

At first, we were able to cope pretty well because the topsoil was fertile. But little by little, the topsoil became eroded, and we found it difficult to produce enough food for the children.

Since they live in an NPA area, I ask about their experience of the NPA.

We need fertilizer, but we can't afford it. The *kasamas*—the NPAs who roam around here—organize people and educate us. With their guidance, we have raised pigs, chickens, and planted vegetables and other crops. With the money we earn we have been able to buy fertilizer.

This year, on the NPA's advice we consulted the owner and reduced the rent from one-third to one-quarter. We are no longer so poor, no? We can buy clothes, keep our children in school longer, and buy some other things we need in the household.

What we most need to buy now is an irrigation pump.

Later, Edith and Lorenzo show me the bamboo "pipes" to water their vegetables they have rigged up in their fields with the guidance of the kasamas. *But they still have to carry the water in buckets from a small stream. A pump could make a big difference. Edith comments on the NPA.*

It's not true what you hear about the NPA up here in the mountains. The NPA is helping the people by giving education, giving suggestions on how to improve their way of living. And the NPA doesn't oppress or doesn't burden the people. Instead they help them. The NPA's don't tell them not to have faith in God. We support the NPA and are grateful to them, and we believe in God. The NPAs don't impose taxes; but the people, through good will, give what we want to give. We give voluntarily, in the form of money or foods— entirely voluntarily.

We belong to a *Kristiano ng Katilingban,* meaning a Basic Christian Community. Every Sunday, we are going to *paimbaon,* a lay people's mass, and we make mass without the priest. We read the Bible, we interpret the Bible in connection with our daily lives, how can the Bible help us. Sometimes, for instance, during the mass we talk about the need for land reform.

Lorenzo brings up the armed forces attack in this area.

It was about June. Fourteen days of bombing took place here. Mortar-shelling everywhere. The few NPA troops tried to defend the people. Fifty-two houses were burnt over there on the ridge. If it were not for the NPA, maybe this house would have been burned too. The military claimed that this is an NPA area and that those fifty-two houses were NPA houses. But they were the homes of poor farmers like us. Only one NPA was killed and one civilian. The people from those houses were evacuated to the barrio. Many now have *nipa* huts donated by Governor Bitay Lacson.

❖ ❖ ❖

In Bacolod, I mention the fifty-two burned-out peasant houses to Father Empestan. He says that during the Marcos period this kind of major military operation—with mortar shelling and aerial bombings—was unknown in Negros. Military operations have become bigger with the Aquino government, he says.

Vicente "Vic" Ladlad
Communist Party of the Philippines
Southern Tagalog and Bikol regions

Vic Ladlad, formerly a CPP/NPA official in southern Tagalog and Bikol regions, and a political prisoner for several years under Marcos, was released from solitary confinement a month after Cory Aquino became president.

Despite, or perhaps because of, what Vic Ladlad has been through, he seems serene and optimistic. He is also very bright and affable. He tells me that a former Peace Corps volunteer whom he had gotten to know "above ground" regularly sent him books in prison, including a number of Food First titles, which he says he read over and over. "These little packages from Chicago helped sustain me."

I'm 37 years old. I am a graduate in agricultural economics at UP Los Baños [University of the Philippines at Los Baños]. I was chairman of the student council in 1970–71 and had been an active student leader before martial law. With martial law and the government imprisoning people without evidence of a crime, I had to join the underground and worked underground until 1983 when I was arrested. I was in prison for three years—two years and nine months of which was in solitary confinement.

Tell me something about your family background.

I am from a peasant family. My father came from a land-scarce province, Marinduque, and settled in Quezon province in the 1920s. My grandfather and my father were able to develop a 12-hectare farm of which 4 hectares were inherited by my father.

In 1966, I graduated valedictorian in high school and found it quite easy to get a scholarship at the University of the Philippines. I was there for four years, and in my third year, the student movement began. I was elected the chairman of the student council and, of course, we had then a progressive student body at the UP. I also became a member of a patriotic youth organization, *Samahang*

Demokratiko ng Kabataan, quite modeled after the SDS [Students for a Democratic Society] in the United States. A year before martial law, I had to quit the school. I was then preparing my thesis to complete my degree. Had I formally graduated I would be a cum laude.

What kind of farm did you grow up on?

I grew up on a coconut farm. In fact, I still know all coconut farm chores. Up to my fourth year in high school, I was making copra during weekends to supplement my earnings for expenses in school. In my college, I had to supplement my scholarship with a gardening job in exchange for free board and lodging.

My mother operates a food *tienda,* or stand, in the town and she used to sell bread in the mornings. I did that too when I was in my elementary grades. But, of course, all this was not enough and in fact half of our farm now is under mortgage. My mother became indebted to a usurer while I was in prison. My sister tells me that my mother pays 40 pesos a day for the interest alone and this has been going on for, I think, three years.

Was this small farm and a bread shop adequate to provide for the food and other basic needs of your family?

Hardly. You see, the peak coconut harvest is from July to September. In the other months, my mother had to rely on borrowings and supplementary income activities. Of course, we were quite lucky because two of my sisters were able to land jobs, however low-paying they were. One of my sisters is a clerk at the Municipal Treasury and she is receiving 800 pesos monthly. Another sister of mine was a teller at the Rural Bank, with a little better salary, but she is now married. My sister at the Municipal Treasury is a polio victim, and she also experienced four months of incarceration because of some military officers seeking revenge against me.

Looking back on your growing up, was there serious hunger in your family?

Not exactly serious, but I remember that we had meat only twice a year, during New Year and fiesta. Our common fare was rice and the least expensive fish.

What led you to join the NPA?

Well, I never had much trouble understanding the basic concern of the national democratic movement, because I grew up in poverty. I was very serious in my study, hoping I could find a better-paying job when I graduated; I wanted to help my mother and my sisters. I didn't have time for *barkada,* or gangs, for

Joseph Collins

Vicente "Vic" Ladlad

leisure. When I found the national democratic movement and its program, I really thought that this is an alternative. Before that, though I was known for my academic performance, I could sense class differentiation among us students. But with the activists I found myself among equals. When I went underground, I first worked in the city, mostly doing education work. I joined the NPA in 1974.

Was there any individual person who inspired you to join the NPA?

You may be surprised, but I found my wife my inspiration. Actually, she was a lot ahead of me in political development. Incidentally, my wife was the editor of the campus paper when I was the chairman of the student council. We were partners when we joined the underground.

What did the work in the city consist of?

I conducted systematic education of recruits into the underground. Mainly clarifying the basic social problems of the country, the alternatives, and the ways to attain them.

And in the NPA?

I was mainly concerned with the political aspects of rural work—organizing, mobilizing the peasantry—not really with the military component of the struggle. Later on, I found myself more engaged in administrative work.

What were the events surrounding your arrest?

One of our personnel was captured, and he cooperated with the military.

Do you know who that person is?

It need not be told. (*Laughs.*)

Is he still alive?

Yes!

Can you describe your arrest?

I was here in Manila for a medical treatment and, in one of the houses I went to, the military operatives came and arrested me. Of course, I immediately prepared myself for the worst because for years so many of my comrades arrested were salvaged. My wife was missing since 1975, and in 1977 alone about a dozen comrades were salvaged. So I assumed that I would be another victim in 1983. Fortunately for me, however, the military authorities in Southern Tagalog were reprimanded earlier for salvaging prisoners. So when I was arrested, I became a good publicity object for the military authorities in that region. I wasn't actually subjected to physical torture except denial of sleep for about a week before the interrogation proper, and after that I was placed in solitary confinement and denied sunning and exercises.

You said that you were a publicity object for the military. What do you mean by that?

The military wanted to exhibit me as a prisoner not subjected to physical torture.

Sounds like a fortunate role given the circumstances, no?

Yes, as I've said, I'm quite lucky because earlier my comrades, including women, really suffered. In fact, there were only two other political prisoners—a coconut peasant organizer and his wife—alive in Lucena when I was taken in. That gives you an idea how many were salvaged.

What were the circumstances surrounding the disappearance of your wife?

My wife was with me in the rural areas from 1973 to 1974. In late 1974, as she was pregnant, we decided to have her area of work be in the city. She gave birth to our only child in April 1975, and was supposed to join me in December. On November 26, she was arrested on her way to a hospital to bring in a peasant for medical treatment. Her relatives—incidentally, she is the niece of a former head of the Civilian Intelligence Agency, the former Ambassador to South Korea, Colonel Nicanor Jimenez—her relatives tried to locate her in different military camps. But military authorities said they had released her in order to persuade me to surrender. But not a word is known about her since then.

After your release, what did you do?

My first one or two months, I was busy responding to invitations to speak. But in April, I started work as a member of a task force for the Philippine Coconut

Authority [PCA]. The chairman of PCA came from our province, and he helped me while I was in prison. The task force was primarily a policy review and policy recommendation body. But I didn't last there, because after three months the Minister of National Defense, J.P. Enrile, put pressure on the chairman to ease me out. I was jobless for about two months, but in September I began working at the UP Institute of Social Work and Community Development. At present, I am the executive secretary of the LAMBAT-LAYA, a network for popular participation strategies.

Did Enrile label you a "red in the government"?

Well, what's quite funny is one of the reasons Enrile was against the release of political prisoners, especially the ranking ones, is that he was afraid we might join the underground, our comrades in the hills. So we told them, Ah, let us see what we could do in the open. So when we were released, I accepted the offer to work in a government agency. But when we were with the government, Enrile complained of us infiltrating the government agencies. So I said, "Well, we can't be in heaven, we can't be in hell, where shall we be?" (*Laughs*.)

Several months later we continued our interview in the Bikol region which, like Vic's native Quezon province, is known for its coconut farms. I asked him about the National Democratic Front, of which the CCP is a key part, and its vision of agrarian reform.

The NDF doesn't mince words when it calls for land distribution. While a genuine agrarian reform would not limit itself to land distribution, I think it is the heart of the matter. There should be land distribution guided by the following principles. First, genuine agrarian reform stands for the policy of land to the tiller, those who work the soil must own the land. Implied in this, of course, is that the absentee landlords are not entitled to long-term ownership of land. Second, genuine agrarian reform means distribution of land for free. If the landowner is to be compensated at the fair market price as the newly ratified Constitution provides, it would mean that we are still maintaining the same inequitable distribution of wealth. And I think the third basic characterization of a genuine agrarian reform program is peasant power, meaning a share in the management of political affairs of the nation. One of the reasons why past land reform programs failed is that the farmers or peasants have no political power. So the landlords were able to dictate the terms that they want—for example, in deciding which crop lands are to be subjected to land reform, in the evaluation of lands to be paid for by the peasants. So the NDF believes that the political power of landlords must be curtailed and that of the peasants must be enhanced. So without addressing the problem of political power, there cannot be genuine agrarian reform.

How do the peasants get a say in the nation's political affairs? How can that be accomplished?

I think there are at least three ways. One is through federated peasant associations that should get representation in whatever political bodies are to be set up on the national, regional, and provincial levels. Another one is through the electoral process. While I don't see a real radical change by participating in electoral struggle, it would pay for farmers to elect their representatives, for example, in the coming congress, not really to initiate radical changes but to be able to express peasants' aspiration and urgent demands. And I think the third way is for militant farmers really to support the all-out effort by the NDF to change the make-up of the political configuration in the country.

We shouldn't forget that one of the achievements of the peasants' movement in the Philippines today is having brought to the public, brought into focus, the question of the land problems.

Actually, today, peasants, the organized peasants in the NDF areas like here in Bikol, have been implementing quite extensively a minimum land reform program—essentially, reduction of land rent. The landlords, in fact, in NDF areas, have come to some sort of a *modus vivendi* with the peasants and the NPA. Rather than lose their lands altogether, the landlords now prefer a reduced income from their land. Of course, this attitude stems from the fact that they could not simply wish the NPA to vanish. The landlords now realize that for the most part of the countryside, the NPA is there to stay. Also, the landlords have come to realize that, really, the peasants have gained in political awareness. At first, the landlords were surprised, taken aback at peasants having shouting matches with them, because it used to be that tenants, for example, were so shy and complacent, even resigned to their lot. But with the onset of peasant organizing and other activities, these tenants have become outspoken, and even would lead in demonstrations and delegations to negotiate for reduced rents.

In the NDF areas, the NPA areas, there has been significant change in the sharing system. Now, to a certain extent, the NDF is addressing the problem of productivity: how to increase farm production now that there have been significant changes in tenurial relations.

Many landowners contend that landless people would not know what to do with land if it were given to them and that agricultural output would therefore plummet. Is there any danger of that happening?

I think it depends on the area. In areas like Batangas, Laguna, and Nueva Ecija,

A regional commander of the National Democratic Front in rebel-held northeast Mindanao trains organizers who will work in "white zones" outside their control.

the peasants are quite knowledgeable about crop production for market. In other far-flung areas, the peasants would tend to produce only rice and some vegetables. In those areas, assistance will be needed in this regard. People's organizations in urban centers have begun setting up institutions that mobilize scientists, researchers, technicians from universities, such as the agricultural college, to help the peasants improve their use of their resources and plan their cropping patterns. There has also been some attempt at linking peasant cooperatives with businessmen in Manila to market peasants' produce. Of course, this start is only on a modest scale.

Money must go for helping to improve farmers' productivity, for setting up cooperatives, for providing credits for farm inputs, and other such concerns, instead of borrowing billions of pesos from abroad for compensating the rich landlords.

How would an NDF-supported agrarian reform affect production of exports like coconuts?

Well, of course, we cannot simply disregard production of coconuts, and 70 to 80 percent of coconuts are for export. What we want is to stop the increase of the amount of land devoted to coconuts, and possibly diversify some of the lands now planted with coconuts. But I'm not against the export of some agricultural products. I am only against a strategy that relies primarily on export of products without considering food self-sufficiency and the industrialization of such crops as coconut. For example, instead of exporting coconut oil and copra, we could intensify the effort at processing these into industrial products such as chemicals and cosmetics.

Getting back to land reform as such, is there enough land to redistribute to the large number of peasants?

Agricultural lands in the country amount to at least 12 million hectares. Peasant and farm workers would be equivalent to eight to ten millions. So if the total agricultural land would be redistributed, at least every peasant or farm worker would have a minimum of 1 hectare. So there's enough farmland.

But in the long run, of course, peasants could not subsist on a hectare, especially given that they have to rear their children. What the country needs, therefore, in addition to land reform, is the development of industries to siphon the labor surplus out of the countryside; otherwise, there would be too much population pressure for the existing land. So the problem of scarcity is not critical, at least not now.

How do you get from land redistribution to industrialization?

I think the approach could be two ways. One is to begin industrializing produce from the countryside and the other is to set up industries not really connected with agriculture. For example, coconut products could, instead of being exported in raw forms, be processed. The same is true with fish. Imagine, the Philippines imports canned fish! The other approach is to set up manufacturing industries. Of course, not necessarily airplanes or robots, but simple materials like spare parts. Would you believe that the Philippines imports even gaskets for our gas stoves? Producing such things here would provide impulses to develop other branches of the industrial economy.

Industrialization can obviously be very capital-intensive. Where would the money come from?

If you study the liquidity of Philippine banks, you will be surprised at the big amount of money that's unused or underutilized. We have enough money. Other than that, I am for a limited form of foreign assistance, especially in technology. I think some European countries like Sweden could be of help. No one should worry about the nationalists closing the door of the Philippines to foreign capital and technology. Even China now courts foreign capital, but of course on terms that China wants, not the other way around. In a country like the Philippines, you see, we have the foreign capitalists imposing the terms that they want. You'll be surprised to know that Dole and Del Monte were able to get tens of thousands of hectares of land almost at the cost of a song.

We are for supporting Filipino capitalists, even assisting them in viable projects. The economy that we want could be termed a mixed economy, where there could be significant state sector, but undeniably the role of private capitalists is very important. Not only the existing capitalists, but even the aspiring ones, for example, all small commodity producers, even Filipino professionals. Of course, in Philippine politics, there are some groups that are for socialism at once. No, I think the February revolution illustrated how significant and important is the role of the middle classes, even professionals, in mobilizing for social actions and that includes industrialization, the mobilization of capital, and technical know-how. I would assume that the Philippines would have advantage over China when it began its economic modernization program in 1949. For instance, we have plenty of college graduates, engineering graduates, who are now, because of lack of opportunities in the country, simply working as domestic helpers in Europe, in Singapore, in Hong Kong.

You come from an area of coconut plantations. Many would argue against land reform, saying that it would destroy the economies of scale you have with plantations.

But if you look at the different coconut farm sizes you will find that there's not much difference in yields between big and small farms. Why? You see, coconut farming is one type where farm mechanization is quite hard to do. You can't use a tractor or other farm mechanical device to harvest coconuts. So whether it is 100 hectares or 2 hectares, that wouldn't matter. You'll have the same harvest, the same productivity. It might surprise you, but coconuts are the least fertilized crop. The landlords simply wait for their share every harvest time. There's no input to increase productivity coming from the landlord. So many studies have shown that in coconut areas, economies of scale cannot be found. Anyway, genuine land reform does not necessarily mean dividing up a plantation, such as a sugar plantation, where through mechanization you might have a certain economy of scale; such plantations could be turned into cooperative farms. Land reform in the areas of the giant Del Monte and Dole plantations could take the form of state-owned farms that would include the industrial parts, the processing plants, not simply the farms. Even then the production part might be cooperativized.

Vic Ladlad, like many, sees the history of his country through the optic of the peasants' struggle over land.

The Philippine revolution of 1896 was a struggle against Spanish colonialism. The peasantry responded with the call to seize and distribute land. In fact, many friars were killed because of their being landlords. In the 1930s, there was extensive peasant unrest and armed peasant rebellion in central Luzon. In the 1950s, the Huk rebellion was essentially a peasants' struggle over injustice in the rural structures. The NPA was primarily established to struggle in response to the peasants' demand for land.

❖ ❖ ❖

In January 1988, I make contact with Vic Ladlad in Manila. He suggests we meet at a McDonald's. He tells me that because of threats on his life, he has reduced his public visibility. He will be doing educational work with peasant organizations in different parts of the country.

Ka Francis and Ka Al
NPA agronomists
Albay province, Bikol region

*I*n Albay province I am invited by the NDF/NPA to go underground to see for myself the "minimum land reform" underway in "NPA-consolidated areas." Over six days' time I hike to various small villages with Ka Al and Ka Francis, agronomists and socio-economic staffers for the NPA. They both are agreeable, bright-faced fellows in their late 20s, with a good command of English. Al and Francis ask me not to photograph their faces. From one trail we get a postcard-perfect view of Mount Mayon, and Al asks me to photograph him facing the volcano, back to me, rifle slung over his shoulder.

On the final day I interview them. We start with Francis talking about his background.

I was born twenty-six years ago, here in the Bikol region. My grandparents were poor peasants. They lived in Albay province near Legaspi, but that's where the Japanese invaders first landed, so they fled to Camarines Sur [another Bikol province]. They cleared and cultivated some forest land. Eventually after liberation, they got titles to the land from the government. After the war and in the 1950s, they planted mostly coconut. And they sold lumber.

From the viewpoint of revolutionary analysis, my parents now are in the upper strata, the landlord class. They have about 69 hectares in different locations, the largest being 30 hectares. They have tenants, and they hire laborers to help with the gathering and the processing of the nuts. The sharing system is 60 percent in favor of my father, and 40 percent to the tenants.

Coming from the landlord class, how did you wind up in the revolutionary movement?

It's because I was away from my parents. (*Laughs.*) I went away to college. That's the foundation at least. It's your immediate environment that contributes to your perception of things. This was particularly true at the UP Los Baños

Joseph Collins

Ka Al

[University of the Philippines at Los Baños]. Student activities at that time had a certain momentum when we entered in 1977. It was a time of massive boycotts and all sorts of demands by the student council. Why is the budget for the military so much higher than for the public schools, especially for our institution, the government university?

At the university, how did you first come into contact with the underground movement?

Actually, it was through a legal organization of Bikolanos, which developed into a politically motivated organization and in a sense was infiltrated by the communists. After two years as an activist with this legal organization, I got involved in the underground student movement of the KM, the Patriotic Youth [*Kabataang Makabayan*]. So behind the legal organization there was an underground organization, the KM.

I assume that when you came to the university you had no intention of being a political activist much less of joining an illegal underground organization. Tell me more about how you got involved.

When I came to UP Los Baños, my thinking was that I would graduate in four years. In high school my first two loves were sports and academics. I was an athletic type, and I used to play basketball. My heroes were Wilt Chamberlain and the Celtics. In college, at first I used my free time to play, to keep physically fit, but then you get close to many in the organization of Bikolanos. And then later you come to know that they are part of the movement. And they are ... are so inspiring. And they—how to term it?—wake you up: Why are so many Filipinos hungry, poor, suffering, and yet there are some who are so rich? That very basic difference in society, and that was the focus of readings—we even read things from Food First—and discussions within the organization itself, leads you into a deeper involvement until, before you are aware of it, you are actively working in the movement.

Were the people in the movement suspicious of you because of your class background?

A social investigation is done before you're invited. I was aware of it. It was almost one year before I formally entered the underground organization, the KM. They kept on investigating my background.

What were some of the political activities that you were involved in during your time at UP?

I held some responsibilities within some legal organizations, for example, the student council, and with some alliances formed around various issues and demands. After a year or two, I became more involved on a low-profile level with the underground. I was doing education, building the cells of the KM. Other people were doing the above ground work.

There was a gradual development in my work. For example, from a single underground cell, I later came to have the responsibility of handling larger groups of cells. In that process, aside from being in the mass organization of the *Kabataang Makabayan,* I was as early as 1980 invited to become a candidate member of the Communist party. I became a full-fledged party member by 1982.

Did your parents know about what you were doing and, if so, how did they react?

When I was in high school, my mother was interested in having me become a priest. She wanted to put me in a seminary. My father wanted me to study in a private school but not in a seminary. For a while, I too was interested in being a priest. Since my elementary grades I used to go to religious schools, a Dominican school, and then in high school it was a Jesuit school. But my father said that it would be better for me to take up agriculture. He's a *hacendero;* so in the future he planned for me to manage our farms. So I took the entrance examination and took up agriculture at UP Los Baños.

Generally, they have accepted my ideas. Still they have their reservations, even now. In the whole family, we are eleven, and I am the seventh child. My elder brothers and sisters, they still ask help from our parents. So my parents see me as a certain hope to help the family, and to help my younger brother and sister to finish their education. But when I involved myself in the underground, it seemed that their hopes and plans for the family were all crumbling down.

Back to your university experiences. Tell me more about how the movement recruits on campus.

One way is drinking, drinking beer. Al is good at that. He is a good organizer during a drinking spree.

Al joins in.

That's true. During our college days, Friday afternoons after a hard day of class work is a good time for relaxation, and that is a very good time for activists in the movement. That's one way. But in reality there is, you know, a problem with this approach: Sometimes they're too drunk.

Anyway, there are other approaches. Actually, during any mass rallies or even sports activities, you chat and say what you think is happening in our country. You spot someone receptive to what you are saying. You let him know that he is not alone in his way of thinking. Eventually, you invite him to join an organization, to join an NDF cell.

Al, to catch up with where we are with Francis, can you talk about your background?

My father was once a schoolteacher. My mother is a simple housewife. We are seven in the family, and I'm the youngest.

My grandfather was a farmer, and my parents were raised in a farming community. I grew up in the town center, but still we have a small piece of land where after classes or during Saturdays, Sundays, I cultivated some vegetables. But that's not really the thing that makes me decide to go to UP Los Baños to take up agriculture. It's my friends, you know, my best friends were eager to enter UP, and I didn't want to be separated from them.

How did you first make contact with the movement? How did they recruit you?

My sister was a member of the organization where I also later belonged. And she was, as far as I know, also a full-fledged member of the party at that time. I assumed that the members of the organization knew that my sister was talking to me and they joined also in recruiting me. I entered the organization in 1978.

Which organization? Is it a legal organization?

Yes, it is a legal organization. I'm not naming it for security reasons.

Working with this organization, how did you end up in the underground?

I ended up in the underground when suddenly, one day, one of my brods [brothers, buddies] invited me for some sort of informal talk. We discussed a lot about how I perceived Marcos and how I looked at the military; how I perceived the national situation. I always answered him negatively. So he said, "Would you like to join an NDF cell?" At first, I was afraid. The first thing that entered into my mind was that I might be ruining my studies if I go fulltime in organizing. But I managed to regain somehow my composure. And I answered him, "Yes, I'm willing."

When you were invited to do political work, what motivated you? Was it Marcos?

It was the press. At that time it was so controlled. I can't take what they are writing. I think it is no exaggeration to say that it is an insult to my sensibility. I wasn't born yesterday. I know what's happening. I know the reality, and yet they are projecting a very good image. I said to myself, Why are they doing this, when in fact it is the other way around? It is not the true picture of what's happening here in the Philippines. They'd say, We are in the New Society now, so everything is fine and everyone is disciplined. Crime is less; graft and corruptions are decreased. But I heard from among my friends that they are not going to report for work, that they just report on the 15th and 30th, and yet they will receive their salaries. So I have the feeling that graft and corruption are not reduced, but instead growing.

This question is for both of you. How did you perceive the communists before you joined the movement?

FRANCIS: I was molded by reading in school, by the black propaganda, by the anti-communist hysteria. You know, I might think that the communist philosophy in a sense is good but its practice is bad. Little by little, my confusions were cleared up, although up to now I find some differences in theory and practice. Take democratic centralism within the party. In practice, there's too much centralism and not enough democracy.

AL: Yes, I also had strong anti-communist ideas because of what my mother is telling me: The NPAs are the oppressors of the people; they are the bandits.

Al, do your parents now know of your activities?

No, not yet.

What do you think would happen if they found out?

They will probably have a heart attack.

Francis, how is it that you are here in the countryside with the NPA?

Usually, in the student section of the movement, we have the feeling that the highest stage of struggle is in the countryside, and in the armed group in the countryside. For five years, I was assigned there in the same territory. There came a time that I was bored with the work. The hassles of talking with the intellectuals, the theoreticals. In practice, they are afraid of joining the armed struggle, of joining the NPA.

By 1983, I gave in to the mounting pressures from my sisters and parents to finish my studies. So from time to time, in the urban part of this region, I work implementing some projects. But then, after a year, there is still lacking—what should I call it?—a fulfillment of myself. Since 1985, I am here. And in a sense, compared to the past activities, it has made for more meaningful work, more significant and more deep than the not superficial but limited legal work. It's a sacrifice to work in the countryside, but a sacrifice with fulfillment.

Could you say something more about those sacrifices?

For one, there's a sense that you are isolated. There's a distancing from the local peasant cadres, at first. You are in a sense outcasted from the movement. That was my first impression. But then after some reflections and actual integration, I came to realize that it is the effect of not knowing really what's in the peasant cadres' minds, their way of thinking. So, in essence, you have to change your thinking and perception. There must be some adjustments so as not to frustrate yourself by having such very high demands and expectations. You must go along with the people. That's one sacrifice, one within the party.

A second sacrifice of sorts has to do with the peasant organization here. My first impression was they are always waiting for the party's directives. So I said, For the past seventeen years, is this the type of people we are organizing—too dependent and too passive, just waiting? But you come to realize that it is a very long process with these kinds of classes—for them to really assert or to express their own ideas, to see that they have their own power even without the NPA or even without the party, that they have their own sentiments, their own ideas, their own hopes. So that's the second one—frustration. And there are others. (*Laughs.*) But I guess these are the two glaring ones.

Soldiers of the New People's Army in training in Albay province in Bikol. The NPA is estimated to number 30,000 fulltime and parttime guerrillas, mostly the sons and daughters of landless rural families. The NPA is active in 67 of the country's 73 provinces.

What are other sacrifices?

You have an abnormal life. That abnormality can be felt in many ways. For example, in your usual eating habits, it's a sacrifice. Outside you can have fresh fish, a beer or two, and all those good foods. But here it's a sacrifice in that sense, no?

But beyond that, you make yourself dependent on the development of the whole revolution. For example, you can't just go and act on your own ideas without, let's say, going along with the pace of the revolution. Meaning you can have so many good and fanstastic ideas, but it's futile. So it's a sacrifice in terms of the bourgeois idea of having the individual excel. You have to make yourself a part of the whole movement; you have to submit yourself to the party's program.

Al, does the movement, especially being fulltime underground, affect your life with your wife?

Actually, we see each other for a couple of days within a month. Because I am fulltime and she is also working as a legal fulltime, and her time is needed there and all my work is here, we are not expecting that we will be together more—you know, live a normal life as most couples do. But we are still happy with such an arrangement.

Did you meet her in the movement?

I met her in the movement and we were wed in a party wedding.

Did you also have a church wedding before a priest?

No, not yet. We are planning to, so that our parents call us as husband and wife. Right now our parents think that we are sweethearts; so we still sleep in two separate beds and two separate rooms.

Do you have any children?

None yet. But we plan to after our church wedding.

Francis, can you too tell me about the impact of the movement on your personal life, your relationships, that sort of thing?

Actually, there are some couples who are matchmaking me with many comrades. For example, one doctor in Manila would like to transfer here in Bikol so as to get expertise in working with the NPA. But they also want to match me to her. But I said it is not good because a relationship is four-dimensional. I mean, it's personal, political, sexual ... and what is the other? I can't remember now. Anyway, what usually happens in the movement is the political dimension plays the biggest role. But you cannot plainly negate the personal interest. For me, the female has to be complete, not handicapped; at least, she should be not married or widowed. One week ago, a comrade in another district talked with me and asked, "What are your plans, what are your tastes in a girl?" Because there they have two female comrades who are prospecting me. So the two comrades are asking the help of this comrade to investigate me. So I tell him these are my habits, my tastes, and such things. That's the way we do it in the revolution.

What does the socio-economic staff do?

AL: The socio-economic staff is involved in training, specifically technical training and leadership trainings of farmer organizations and individual farmers. We also are involved in introducing ecologically sound projects that are, at least, accessible to the poor. Simple projects—animal caretaking, plant production, and food production. But right now we are still on the small scale. We recognize that we should start small with a very high tendency of success, rather than start with a very big endeavor which we feel could be prone to failure or much lower success. We are also involved in social investigations of the communities in which we work and in doing some work with the comrades in the territory, especially education work along socio-economic lines.

FRANCIS: Actually, when we say socio-economic work, it is essentially another term for national democratic revolution. Socio-economic work is only an academic term. It's real essence is changing the lives of the people. For the Marxist, essentially, socio-economic work means changing the relations of production to more democratic ones and to advance, to develop, the forces of production. To put it simply, change people's lives into better ones. Essentially, it is the creation of political power in the hands of the vast majority of the people. For anything to be developed, there first has to be control in the hands of the people. So, essentially, the revolution's idea is for the majority to control, not the few, which at present is the state of affairs, economically and socially.

But if we must distinguish socio-economic work from, say, other fronts of work—for example, military work or educational work or any other kind of work in the revolution—then at this stage let us say that it is the same as production work. The NPA tradition was not only a military and political group but also a production group. The NPAs in their free time involved themselves in production efforts. Even the party comrades, they worked in production work. But then for the past years in our region, they are so scattered, the movement's development is so, in a sense, like mushrooms—they just grow anywhere. So there was the need to put up a specific group, the socio-economic staff, to coordinate the efforts of comrades in the guerrilla zones, of organizations, of independent agencies, or of contacts within the government. So, for the past year we have lain the foundation to systematize these efforts of the party and the people.

AL: There is still another rationale for the formation of the socio-economic staff. We recognize the fact that as our military formations grow larger we really rely on the support of the masses. We recognize that there will come a time when, if we don't really pay attention to increasing their incomes, perhaps their ability to support the revolutionary movement will wane. We help the farmers' get a bigger share of their production, and we help them increase production, not merely to raise the farmers' standard of living but primarily so that they can support and sustain the revolutionary movement until we seize power.

What do you see yourselves doing after victory?

FRANCIS: I take the perspective that winning victory is easier than reconstructing society; so I guess after victory there is still a lot of work to do. It is not the case that after victory you have finished the job. It is more demanding to reconstruct the economy, the society. The experience that we are now accumulating could be a big help to further develop and advance the revolution. After winning this national revolution, what we have in mind is the perspective of a socialist society, although there could be a transition of experimentation, some sort of mixed economy.

AL: Well, I do hope that one day I'll lead a normal life, one day after the revolution. Probably, I'll be involved much more in just what I'm doing right now—preserving, protecting, perpetuating the gains of the national democratic revolution, in helping the people have access to food and jobs.

FRANCIS: Sometimes I have the notion that maybe after victory at least there could be time for you to fully develop yourself, for example, if you still have the aspiration of completing studies in your field. Further study could be a help in the building of the country. So, after the revolution, there could be the possibility that I could have a plan to study further in the field of agriculture.

Any number of times this week, and again today, both of you have mentioned democracy. You have a great deal of experience here at the grassroots level. How would your notion of democracy differ from what Cory Aquino talks about?

AL: I think democracy is defined in several ways, depending on who defines it. For the rich, I should say "democracy" is some sort of a freedom to accumulate more wealth. But for the poor majority, democracy could be seen as when all our people readily have access to food, to jobs, to justice. We can't say that we are free, if our people are still hungry, the oppressive structures are present, and the lands are being controlled by the minority of our people. Democracy for the Cory government is the freedom to continue to exploit the vast majority of our resources, the people. For the Cory government, there should be no dissent, no one should rise up and say, "We resist." So for me to think that this community is a democratic community, that this nation is a democratic nation, the people living here should benefit from what the lands produce. They should never go hungry.

The time has come for goodbyes. Al, Francis, and I agree to keep in touch. I promise to send the photos of the peasants I have taken and some Food First books. Al gives me an "above ground" address. He says that he will send some regionwide data on the NDF/NPA minimum land reform for my book that they are to pull together at a party seminar the next month.

In a letter I receive shortly after my return to San Francisco, Al tells me he has received the books I sent in Manila and is happily spending a few days in a safe house in town, with his wife, reading them. He also tells me that it was a good thing we left "the area" when we did. The next day, the military, guided by an NPA soldier who recently had surrendered, came to one of the barrios I had visited. They interrogated several peasants I had spoken with and hit them in the stomach with rifle butts. In the next barrio, the soldiers killed some pigs and chickens and ransacked the houses, breaking the drinking glasses and plates. In the village where I interviewed Al and Francis, the military entered and opened fire on unarmed peasants, killing four, including an 8-year-old boy who was shot in the head while cooking rice.

Ten days later I hear again from Al. One of the other members of the socio-economic staff I had briefly met was in town one day and was "fingered" and fired upon simultaneously by seven military and police. He died, Al notes, wearing a red polo shirt that one morning I had accidentally left behind. Soon he hopes to be able to collect and send to me the regionwide data on NPA land reform. "Also someday I hope to see you again and pose for a photograph without facing Mayon Volcano!"

A week later, another letter arrives from Al. He has received a large envelope with photos in it, but he fears that it has been tampered with. He is worried. Would I please immediately write back, listing the photos I sent? I should use a different name and address and "destroy" the ones he had given me. I realize that it never occurred to me to make a list of the photos I was sending. In a "P.S." Al says that Andro, the NPA soldier who was my bodyguard during my visit, likes his photo and asks that when I come back I bring him a pair of Levis, size 28.

❖ ❖ ❖

Weeks pass and I don't hear anything more from Al. Then one day I receive a handwritten unsigned note postmarked Legaspi City (Albay) but without a return address. It reads "Ka Al, Ka Francis, three other members of the socio-economic staff, and Andro were ambushed and killed by the military in May. The military found in Al's backpack photographs of a 'foreigner.' "

Six:
MISPLACED INDUSTRY

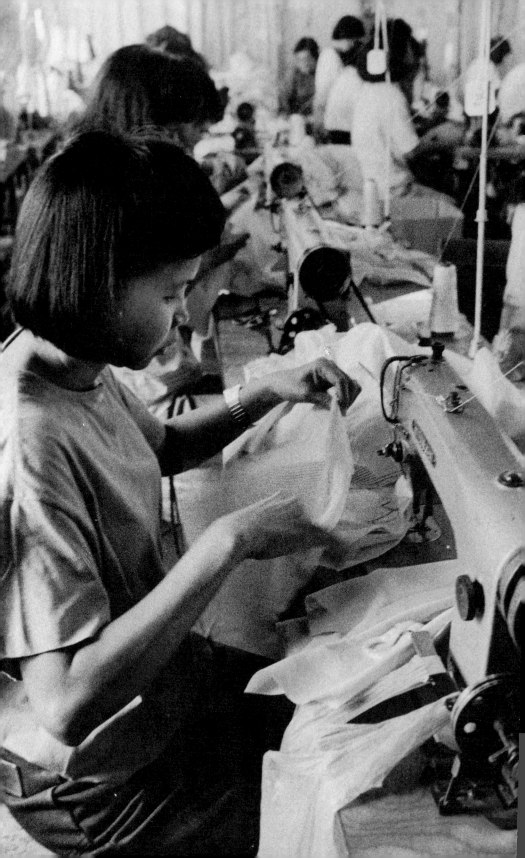

The Aquino administration's strategy for addressing the nation's widespread poverty has not been one of democratizing the land and other productive wealth. Instead, Aquino has chosen a policy of "economic recovery" based on the assumption that recovery can be achieved only with the help of foreign capital.

The first consequence of adopting the strategy of wooing foreign capital was that Aquino immediately committed the government (and people) of the Philippines to honor every foreign obligation incurred by the previous regime. This is no small commitment. The payments on the over $25 billion in loans under the Marcos regime consume 40 percent of the earnings from all the sugar, coconut oil, and other exports from the Philippines.

Almost all of this massive debt resulted from the billions swilled during the Marcos years, in largely nonproductive ventures. Many of the loans are patently outrageous instances not only of irresponsible borrowing but of irresponsible lending. It is worth a close look at one such loan—$2.1 billion for a nuclear power plant—to judge mortgaging the Philippines' economic future to pay off the boondoggles of a corrupt regime.

Westinghouse, for double the bid made by rival General Electric, constructed one of the most expensive nuclear power plants in the world in Bataan, across the bay from Manila. The plant is located within less than one hundred miles of four active volcanos, on the shoreline forty-five miles from an underwater fault line (earthquakes and tidal waves are frequent in the archipelago), and six miles from the nuclear weapons stored at the U.S. naval base at Subic.

As if this site were not enough to terrorize anyone, Westinghouse unloaded a reactor that had been certified defective by the Nuclear Regulatory Commission. Westinghouse awarded, without competitive bidding, a cost-plus–fixed-fee contract for all site construction to Herminio Disini, the husband of Imelda Marcos's cousin and Ferdinand Marcos's golfing partner. Disini obtained a government loan to set up a construction company for the project. Westinghouse paid a commission of nearly $80 million to Marcos through Disini, which was spirited away into secret Swiss bank accounts.

One auspicious element of this otherwise outrageous story is that the plant provoked some of the largest popular demonstrations during the Marcos regime (widely considered the precursor of the February 1986 uprising). Combined with the NPA's blowing up of the plant's electric pylons and lines, the protests delayed the installation of the plant's fuel rods. Subsequently, the Aquino government has indicated that the plant will never operate.

Nevertheless, under the Aquino government's economic program, the Philippines continues to pay $140 million annually in interest on the loan for the plant. The money goes to a Citibank-led consortium and to the U.S. Export-Import Bank. Ex-Im Bank's then-chairman William J. Casey, a Marcos loyalist to the end, was the staunchest supporter of what was the largest loan deal in the bank's history. The payment of $140 million a year is more than the government's annual health budget—in a country in which one out of three persons suffers from tuberculosis.

Many people would suggest that Aquino, especially after the internationally notorious corruption of the Marcoses, could have made a compelling case for the selective repudiation of the foreign debt. This strategy was proposed by her minister of economic development. Instead, while Aquino has gained some modest debt "rescheduling," the Philippines government has signed on for a policy that not only burdens Filipinos with the mistakes of the past but offers little prospect for success in the future.

Even the most faithful adherence to the rules of the game will not change the fact that, with the international debt crisis, western banks have been sharply pulling away from third-world lending since the mid-1980s. New bank loans to the third world declined from $35 billion in 1983 to a mere $3 billion in 1985, with a significant upturn unlikely. Similarly, foreign investments in the third world declined from $14 billion in 1981 to less than $9 billion in the years 1983 to 1985.

For the foreseeable future, the money flowing out of the Philippines to service existing foreign debt (projected at $13 billion for the period of 1987 to 1992) will far exceed the most optimistic projections of foreign aid. In 1988, U.S. aid (loans and grants) to the Philippines totaled less than $380 million, compared to the $2.3 billion the Filipino people paid in interest to foreign banks. Nearly half of the U.S. aid goes directly to the Philippine military, to fight the rebellion in the countryside.

Under the Aquino "economic recovery" strategy, the government will need to do all it can to promote exports. But promoting exports tends to put more land into production of luxury export crops instead of foods needed by most Filipinos. Promoting exports plays into the hands of those fighting the redistribution of agricultural resources away from the wealthy oligarchy and allied foreign agribusinesses. Further, exports of Philippine products, from the land or from manufacturing in export processing zones like those in Bataan, have no chance of being competitive unless wages are held down and the fields and factories kept union-free. Finally, the world markets for much of Philippine exports are shrinking, and output by rival exporting countries is increasing.

President Aquino also readily implemented the World Bank-prescribed pro-

Leo Esclanda

The Bataan Export Processing Zone (BEPZ), an 850-acre industrial park. Multimillion dollar public investments in subsidized facilities together with tax exemptions and other privileges are offered to lure export-oriented corporations.

gram of trade liberalization, lifting tariff and other barriers on a wide range of imports from multinational corporations. The Philippines is thus ever more trapped in the role of supplying raw materials and importing finished products.

The Bataan Export Processing Zone

The Bataan Export Processing Zone (BEPZ) is an 850-acre industrial park located on the southern tip of the hot and hilly Bataan Peninsula of Luzon Island. It is built upon the scene of General Douglas MacArthur's "last stand" against the Japanese Army in the early days of World War II.

Modeled after Taiwan's pioneering Kaohsiung "export platform" (in operation since 1966), the BEPZ was created by presidential fiat two months after Marcos declared martial law in September 1972. Corporations that exported at least 70 percent of their products were rewarded with a number of incentives for relocating to the new enclave. The most important incentives were exemptions from taxes and duties, ready-made factory facilities for nominal rents, access to good roads, a port, electricity, and—thanks to martial law—a strike-free labor force.

In its peak in the early 1980s, the Bataan Export Processing Zone, situated beside the once sleepy fishing town of Mariveles, was home to fifty-eight export enterprises employing 29,000 workers, about 80 percent of them women aged 15 to 24. By the time of my visit (1987), only twenty-eight companies were still in operation, and the number employed was down to 12,000. Once touted as the showcase of the future of the Philippines, the BEPZ had become, in the words of visiting journalist Jon Miller, a weed-choked monument to a national economic strategy favoring export-oriented industrialization over the development of small scale industry for domestic markets."

The manufacture of labor-intensive products like garments, electronic goods, and sporting goods for export was the road to development prescribed for the Philippines by the World Bank. The BEPZ was to be the spearhead of this strategy. But by the mid-1980s, a number of flaws on this path to development were evident. These flaws were nothing new to the Philippines: they were just the latest variation on the inadequacies of the elite-controlled, export-oriented economy that has been imposed on the Philippines since colonial times.

The development of the Bataan Export Processing Zone has brought with it the following problems.

❖ The competitiveness of Philippine manufacturing on the world market depends on paying low wages to the work force. Keeping wages and benefits low inevitably requires the repression of labor organizing. The very social and economic structures that generate a large number of economically desperate people become the country's comparative advantage. The BEPZ needs to maintain this advantage rather than increase people's well-being and control.

❖ The BEPZ has attracted enterprises that mainly specialize in assembling imported components. This process has not stimulated the emergence of complementary local industries, added greater value to local agricultural products, or transferred industrial technology to the Philippines.

❖ The foreign exchange the BEPZ has earned is minimal; approximately two-thirds of the value of its manufactured exports comes from imported raw materials and only one-third is value-added in the Philippines.

❖ The export-oriented industrialization strategy has involved large infrastructure expenditures by the government on behalf of private, mainly foreign corporations. A considerable chunk of the Philippines' $30 billion debt was incurred to provide infrastructure for the BEPZ. The inoperative $2.1 billion Westinghouse nuclear reactor in Morong, Bataan, for example, was meant to service the BEPZ. The Zone has operated at a loss since it was opened.

❖   The trends in world market conditions beyond the control of the Philippines doomed the BEPZ from early in its history. Stagnating world trade and rising protectionism in prime markets like the United States make the import of manufactured goods from the third world increasingly difficult. The Zone's exports have decreased from $160 million in 1982 to $60 million in 1987.

The BEPZ was premised on a low-paid, strike-free labor force. But in 1979, the workers at the Ford body-stamping plant launched the Zone's first strike. In succeeding years, the mostly female labor force that was once represented to foreign investors as docile, has stood in the forefront of militant labor unionism in the country.

It is not difficult to understand the workers' determination to defy the presidential decree banning strikes in export industries. Their working and living conditions are, in the words of one U.S. investigator, reminiscent of the early days of the Industrial Revolution in England. Illnesses from exposure to chemicals in many of the industries are commonplace: upper respiratory and throat infections in apparel factories, sinusitis in footwear and leather plants; eye irritations and hypertension in electronics industries, and conjunctivitis in plastics and metal fabrication factories.

Workers continue to struggle for a living wage and decent working conditions under the Aquino government, as interviews with some of the workers show. Yet, like workers in other third-world countries that have adopted export-oriented strategies of development, the BEPZ workers are finding that strikes and other traditional workers' weapons are increasingly ineffective against the exceptional mobility of multinational companies. This power was underlined by one executive in Manila: "We tell the government, You've got to clamp down [on the workers] or we threaten to move elsewhere. And we'll do just that. There's Sri Lanka ... now China too."

Dioscoro Calimbas
Shopowner and Catholic activist
Mariveles, Bataan Peninsula

D *ioscoro Calimbas has opened a small dry goods shop in the front part of his house. It's late one afternoon a few days before Christmas, and the shop is full of women customers. Nonetheless, the tall, thin Mr. Calimbas sits down with me in the living room, right off the shop. We talk over a couple of soft drinks, as his wife and daughters wait on the happy-sounding customers.*

I am the president of the parish council of Mariveles, and I am the vice-president of the PERES, the provincial ecumenical organization.

My family is from here, from Bataan. During the war, my family moved to Manila because this was an American base. I was born in Manila in 1943. Bataan was the center of the retreat of the American soldiers. That's why so much devastation happened here in Bataan, specifically here in Mariveles. No building was left untouched by the war—including the church, the hospitals, and everything that was built. Formerly, this was a fishing village.

My father was a farmer from a farmer family. My mother was a public schoolteacher. I went to elementary school and high school here in Mariveles, and then I went to Manila for my college. At one point I entered the seminary, but I was not chosen.

How did you view the coming of the export processing zone?

Being president of the parish council when the BEPZ was being started here opened my eyes. First, because it involved the displacement of the indigenous people in the surrounding areas—the farmers and those who had been doing farm work in the areas that were going to be the Zone. Four *sitios* [settlements] were moved, people living off the soil. The farms were about to be harvested of rice when the government bulldozed the area. Not even a single cent of compensation was paid to them; some died clamoring for it. Those people who were brave enough to fight, to register their protest, were picked up and detained. That was how the BEPZ was started.

We even held rallies against the planned Zone. It was very hard to be against the Zone. Even before martial law, it was risky. That's why so many of us were picked up. I don't know why I wasn't one of them. Specifically, the young men of the community, including my brother, my relatives, were put in jail.

Has the Zone been an economic success?

The Zone is a success for the foreign capitalists, probably. But look at the community, compare even the physical appearance of the community before the Bataan Export Processing Zone and now. Before, we had a very quiet community, with job opportunities and good relationships among the people. The community before the BEPZ was self-sufficient enough to have potential for progress in the big shipbuilding industry, the farms, the fishing.

At first, most of the people here were quite happy at the prospects of the Zone because something new—and foreign—was being introduced. Filipinos are really culturally dominated. Filipinos are so much Americanized in their thinking that everything that the foreigners say is the best; everything imported is good. And this includes the poor, especially when you dangle in front of their eyes the so-called economic benefits that the Zone would provide.

Now people are slowly finding out what the community has been reduced to. First, a big slice of their area—a potential for income-generating projects for their municipality—was taken away by the national government. They are not paying real estate tax here in the municipality—nothing. So the income of the municipality was considerably reduced. We cannot even afford to fix our municipal roads. And second, the influx of workers here—we were not prepared for that either. The community atmosphere was so much altered. So much so that there are community problems in the peace and order situation that include vices and all the defects of sudden urbanization. Before we could leave clothes hanging outside to dry; now the next day you will find nothing. And before we could leave our windows open; now you cannot. Now there are so many robberies and holdups happening. The Zone brought us more problems than if we were left alone here.

Actually, one of the biggest defects is that we were not prepared by the government. They just forced the Zone here, and we were left on our own. Most of the workers live in the *poblacion*. We were not prepared for it. We have so many makeshift houses, and the majority of the houses are subhuman conditions. We have many fires. Everything was done in a hurry just to accommodate the Zone.

In your view, the local economy has actually deteriorated since the Zone came in?

Our economy is so dependent on foreign investors. With the slightest twist of a foreign event in another land, we are affected. In the 1980s with the Zone going down, we have so many problems. There are now many unemployed people in Mariveles. And now the Zone is trying to minimize the number of local people getting jobs in the Zone. They find the transient workers more manageable than the local workers. The workers here can fight for their rights. They live here, while those transient workers are manageable in their thinking.

So many former workers are now unemployed, because before there were fifty-eight companies, now there are only twenty-seven. There were about 35,000 workers at the peak. These workers left their hometowns poor. It is basic in the Filipino to be ashamed to go back unimproved; so they stick it out here in the hope of finding another job.

The Aquino government says it is trying to stimulate other economic activities, but they will find it hard, because actually they are following the same program with new clothing. The announced economic program of the new government has the same basic elements reducing the economy to a raw-materials-for-export economy. In agriculture, they have even fewer plans for industrialization. The Aquino government is for all-out compliance with the economic policies of the International Monetary Fund–World Bank tandem, orienting our economics ever more toward export promotion. There is no change—the same technocrats, the same policies, the same lenders, the same controllers. We could name so many business opportunities here that could very well be handled by local entrepreneurs, but they are handed over to multinationals. And to develop a nationalist economy would entail a redistribution of control over wealth—the whole setup. And the government is not going to do that.

Have local businesspeople benefited from the Zone?

Mariveles is a very poor town. There are no managers from Mariveles. There is really no elite class. The managers do not go to our church, they have their own there on top of the mountain. They say it is much nearer to God, I don't know how.

Mariveles is a town with a reserve work force. It is reduced to being like South Africa with its Black reserve labor force—that is the picture we are getting.

What we can be proud of here is that unionism started in Mariveles. I'm glad to say that we are part of the development of unions in this part of the world. The parish council—upon the introduction of the BEPZ, because we could not do anything to stop it—we decided on another strategy. We phoned first a labor consultative council so that we could analyze the situation and help organize a labor movement within the BEPZ. We helped financially. We helped in building facilities. When, under martial law, strikes in export-related companies were banned, the first strike was held with the help of the community, with our help.

I want to appeal to the American people, specifically the American businessmen, to have more social conscience. It is not bad to have profits, but to profit at the expense of the very life of the people, of struggling people, is bad. No, we would not have the multinational corporations closed down. We accept the reality of foreign capital in the Philippines. What we are struggling for is more consciousness on their part toward the Filipino—specifically, higher wages or a just share in the profit so that we will be able to live decently.

When they put up the BEPZ, most people here were still under the chocolate Joe mentality [the fond view of Americans, especially of GIs]. Well, that mentality has changed significantly. I speak of the Catholic people; I don't know about the other sectors. There is growing support for real change, because the real role of the U.S. is slowly unfolding. And thanks to the past regime, it has accelerated. The politicization of the Filipino people, of the people of Bataan, was much faster during the past regime. And the capacity to analyze is carried over to the new regime so that they can see that there is a very bad trend already in the new government.

Lucy
Garment worker
Bataan Export Processing Zone

ucy is a young, earnest woman with a big smile. I meet with her at dusk in a small wooden house in a crowded working-class neighborhood in Mariveles. She shares the house with several other women her age, also factory workers. It is mid-December, and, as Lucy and I talk, dozens of children are on the unpaved street outside her window, singing Christmas songs, including the Filipino favorite, "I'm Dreaming of a White Christmas."

I'm a worker in a garment factory owned by a British multinational, Intercontinental Garment Manufacturing Corporation. It sells jackets, coats, especially winter coats, and it has a big business in England. Almost everything is exported—there's not much market for winter coats in the Philippines. We have distribution even in the U.S., and also in Australia. The company has many buyers, like Catalina, the biggest garment company in the U.S., and South America.

I was born in Samal, fifty-five kilometers from here. I came here to Mariveles in December 1975, to look for a job because I saw an advertisement. I got this job; so I've been with the firm from 1975 until the present—ten, eleven years. The first batch of workers have thirteen years in the company.

My father is a farmer. We pay thirty-six *cavans* for 1½ hectares each year. It is very difficult. I work here to send money back home to my parents, and at present I support one of my nieces for her studies.

I am still single. Eighty-seven percent of the total work force of the BEPZ are women. I think 40 percent of the women are single, and 60 percent are married. In the company where I work, 10 percent of the workers are men.

The truth is, our company has the highest wages in the BEPZ, along with one other company, also a garment company, owned by a Hong Kong–British firm.

Bulit Marquez

Members of the Armed Forces try to break up barricades of striking workers at the Bataan Export Processing Zone (BEPZ) in January 1987. On January 31, soldiers fired directly at workers, killing two and wounding twelve. The 80 percent female labor force of the BEPZ, once represented to foreign investors as "docile," has stood in the forefront of militant union organizing.

The wages in our company are higher because of a strong union. If you are new to the company, they only give you fourteen pesos a day. Yes, fourteen. The government wanted to send someone to investigate, but of course the management will not allow that.

Our first strike was last January. After forty-two days, it was successful. There are thirteen hundred workers. It's the second biggest, next to Mariveles Apparel Corporation, with three thousand workers. Not all the workers are in the union, because some are in maintenance or on probation. If you are a regular garment worker and you want to join the union, you can. More than eight hundred workers are in the union. Most of the leaders are women. At present only two men are officers.

What were the issues in the strike?

Wages and working conditions. There are not enough safety devices. Fibers enter our bodies because there are no exhaust fans, or very few. And last summer, especially—it is the time we made winter coats—you can imagine how hot the place is. There is the wool, and there is a foam used to make the coat much thicker; so it's very itchy at that time. And there is much fiber in the air.

We discussed the working conditions with the management. And they improved the ventilation. But the women, the workers, did not accept the disposable mask because it was very hot. If you put it on, you perspire.

Once a year we have medical checkups. That is something the union won. Right now we have eleven workers who are on leave because of TB. They do not receive their full salaries while they are on leave, only partial, from the social security system that we pay into. It is only for 120 days. After two years, if they don't cure their TB, they have a medical termination.

Now with our new collective bargaining agreement, we have it that workers terminated for medical reasons, they will give them twenty days of pay per each year of service. That's the separation pay if you are medical terminated. It's not much, but it's a start.

The workers come from many places. If there is one vacancy, there are a hundred persons. Some apply after high school. There are even college graduates who are applicants. Some management people take advantage of their position. They give priority to hiring their relatives. It is also a way to break the union, because their relatives don't join the union. And management gets workers from the *Iglesia ni Kristo* [a century old right-wing Philippine church, close to Marcos].

There are only three companies, I think, that have no union. One is the United Hong Kong Company. If they know that the workers plan to make a union, they discharge them.

I think it is the situation here that forces the workers to unite and form unions. We didn't come here to form a union. Before I entered the BEPZ, I believed it was a paradise of the workers. But after a year of working, I found out that it is not true. It is the paradise of the capitalists, not the workers.

The BEPZ doesn't work even for our government. The aim of creating BEPZ, according to its history, was so that the government could have dollars and to have a lot of jobs for the workers and to have a provincial improvement of Bataan. But how can you improve Bataan, or this particular area, Mariveles, if the BEPZ itself and the capitalists are exempted from tax? And even the raw materials are all imported, and they are free of tax for six years. And they can say that they did not succeed in their business or lost money, and they get another four years. So, for a total of ten years, they are free of tax. Even after ten, I don't know if they have really full taxes; some of them run away. Very few companies are really in BEPZ for a long time. And if they close a company, and the workers file a grievance to the Ministry for severance pay and so forth, they find that there is a third party—the bank. The bank owns all the machinery.

I was almost four years in the company before I joined the union. I was just an ordinary member. But after two years of being a member, and when I see the situation in my own section, I really found that we have to get everyone organized and aware of the situation. Some of my co-workers are abused at the supervisor's discretion, or sometimes supervisors get angry easily. They do not treat the workers as humans sometimes. So I organized my co-workers, and they said to please stand as a leader so that we can have a good union. Twice the company attempted to terminate me. The workers did not allow it, especially the union members.

Are you still working in the factory?

Yes. I'm a sewer. I sit at a machine, a big machine with a lot of noise. And if you work for eight hours, it gets hot inside your knee, because the motor is near your knee. And all your body is moving. You don't use your mind because the process of production in our company is a modern way: part by part. If you belong to the collar section, you put on collars. In my case, if the production is very near to ship-out, the remaining garment is sewn by me. I'm the one who finishes it.

I work eight hours. Formerly there was mandatory overtime. But now that we have a union it depends on you. But now, because of the crisis, we have no overtime. Now the workers are the ones asking for overtime. I mean the crisis in the Philippine economy and in Mariveles.

Are you making a living wage?

All the commodities here, from food to dresses, cost about 30 percent more than in Manila. The government has estimated that a worker with a family of six would need at least 112 pesos a day to survive. But we earn only 73 pesos a day. That's the average wage in our factory. In some factories, it's only 54 or 53 pesos, the minimum wage. Formerly, with the wages in 1975, we could save a little. Now we get 73 pesos and we cannot save money.

And can you believe that some of my co-workers who are women, they are the breadwinners and their husbands are the ones taking care of the babies? Or sometimes their husband is away in Saudi Arabia or in other parts of the world.

At present, there is a negotiation with the management. Until now, they discuss only the men topics. But we put in that we discuss a day-care center, because some of the children are being taken care of by their fathers or their grandmothers. Most of them are in the province. So you can imagine how the children grow without their mothers.

Dr. "X"
Provincial doctor
Bataan Export Processing Zone

I meet a middle-aged doctor while visiting the residential and commercial area within the Zone, near the shopping mall. The mall is eerie, unforgettable: built to look stateside, it is half-finished, and there is no evidence that construction is still going forward. Only a few food shops and the movie theater seem to have been opened. Escalators are in place but are covered over with construction rubble.

The doctor says he will talk with me, but asks me not to use his name. "Simply call me 'Dr. X, a provincial doctor'." He has been practicing as a government doctor in the Zone for eight years, and also has a private practice in Mariveles. He has lived in Mariveles for twenty-two years and has seen it "change from a sleepy town into an industrial town."

Most of my patients are workers in the Zone. They can come to the community health center during office hours for free consultation and free medicine, if we have it.

The workers are mostly workers in garment and electronics companies. Most of the diseases I encounter are respiratory diseases due to inhalation of fibers and small dusts. Often the exhaust systems in the factories are very poor. The temperature—hot—is good for the products but not good for the workers.

I gave some companies, like companies producing electronic chips, suggestions to prevent too much inhalation of plastic products—mainly proper ventilation and masks that are good, that are not readily available in the market. Most workers only use a piece of cloth tied around the head. That's all. Well, I think these companies say these good masks are too much of a price, and instead they provide surgical masks. I still encounter too much dust from the polyvinyl plastics.

The Zone management will tell you that there is an excellent hospital. But none of the workers can afford it. Therefore, we have organized a group to try to take over the hospital. We have learned from our studies of the hospital that it does not pay the rent but is subsidized by the government's Export Processing Zone Authority. That's why we are wondering why the charges are still high. It is run by a private corporation, but it is government-owned. The building and all the equipment are given free to the corporation to use. So you would expect the charges to be lower than in other hospitals outside the Zone; but instead they are as high as the private hospitals outside.

Do workers have health insurance?

The workers have this Medicare, but it's not enough for hospitalization, except for the middle management, probably.

The group I am now involved in, we want to take over the hospital and make it nonstock, nonprofit. We want to lower the charges and improve the quality of service. We want hospitalization to be affordable to the workers and, if possible, we would extend this to the indigent people around because we have lots of people here who can't find work in the Zone. They don't earn as much as the Zone workers do. Anyway this is not all the change we would like to make, but probably it is a start.

A big problem for the workers here is the price of medicines. That's a big problem for ordinary people. You know the economy of medicines is different from that of ordinary food and clothing. The multinational pharmaceutical companies price medicines to be level with prices in other countries. And these multinationals import all the medicines. Probably many of them could be made from raw materials from here. But instead of producing medicines for Filipinos from Filipino raw materials at affordable prices, we have this Zone here producing athletic goods and suits and gloves for rich foreigners.

What about outside the factory—the living conditions in the Zone? Are there health problems that come from the living conditions?

Congestion is a health problem in the Zone because of the influx of workers during the time the Zone was booming. The houses are occupied by many people. Also there's been a sudden change of culture. These things influence the higher incidence of diseases, not only physical diseases—viral or bacterial diseases—but mental diseases. So we have higher incidences of suicides, abortions, drugs, alcohol. Now we especially have lots of drug addicts in Mariveles. Among the younger groups of workers, those who should be high school students, there are those who are drug addicts. They use cough syrup, marijuana; there are some who use injections, but most use cough syrup and drugs like tranquilizers, depressants, and speeds.

Despite its problems, do you think the BEPZ is worthwhile for the Philippines?

I know it is said that the BEPZ is a dollar earner. But the dollars do not go to the Philippine government, they're transferred to the mother country. If you examine it, I think ultimately the BEPZ is not helping the national economy. This is my opinion.

You saw the shopping center. It's always been a ghost town. Lots of people earned from its construction. They don't think of the importance of the area to the community; they just think of the cut. (*Laughs*.) It was a corrupt project. Yes, it is showing movies. The Zone workers can afford the movies sometimes. Even people from the *poblacion* come here to watch a movie because Filipinos, you know, stick to Tagalog movies, especially the movies of Dolphy, Nora Aunor. Filipinos are very fond of these artists. It costs about six to eight pesos. The bowling lanes? Probably only supervisors use them. Maybe some workers once a month, they can afford to play there. They play especially when there's a tournament because the management pays then.

Jones Albanza
President, Chamber of Exporters and Manufacturers
Bataan Export Processing Zone

Mr. Albanza sits in his office of the firm he runs. The firm's factory turns out "embroidered goods, beaded bags, and other top-class fashion items for Dior, Gucci, and the like for export to the USA, Japan, and Europe." Mr. Albanza is proud that all the work is done by hand—the hands of a couple hundred young women. Through a long glass wall running along one side of his office, he can see the women sewing. As I enter through his secretary's office, the workers catch a glance of me; they giggle.

Why has the number of companies in the Zone gone down from more than fifty to about thirty?

For various reasons: the economic condition, the political situation in the Philippines since the start of the 1980s has seen tremendous changes, and, more often than not, negative changes—and the situation worldwide also.

Then there is the growing labor militancy and labor unrest here in the Zone. Companies like Wilson Electronics, for example, have been pushed to the edge of deciding to move out, because of the labor problems that they have.

But generally, the moving out of investors here is attributable to the government. I'm speaking particularly of the Zone authority, but even of the entire government machinery during the time of the old regime of Marcos. The Zone administrators during the past five years are politicians and technocrats. Probably, there needs to be an entire reorganization or revamp of the government machinery that takes care of the export processing zones.

What would the new government need to do to revitalize the Zone?

First, the government has to improve the economic and investment climate, as well as the political situation here in the Philippines. Two, an EPZ in the

Philippines does not enjoy incentives on par with others EPZs in the world. You have to orient yourself to the needs of the Zone enterprise in terms of services, facilities, procedures, incentives, and benefits. Then you would be able to encourage and put more confidence in those who are already the EPZ, and further encourage others to come over.

We sometimes go days without electric power. Two weeks was the most. Then we have scheduled repairs, maintenance, and power brownouts due to the main supplier, which is the National Power Corporation itself. If you don't have power, your factory won't run even if you have cooperative workers. The underground power system for this Zone was laid in 1972–74. I don't think there's any proper maintenance program. So you have obsolescence, or breakdown of power facilities.

The other factor is the labor sector. This consists of radicals, moderates, or whatever. We know for a fact that one of the labor sectors here in the Philippines does not favor the EPZ concept, or does not favor multinational corporations. Their motive has been since the start to destabilize the EPZ so more companies would move out, more people won't have jobs, and so on. So I think it's very difficult to put things in the proper perspective in the light of what's going on now. But you can only start with the government sector.

Why are labor unions so active in the Zone?

Well, there are a lot of reasons. One, industrial relations are not always working out perfectly, considering the cultural differences a multinational firm has with the labor sector here, and considering that managers perhaps are pushing through corporate programs which may not necessarily be congruent with the aspirations of the labor sector within a particular factory.

Two, the uncertain political situation. You see, one of the attractions to the multinationals was that there were no strikes during martial-law time. But martial law lasted only until the late '70s. So the lifting of martial law and the normal course of the antigovernment, anti-Marcos protests, and so on, by nationalists would definitely be a big factor in the militancy of labor. So the real reasons we have unions are all political reasons—Marcos, and the leftists within the country who would not want the EPZs to thrive because they are antimultinationals. They have these hard lines since before any experience of the multinationals.

You have to add in the weakness of the government. There's no firm implementation of laws and no clear-cut policies. You have the laws to deal with labor there, but it's just a piece of paper. Sympathy strikes, for instance, are illegal, of course. But when you don't apply the law firmly, it might be misunderstood as weakness and definitely your enforcement of all vital laws vis-à-vis labor tends to be eroded.

Why are there so many sympathy strikes?

Well, as I say, the government hasn't been firm enough. Then you have a situation here where companies are clustered together in one small area. If you have foot-loose industries within that area who do not take care of their workers as properly as you would want them to, then it seeps down to other companies, even those who are treating their workers well. So it becomes a major issue against management as a whole by the labor sector. Especially if labor is infiltrated by more radical and more militant groups, then it would be very easy to convince the workers to join their cause.

Then you would also notice the social problems that we have here. This area is a substandard town relying on fishing as a main livelihood. This is a sleepy town when they started putting up the Zone here. On hindsight, this first EPZ was established by enactment of law; definitely it was a political decision at that time to put it here. It was before martial law, so they had to contend with what was already in this area. They actually had to move hills and cover rice fields to create this industrial estate that we have now. The social amenities, support manpower, and facilities and auxilliary services that should be present in an industrial estate or EPZ are not there. You have to create these. But the government can only do so much. They were concerned more with the infrastructure, not with putting, what I would term, a "soul" in the community. The town should have grown in level or at par with the developments here in the EPZ.

Aquino has changed the administration, but it's the same banana—they're still politicians. Sure, the new government has plans for developing new services and facilities here. We've heard it for a long time. Unless we see it, we won't believe it. They need to start here at the top. Get somebody who knows EPZs in other countries and knows why they are successful. It's a fact that we're one of the pioneers in the EPZ in Southeast and South Asia—EPZs since 1972. That's fifteen years of experience in EPZ. I don't understand why we are deteriorating while other countries' EPZs, which have existed for five or seven years, are already successful. It's not just putting these facilities here, you know. That's a mistake to think that you put 100 percent class A facilities, inviting investors, you give all the incentives and then they would come in. No. It needs a continuous process of trying to find out what works.

How about your company? Is it doing well?

In my firm we're doing all right. We didn't have any strikes, our relations are okay. It's a matter of trust, respect, and confidence in each other. They haven't even joined sympathy strikes. If the federation calls for it, they come to me and arrange with me that they would go on overtime before any sympathy strike just in case they would be pressured to join it. So they come to me and we make arrangements.

Dr. Melba Buenaventura
Mayor
Mariveles, Bataan Peninsula

*M*elba Buenaventura is a Cory Aquino look-alike, eyeglasses and all. As we talk in her office, I find myself wondering if the color photo of a woman speaking at a podium, hanging on the wall, is the president of the Republic or the mayor of Mariveles.

I ask the mayor what has been the impact of the Bataan Export Processing Zone on Mariveles.

I came here way back in 1964. I found that this town was really a very rural area where the livelihood of the people were fishing and farming. There were also people who were working in two government enterprises, shipbuilding and quarrying. So life here was so simple and peaceful. That's why I chose to live in this place and serve the people of Mariveles, rather than practice in Manila and earn more.

So your dream was shattered?

Yes. That is one of my frustrations. In 1970, came the people in the government destroying farmlands, cutting down trees, moving people out of their areas—people who have lived there since their birth. I can say that the people of Mariveles were not ready for the government industrialization. There was some resistance, but who can resist under martial law? I knew what it would be for some people, for professionals like us. But those people who were dislocated and displaced from their livelihood, what would happen to them? And there are more of them than professionals like us. So even though they say that the BEPZ, the industrialization of this area, would lead to progress and development, I didn't believe that so much.

With the development of an area, the question is who benefits? Now in this case, the poor people did not directly benefit. Many even lost their livelihood.

It was those people who have the capital to put up businesses who benefited. So business was monopolized by the rich.

These were people who came from the outside?

Yes, mainly. These people who came from the outside to Mariveles were those who benefited from business.

Another problem which involves the municipality is that by Presidential Decree 66, the BEPZ is exempted from taxes of all kinds. So all the benefits we derive from the BEPZ are indirect—we benefit only from the licenses, the taxes, from the businesses here in the town. By another presidential decree, the taxing power of the municipality is not authorized inside. One other power they have is the police power, because the zone administration has its own police.

Because of the sudden influx of people coming from different provinces and regions, we cannot give all the basic services that are needed by the people. We were not prepared as a municipality to give basic services like education, health, and infrastructure. People are coming in all the time and they add to our unemployment. Our problem is not organic. It is not from within. All our problems come from the outside.

There has been an imbalance of development. The community of BEPZ became overdeveloped, leaving Mariveles as a very much undeveloped area. Now you can see the difference very clearly.

I must say, having visited export processing zones in other countries, I never have seen a zone with such a high level of labor-union activity.

That is one reason why in the last five years so many companies have packed up and closed down. And this has had a very big effect on the municipality. And I hear that there will be more companies closing next year, about six. I was really puzzled why, with the wages that they receive, they are not contented with the work. Their minimum wage is fifty-three pesos, and that is much more than government workers make. It is the workers themselves, not management, who trigger these strikes. Also, there are people who are interested in eliminating these multinationals and who are infiltrating these laborers, in order to use them to help in their cause.

What is your own view of the multinationals here in the Philippines?

There are many Filipinos who are critical of the multinational foreign companies. But I welcome foreign companies because Filipinos cannot stand on their own. I know that. Especially when it comes to our economy. Where would we be without foreigners? I am with the opposition, you know that. But when it comes to the multinationals, and the bases, I am with the president.

Rodel Cruz
Union secretary, Manila Apparel Corporation
Bataan Export Processing Zone

I meet Rodel Cruz, who appears to be in his late 30s, in the small union office on the ground floor of the Manila Apparel Corporation. It is break time, so there are many workers, men and women, inside and outside the office, talking with each other. As the break ends, Mr. Cruz suggests we walk around the factory.

The factory has two stories, each mainly a huge shop floor with high ceilings and low-hanging fluorescent lights. Many workers, mostly women, are busy at work at long tables, cutting cloth according to patterns from huge bolts of material. Others are sewing the pieces together. Men are doing the final pressings and carting the finished suits on racks across the factory floor and onto trucks, which, Mr. Cruz tells me, will go to the port in Manila and then on to the United States. The women sew on a number of brand labels, including Sears and Macy's.

How long have you been working in this factory?

About nine years.

Do you still work on the line now that you are the head of the union here?

Yes, I work on the line fulltime to support my family.

Mr. Cruz is eager to know how much one of the suits they are making for Macy's would cost in the United States. It is a three-piece silk and wool suit with a highbrow label on the inside jacket pocket. I tell him, at least $350, probably more. He makes a note of that in a little pad. I ask him how many hours of work go into making the suit, from cutting the bolt of cloth to rolling it onto the truck.

I think it would take about three hours. Even less because in Coat Unit 1, there are around five hundred workers, and we produce around sixteen hundred suits every day—only in Coat Unit 1.

And the average pay per hour?

7.35 pesos, which amounts to about one dollar to make the suit.

The mayor of Mariveles and the head of the management association in the BEPZ say that the true purpose of the unions here is to destabilize the Zone, that you are really for the closing down of multinational companies, here and throughout the Philippines.

I'm not surprised that they tell you that, because in this country, if you fight for your basic rights, they will say that you are communists, that you only want to destabilize the country. In fact, we are fighting for our legal rights. We only want to have job security, good salary, and at least to have the right to strike when we vote to strike.

Don't you have the right to strike, now that Marcos has fled?

If we satisfy a list of conditions, like give thirty days notice. During a strike, the management can export their products freely and they can bring in raw materials freely.

You mentioned job security as your first demand. Have you had layoffs here?

Yes, we have layoffs and temporary layoffs. When there are no job orders, we are placed under forced leave without any compensation. Like this year, we have an average of forced leave of five to six months without compensation from the management or even from the government. In Canada, where when there is forced leave, the government gives a 60 percent subsidy to the workers. But in the Philippines, nothing.

Primo Amparo
Chair, AMBA-BALA labor alliance
Bataan Peninsula

I meet Primo Amparo at the big Lotus factory where he works. The factory makes Reebok and Nike shoes for export. AMBA-BALA is the alliance of twenty-three labor unions, mainly in the BEPZ, and constitutes the Bataan provincial chapter of the national labor alliance, the KMU.

I was born in Quezon province, which is more or less twice the distance from Manila to Mariveles. My father was a coconut farmer and had a rice field. One afternoon, when I was in elementary school, my father died while he and I were making copra on our coconut farm. He got a stomachache, and then after several days died. He was 48. Someone says it was the effect of being struck in the stomach by the butts of the guns of the Japanese soldiers during the occupation. Anyway, we were forced to sell our land in order to pay a loan from the bank. That's why I'm here—I had to look for a good job because I'm the eldest; I'm the breadwinner. I have five brothers and sisters. I was 18 years old when I left for Bataan.

What was it like looking for a job in the BEPZ?

I came here in 1978. Actually, when I first apply in the factories, it is very hard to get a job if you have no backer or any management backup. But because I am good at sales talk—I was student leader even during my school days—I introduce myself to everybody, I'm Primo, and so on and so forth, and I made some friends. Finally, I met one of my schoolmates who was fourth year high school when I was in second year. He accompanied me to the personnel officer of the Lotus factory I work in now.

I start as a worker, but I have an initial idea when I go to the factory to form a workers' organization. But I do not know what kind of organization. I have no definite information about unions, but because I was a youth leader I wanted

Jun Cañete

Primo Amparo

to organize workers into an organization. My father was a *barangay* leader even from a young age. I just picked up my desire to organize from him.

As early as 1978, workers in some of the factories at BEPZ start to organize their unions. There were so many forced overtimes, and the minimum wage was not being implemented by some companies—even now in a few companies. And the working conditions inside the factory are very hazardous to the health of the workers—chemicals, no safety devices, hanging objects which commonly cause accidents, and often a finger gets cut in the cutting machines, especially because with the mandatory overtime the workers become sleepy. And then the factories have their forced leave, or temporary layoff, because of the foreign market conditions.

Was it difficult to organize unions?

The managers make so many moves, they try everything to prevent us workers from organizing our unions. Sometimes they terminate the leaders. Sometimes they pay the leaders. And many other tactics. But the workers assert their rights, and as early as 1978, some unions were being recognized at the BEPZ. In 1979, a first strike was done by the workers of Ford. And in 1982, strikes really hit the BEPZ because of these working conditions and the managers trying to bust the unions. So more strikes arise because of their efforts to prevent the workers from self-organizing.

During several strikes, we were struck by the hose of the fire trucks and the truncheon. In 1984, they even fired guns, but they did not shoot us, they just shoot up in the air.

I was one of the organizers of the union in Lotus. It was founded in 1981.

Do you still work in the plant?

I am still working at Lotus, but I am working if I have time to work. I don't report if I don't have time because of union work. We have an agreement that this is one of our labor privileges. Actually, management is requesting me to be present in the company because it is very hard for them to talk to the other officers. They think that anything I say is final. Actually, it is very easy to deal with me, even though I am representing the genuine interests of the workers. Before, management had a misconception of genuine unionism, because if you are introducing the union, you have to show strength. And, of course, the mass actions or concerted actions are always there to show that strength. We have already shown to them that we can control the factory, we can control the production, and we can control our members. So now management can't do anything but to ask what we will do. We cooperate with them because, even though our aim is to topple the multinationals here, we must still work with them because we are organizing other workers in other factories.

How many workers have you organized?

More or less all the Lotus workers are organized; we have 960 members out of 1,100 workers. The rest are middle management and they are already semi-organized. If they have a problem, they consult us. (*Laughs.*) There are Filipino managers and Korean ones. The top manager is Korean.

How did you form the alliance of labor unions?

In May 1982, during a strike here at Inter-Asia, they passed National Law Number 227, whereby the management can have free ingress and egress during a strike. So our strike would have no effect. But with that kind of harassment the workers at Inter-Asia had even a stronger determination. The management cannot move their picket until all the workers were put in jail. By that time, all leaders of the unions in the BEPZ called for a meeting. That was when all leaders unite to launch a sympathy strike, so that was the formation of the AMBA-BALA.

Have things changed since the fall of Marcos?

In the months since Cory became the president, layoffs are very rampant at

BEPZ. Last January to March, twenty-five thousand workers were laid off—not for that whole period, but sometimes fifteen days at a time, like that. I think it is not related to the political situation. We asked for a dialogue with the EPZA investors. They say they cannot avoid these forced leaves, layoffs, and other problems, because they do not control the market. If they are in the foreign market, they cannot avoid these problems.

We union leaders, together with the others workers, discuss these matters. It is very complicated, of course, but I think the root problem is dependence on exports. Now making it worse, this government's policy is to open the doors even more to imports, as the IMF–World Bank want. Another problem is that we are just assembling these parts, we import all the materials, even though we have the raw materials in the Philippines, but they are not developed.

Another problem is these underdeveloped industries—like the textile, polytextile—cannot compete with the multinationals whose products are pouring in. These local markets and local industries will be taken over by the multinationals. Our underdeveloped industries do not grow; they are being eliminated or absorbed by these multinationals. The multinationals get these Filipino managers, Filipino dummies, who have a small share of the investment. These Filipinos are the ones who make the laws, and they make laws to protect their interests here, in favor of their investments and therefore the multinationals. These multinational investments here must be made to benefit Filipinos by way of transferring technology, and these investments should be for a permanent market, so that there'll be steady jobs for the workers. And another thing is that the technology after a specified time should be Filipinized.

Our main objective—in order to solve the root problem—is to work for national industrialization. This is our main focus of struggle. And to have national industrialization, we join in the struggle of the farmers for genuine land reform. Because when the elites and the multinationals control our agriculture, our agricultural products go for export and we do not have raw materials to be processed in industry. Also, industry here will not bloom, because we don't think we have a market here because of poverty. So that we can have good purchasing power for all Filipinos, we have to uproot joblessness and landlessness.

Do you wind up being treated as subversives?

Of course. We are all the time tagged communists or subversives. But we are ready to explain that we start with the objective conditions of the workers and the ordinary people. And the very first thing we explain to people is that we respect everyone's religious beliefs—we must not talk about religion, but we must talk about the causes of our problems. We must respect your belief and the beliefs of others.

There is not as much harassment now, because when a picket of the workers is harassed, automatically there will be a sympathy strike in other factories. We do consider just a little that this is the fruit of the February revolution. But our office has been bombed. We have some idea who did it, but we cannot pinpoint the suspect. The government is not actively investigating. We have followed up again this week, and they encouraged us to give a statement. But they conduct just a little investigation. Also, a generally reliable informer says that one of the military here, suspecting that this AMBA-BALA is related to the NPA, was behind the bombing.

❖ ❖ ❖

Four weeks later, police and military fire into a demonstration of striking workers in the BEPZ, killing six.

Seven:
U.S. MILITARY
PRESENCE

From the moment Commodore Dewey sailed into Manila Bay in 1898, military occupation has been the core of the U.S. presence in the Philippines. Few Americans have even heard of the war between their country and the Republic of the Philippines. It is not mentioned in our schoolbooks. And yet, it was a very real war: 126,458 American soldiers were shipped all the way to the Philippines for combat in what the U.S. War Department termed "an insurrection," as if, as writer Stanley Karnow observed, the Filipinos were rebelling against legitimate U.S. authority.

The three-year Filipino-American War started in 1899, the year after the brief Spanish-American War. Through their own military efforts, the Filipinos had already broken the back of Spanish rule in rural Philippines, and the Spanish forces had taken refuge in the walled inner city of Manila. Dewey, the commander of U.S. forces in the Philippines, with no foot soldiers to fight the Spanish on land, induced General Aguinaldo and his Philippine nationalist army to be his ally in the American war against Spain.

Spain, to save face by surrendering to U.S. forces under Commodore Dewey rather than to the *indios*, arranged a mock battle with U.S. forces. Six months later, Spain signed a treaty ceding the Philippines to the United States for $20 million.

This was outright theft of the fruits of victory from the Filipinos. During this six-month period, the Republic of the Philippines had already been established with an advanced constitution (including a bill of rights), a popularly elected Congress, a president, an army, and local governments. While the U.S. Senate debated the highly controversial treaty, President McKinley ordered the War Department to extend the military occupation of Manila to the entire archipelago. Recognizing that U.S. claims of being an ally in the Filipinos' fight for freedom were hollow—as well as U.S. denials of any ambitions to possess colonies like the European imperialist powers—the fledgling republic again took up arms for its independence. Filipino resistance promptly took the lives of American soldiers, which no doubt swayed Senate votes.

America's First Vietnam

The U.S. waged a brutal colonial war, what some have called "America's first Vietnam." The U.S. military uprooted whole villages, driving the people into "reconcentration camps," where starvation and disease killed tens of thousands. U.S. forces turned cultivated areas into scorched wastelands, torturing and killing prisoners, massacring entire villages in retaliation for the killing of a single American soldier.

© 1900 by B. W. Kilburn

"Our boys entrenched against the Filipinos" (1900). More than 125,000 American troops fought a three-year war to bring the Philippines under colonial rule. As many as 600,000 Filipinos, mostly civilians, died in a war now largely forgotten in the United States.

U.S. Army records indicate that more than sixteen thousand Filipinos were killed, but many respected scholars estimate that as many as a half million Filipinos, mostly civilians, died from combat, disease, and of starvation. The entire population then numbered barely six million. One American soldier wrote home, "This shooting human beings beats rabbit hunting all to pieces." The International Red Cross reported villages burned to the ground, and "horribly mutilated Filipino bodies, with stomachs slit open and occasionally decapitated." General "Howlin' Jake" Smith instructed his troops: "Kill and burn, kill and burn, the more you kill and the more you burn, the more you will please me."

Genocidal warfare comes easier when there is an underpinning of racism. American soldiers commonly referred to the Filipinos as "niggers." President Theodore Roosevelt called them "savages, barbarians, a wild and ignorant people, Apaches, Sioux, Chinese half-breeds." For Roosevelt, "the most ultimately righteous of all wars is a war with savages," which establishes "the foundations for all future greatness of a mighty people." Having commanded much of this war, General Frederick Funston boasted, "I'll warrant that the new generation of natives will know better than to get in the way of the bandwagon of Anglo-Saxon progress and decency." He also hoped, "Uncle Sam will apply the chastening rod, good, hard and plenty ... until they come into the reservation and promise to be good Injuns."

Secretary of War Elihu Root asserted, "The warfare has been conducted with marked humanity and magnanimity on the part of the U.S." A former U.S. Army captain, however, testified in a Senate hearing that General Funston ordered his men to administer the "water cure," to force information from prisoners before they were killed. Several gallons of water were forced down a prisoner's throat, horribly distending his midsection, and then he was repeatedly kicked in the stomach.

In the United States, opposition to the war and the annexation was widespread. Respected public figures spoke out and wrote against the war: intellectuals William James and Charles Eliot; writers Mark Twain and Lincoln Steffens; abolitionist William Lloyd Garrison and reformer Jane Addams; labor leader Samuel Gompers; former President Grover Cleveland; and even the original captain of industry, Andrew Carnegie.

The treaty to annex the Philippines was ratified in the Senate, with the vice-president casting the deciding vote for the required two-thirds majority. Two days before the vote, Secretary Root reported that "an army of Tagalogs, a tribe ... under the leadership of [President] Aguinaldo, a Chinese half-breed, attacked ... our little army in the possession of Manila, and after a desperate and bloody fight was repulsed in every direction." Months later, eyewitness testimony, including that of General Douglas MacArthur, made it clear that the U.S. fired first and received very little return fire from Filipinos.

General Funston regularly blasted his foes at home as being "misguided" and "ladylike." He blamed American deaths in the prolonged war on American critics of the war, and suggested that they keep their opinions to themselves "until every square inch of that territory recognizes the sovereignty of the United States."

A Conditioned Independence

When the United States ended the formal colonial status of the Philippines after World War II, a key U.S. condition was that it retain vast tracts of land for military bases. Under severe economic pressure, the war-torn Philippines agreed, and signed the Military Bases and Military Assistance Agreement in 1947, granting virtually everything that the U.S. War Department wanted.

The United States obtained a renewable ninety-nine year lease on twenty-three military base sites throughout the islands, five of which were fully developed and the rest held in reserve. Included were the naval station at Olongapo—Subic Bay and Clark Air Base, encompassing 135,000 acres of rich farmland in central Luzon. (To this day, the Pentagon is one of the largest holders of agricultural land in the Philippines.) Today, Subic is the home base of the U.S. Seventh Fleet, with its 90 ships and 550 fighter planes, and the largest naval supply depot in the world. Clark is the third largest U.S. air base overseas.

The Agreement created virtual U.S. enclaves in which, for instance, Philippine courts had no jurisdiction. (For a while, the Eisenhower administration went so far as to claim that the base sites were not covered by the independence granted by the United States, but he backed down in the face of protest demonstrations in Manila.)

The nationalist feelings aroused by various incidents have resulted in forty negotiated amendments to the Agreement. The U.S. relinquished a number of the minor sites and, in 1965, the term of the lease was reduced to twenty-five years, after which (1991) the term would be subject to one year's notice of termination by either party. In 1979, Marcos wrested cosmetic changes from the United States: the bases were redesignated "Philippine military bases" over which the Philippine flag now flies.

The Case Against the Bases

Those advocating that the Agreement be allowed to expire make the following arguments.

❖ The U.S. bases act as a magnet for attack—today, a nuclear attack—by any power that chooses to challenge the United States. This makes the bases more of a threat than a guarantee of Philippine national security—a threat to the very survival of the Filipino people.

❖ The Philippines should help form a Southeast Asian counterpart to the fourteen-nation South Pacific Nuclear Free Zone and declare its territory free of nuclear armaments. This is not an inherently leftist position: the Philippine Senate has voted in favor of a ban on nuclear weapons. While U.S. policy is never to confirm or deny that the bases and the naval fleet have nuclear weapons, numerous unofficial authorities confirm the common-sense judgment that there must be nuclear weapons there. The U.S. position—that the question of nuclear weapons in the Philippines is not the business of Filipinos—is an affront to Philippine sovereignty and complicates relations with its neighbors.

❖ Since 1900, U.S. military bases in the Philippines have been used as major launching grounds for every U.S. intervention in other parts of Asia, from China to Korea to Indochina. The Philippines is thereby drawn into

Ramon Acasio

USS New Jersey in Subic Bay. The naval station at Subic is the U.S. Navy's most important overseas base. The "forward base" of the Seventh Fleet, it is the springboard for U.S. naval deployments in the Indian Ocean.

conflicts not of its making, as well as into the suppression of popular movements elsewhere.

❖ The rent paid to the Philippine government for the bases is grossly inadequate. Officially, the U.S. denies that it pays any rent, claiming rent-free rights. The 1983 amendment to the Agreement, which calls on the "best effort" of the U.S. president to secure from Congress $900 million over six years in "security assistance" (military assistance and U.S.-administered economic "development" in the vicinity of the bases), is regarded by the U.S. as a voluntary commitment. Far greater amounts are paid as rent to countries such as Greece, Spain, and Turkey for hosting U.S. bases.

❖ The bases exploit the impoverished condition of Filipinos through the concomitant "entertainment" industry. Olongapo City, once a farming and fishing village adjacent to Subic Bay, is now the site of 500 bars, nightclubs, massage parlors, and hotels. As many as sixteen thousand women work as "hospitality girls" in the entertainment industry. Most have been made virtual slaves to the club owners, some of whom are retired U.S. military personnel. Twelve of these women in 1986 tested positive for the AIDS antibody. Hundreds of Amer-Asian children are born each month. There are about three thousand abandoned children. The U.S. Embassy states that "any damaging or disruptive social behavior [near the bases] is likely to remain ... until human nature changes."

❖   As part of the Agreement, the United States provides military assistance in the form of weaponry, training, and advice to the Philippine military, and thereby directly intervenes in the internal affairs of the Philippines. Currently, U.S. forces are aiding and abetting the counter-insurgency campaign of the Philippine armed forces. Both Subic and Clark regularly train Philippine commando troops. (In 1987, the National Democratic Front publicly warned that American personnel directly involved in the country's civil war will be considered appropriate military targets by the NPA. In 1989, the NPA "executed" Col. James N. Rowe, chief of the ground forces division of the Joint U.S. Military Advisory Group in the Philippines. The NDF issued a statement saying that it was "determined to make U.S. imperialism pay dearly for the continuing stay of its bases and its escalating intervention in our people's affairs.")

❖   While the U.S. government argues that the bases are a boon to the Philippine economy, studies by opponents indicate that converting the base sites and facilities into civilian uses could make a great deal of economic sense. Ultimately more, not fewer, Filipinos could be employed. For instance, Subic could be made into a commercial, year round ship-building and ship repair facility, and farm land and other untapped natural resources at Subic and Clark could be put into production.

Wedded to the Status Quo

The bases are at the heart of U.S. concerns over the Philippines. In effect, U.S. policymakers would have us Americans identify our "national interest" in the Philippines with the continued presence of these bases. Democracy, freedom from hunger, and nonintervention take a back seat to the bases. No matter how many Filipinos live in fear, are driven from their homes, and are tortured and killed, the only thing that really counts for the U.S. government is whether it can keep its bases. Indeed, President Reagan, pressed by reporters to explain his continued support for Marcos in the wake of evidence of massive electoral fraud, answered that nothing there is more valuable than the bases. His response typifies the thinking of decisionmakers of both the Republican and Democratic parties for decades. In 1972, American officials told *The New York Times* that the bases were the chief reason for U.S. support for martial law in the Philippines under Marcos. A 1973 staff report of the U.S. Senate Committee on Foreign Relations concluded that actions in support of martial law would give the impression to the world that "our military bases and a familiar government in the Philippines are more important than the preservation of democratic institutions." In 1987, Secretary of State George Shultz, referring to the Aquino government, said that the U.S. would "have no qualms about destabilizing the present government" if the future of the U.S. bases was in jeopardy.

Two decades ago, Senator William Fulbright understood the implications of the U.S. commitment to its bases in the Philippines: "Is it not inevitable that because of our presence there and with this purpose, we would always use our influence for the preservation of the status quo? We will always resist any serious change in the political and social structures of the Philippines Government, [a policy] which is very likely to be, in the long run, a detriment to the people of the Philippines."

Jimmy Mendoza
Secretary General, PDP-Laban
Olongapo

Jimmy Mendoza meets with me in the City Planning Office of Olongapo. It's a Saturday afternoon, and we are the only ones in the office. Jimmy came to Olongapo in 1966, during the Vietnam War, to work with the U.S. Naval magazine, where they stockpile weapons from small arms ammunition to guided missiles. He quit in January 1972.

I came from a peasant family in Pampanga. My grandparents were tenant farmers. My father also worked as a tenant farmer, until he left the farm to become a worker in the town proper. My father also worked on the base when a Hawaiian company was still constructing the base.

In high school, I was president of the student council, and I was also editor of the school paper. Later, I went to Manila to work while I studied at the University of Santo Tomas, a Catholic university. My family is very devout Catholic, very conservative. What I earned was not really enough to get me through my studies. So I quit college and just worked. I took one of the tests they give to prospective apprentices inside the base. After one year, I got this card from the base asking me to report. I was interviewed, and they took me in as an ordinance learner.

Especially at that time, it was some status symbol to be working inside the American base. A lot of friends in the province really envied me when I got the job. As a matter of fact, there were nine of us friends from the same town that took that test, and I was the only one who passed. That's also the reason why my parents were mad when I resigned after five years.

What did you do on the base?

I started working on small arms. We would segregate small arms ammunitions from the ships that came from Vietnam—mark them and prepare inventories, things like that. And then I was assigned to a shop called a product shop where we did rehabilitation of projectiles. I was assigned to the guided missiles division after I got what they call a confidential clearance. They did some background investigation on me that took almost two years. They interviewed everybody—even my grade-school teachers and all the boarding houses I lived in, in Manila.

Did the work influence your political perspective?

Remember, at that time there was a very strong antiwar movement in the States, and a lot of these GIs, the servicemen I worked with, were against the war—most of them, in fact. So during break times we'd talk about the war. I kept wondering why most of them seemed to hate what they were doing, and why they were here in the first place. So I got to thinking about the kind of job I was doing. I think the turning point for me was when one of the officers we had then—his name I think was Gunnar, he was a gunner, you know—he was boasting about how effective the weapon we were working on was. He told me they call it the weapon with its own brain because it sees its target and almost never misses and it could "blast these goddamn Vietnamese to pieces." So that's when I started worrying about the implications of my job. I was involved in this killing of people.

When I'd go home to the province on weekends, some of my friends there were already talking politics, and so I started thinking politics at that time. I told myself when change has got to be made, somebody's got to start it all. I started organizing in Olongapo among students.

By the middle of 1971, we already had a very good movement going here. We already had organized ourselves into a political organization. And then when Jane Fonda visited Vietnam and stopped over in the Philippines, we invited her to come over to Olongapo and help us. I was her host when she came over. They did a show with her group. After, we went to a bar and had discussion groups among the GIs who attended the show. We expanded to a point where we would hold rallies and demonstrations near the gate and American GIs would join us, and these GIs were also arrested and some were courtmartialed. It became necessary for us to ask for legal assistance from other groups in the States. There was this group called the National Lawyers Guild and they sent us three lawyers to help us out with the GIs who were being courtmartialed.

Was it difficult to work at the base and do political organizing at the same time?

I decided that the movement work I was doing was no longer a parttime thing—somebody's got to work on this fulltime—so I quit my job on the base. At the time, the biggest and most well-organized youth organization was the

Jun Cañete

Jimmy Mendoza

KM, the *Kabataang Makabayan* or Patriotic Youth. Every time I would go to Manila—there were so many rallies going on in Manila at that time—most of the manifestoes I got came from this organization. So when I came back, we decided to form a chapter of the KM here. Our organization grew so big that we are now able to look back, my friends and I, and smile when we talk about our first rally. Our first rally was really small—there were nine of us. That was in early 1972. There were more military tailing us than we were.

Did the military step in to harass your organization?

When martial law was declared, I was on the military's list—they used to call it the order of battle—of the most wanted political dissenters at that time. So I had to, we had to, go underground. I got arrested in 1973, about a year later. I was tortured, and I was in jail for a few months. And then I was finally released. You know why? The solicitor general of Marcos was my cousin. My parents went up to him, and you know how relationships like that are among Filipinos.

When I got out, my wife would cook pancit-noodles and sell them in the slum area where we lived, in Santa Rita. My first job was helping to sell that food. And then we were able to save a little money to rent a small store. And about that time, the mayor here, a certain Dr. Lipomano, gave me a parttime job ghostwriting for him. Later on, they got me a regional position as a researcher/writer, and then I was promoted to assistant city development coordinator. The mayor sent me to the University of the Philippines to take up a special course in urban planning. So, I became the urban planner of the city. That lasted for five years until I left the government and worked with the Water Authority here until 1984.

How soon after prison did you take up politics again?

Although I did not stop in my political work during all those years, it was hard for me, because I was still under surveillance. The most I could do was articulate issues to friends, like informal coffee shop groups, and things like that, until 1980, when I worked with TFD, the Task Force for Political Detainees. Being a former detainee, I thought I should help in monitoring human rights violations, especially here—salvaging cases, and things like that. We organized the Concerned Citizens for Justice and Peace in 1983, and then I joined the Nationalist Alliance for Justice, Freedom and Democracy.

Teddy Macapagal, who was a human rights lawyer defending political detainees, was appointed mayor by President Aquino. He was the chairman of our Concerned Citizens for Justice and Peace group. He took me onto his staff to help them out at the start, because among his friends I was the one who was more experienced in bureaucratic jobs. I recently resigned. That people power thing was a very beautiful thing, where people would be that active, politically, that assertive. But unless it is sustained—it's got to be institutionalized—it will quickly be history. Despite her rhetoric, I think Mrs. Aquino is afraid of people power.

Can you describe your current position?

Now I am the secretary general of PDP-Laban [pro-Aquino party during 1986 elections] for Olongapo City. That helps in building rapport and alliances with the influential figures here, especially the politicians. It helps in a place like Olongapo to do alliance work with the politicians.

When I was with the City Planning Office, I did some research on the history of Olongapo. Right before the turn of the century, the Spaniards had some sort of naval station here. When the Americans took over, they realized the strategic importance of the bay for U.S. economic and military interests in this part of the world; so they continued to use the base. But the real development here happened in the early 1950s. The base was used extensively to support U.S. military activities in the Korean War.

Jimmy stands up and points to a wall map of the area.

This part of the area that is now called Olongapo was, until then, part of the U.S. Naval Reservation, meaning that, although the U.S. was supposed to have granted independence to the Philippines in 1946, the territory now called Olongapo was not included in that independence. An American naval officer—I think he was called administrator for civilian affairs—acted as the mayor. If you're not a resident of Olongapo City, you've got to get a visitor's pass. So it's like entering foreign territory, you have to have a sponsor. In the middle of the '50s, there was a big clamor by the Filipino residents here for a belated independence, for the U.S. to turn over this territory to the Philippines government. In 1959, after some negotiations on the diplomatic level, Olongapo was turned over to the Philippines government and was converted into the municipality of Olongapo. With the job opportunities opening up inside the base and the business opportunities opening also outside the base, that was when this phenomenal growth in population of Olongapo happened. Especially, also then with the Vietnam War.

All the economic activities are geared to providing entertainment for the American GIs who come here, also the civilian employment on the base—that's how the economy is; that's how dependent and unstable the economy is.

When you come to think of it, the reason why people crowd this small, already crowded place is that life is so hard in the places they come from. A friend of ours who used to be dean of the college here made a study of institutionalized prostitution here in 1977. Among other things, he found out that most of the girls who work here come from the most depressed areas of the country. Meaning, if the national government would come up with economic policies that would include the rural economy, there would be no reason for these girls to come here and become prostitutes.

What kind of changes would you like to see in Olongapo?

When I was on the city planning staff in the late 1970s, we came up with a long-term development plan for the city that included looking at alternatives to the base, such as the development of commercial ship repair facilities here. The problem, I think, is that there is not much enthusiasm on the part of the national government for alternative planning. Also, most businessmen here are so conservative. They are so used to the kick-back type of business. That's the type of business we have here, like those carpetbaggers we see in the movies in the U.S. They don't care about the place, they came from other places, they came here just to make quick bucks. During the Vietnam War, all you have to do was set up your table and some women and it could be raining dollars. They've been so used to this type of business that they have their minds closed to long-term type of investments. Some of the businessmen whose business went down after the war, you know what they did? They pulled out all of their investments, the money they made here and took it somewhere else.

The bases issue was a very big issue especially during the Con-Com [Constitutional Commission] deliberation, and even now it's a very big issue here. We hear of many private groups trying to do their own studies on alternatives to the bases. The government is not showing any concern for planning alternatives. I suspect that the Cory government is not really keen on letting the bases go after the expiration of the bases agreement.

I've heard Tony Zumel [NDF leader and spokesperson] say that while, in principle, they're not changing their stand as far as the bases are concerned, it's not a rigid stance. I've been hearing of a possible political settlement. I think one of the main reasons, as far as the CPP/NPA/NDF is concerned, is to

Demonstration against U.S. military bases. An anti-nuclear movement is sweeping the South Pacific and Southeast Asia. Opponents charge that nuclear-powered and armed ships dock at the Subic naval base and that nuclear weapons are stored at the U.S. bases in the Philippines.

preclude a lot of shedding of blood. The CPP/NPA/NDF would agree to some principled settlement with the U.S.

Certainly the U.S. government is trying to improve its image here, to save the bases. This Economic Support Fund in its so-called aid program is more propaganda than anything else. During the Marcos regime, when this Economic Support Fund started, the first project funded by the ESF here in Olongapo was a garbage processing plant—and it's not even working anymore! It had to be built by an American contractor because if it's ESF money, it's got to have a lot of American consultants who do the planning. A considerable part of the fund goes to these American consultants.

For towns around here, they built public markets. I think public markets were easy to build and easy to overprice. It was the politicians who were handling this ESF fund, and they got a lot of fat commissions out of it. There was this one town here where a friend of mine told me that they built this market out of ESF funds. But the rental for the stalls is very much higher, and the vendors now sell their goods along the streets of the town.

How do you judge the popular support for dismantling the bases?

For one thing, not an unusual response of the people, especially those who are not against the bases, is, Where will we get our jobs if the bases go out? So we came up with a policy not to dismantle the bases but to stop storing nuclear weapons inside the bases, like that. Improve working conditions for workers inside the bases. It's more gradual. No one can dispute the fact that if a nuclear accident happens with those weapons stored inside the bases, the people of Olongapo would be in danger. Another Chernobyl, even worse.

Is it known for a fact that there are nuclear weapons on the base?

There are nuclear weapons. As a matter of policy, it is never confirmed or denied by the U.S., but they issue instructions on what to do in case of a nuclear accident.

One thing good going for us here in Olongapo is the fact that there's a growing anti-bases sentiment outside Olongapo, and that really affects people here. They start thinking. Some have already accepted the fact that if the majority of the people in the Philippines want the bases out, there is nothing the people in Olongapo can do. So, during organizing work, we make it a point to educate our people here, tell them there is a growing anti-bases sentiment all over the country. And they can see it all over the newspapers, especially those debates of the Con-Com. A lot of people have already realized that to have an economy based on the bases is not good. They have already realized the instability of the economy of the city, the abnormality of an economy that depends on whether a ship comes or not.

What is in the new Constitution about the bases?

I think that the provision in the new Constitution regarding the bases only provided for the perpetuation of the bases. It is not a victory for those opposed to the impact of the bases on our country. I would rather that nothing was mentioned in the Constitution about the bases, rather than a provision that is so vague and gives so much discretion to Congress on the fate of the bases. To me, that's not good, because of the kind of politicians we have here in the Philippines. I'm sure that most of the people who, because of their economic power, have the capability to be elected to Congress would be pro-bases.

Roland Simbulan
University professor
Quezon City

R oland Simbulan has established himself as the leading scholar on the issues surrounding the U.S. bases. A university professor, he lives in a simple apartment that is part of a large housing complex in Quezon City. He is 32 years old.

In my younger days, I had feelings about becoming a military officer. My dad is a retired army officer. Most of his military career was spent as an instructor in the Philippines Military Academy, which is dubbed the West Point of Asia.

Right before martial law, I was very active in the student council at the university here in Manila. When Marcos declared martial law, I was detained for two years. I was never formally charged either in a civilian court or a military court. I was just put in prison on general violation of the anti-subversion act. Friends and relatives worked for my release and, after two years of being out of circulation, I was finally released.

After my release, I saw the need for solid substantiation of the bases issues. My university has some sort of exchange program and I was for two years at New York University where I finished my masters degree in social sciences.

From a historical point of view, what are some of the important issues raised by the presence of the bases?

Unlike any other countries—whether in Asia or Europe, where the United States has overseas military bases and facilities—the American bases in the Philippines were part of the colonial process here, part of the military occupation by the United States in the beginning of the century. The bases, in fact, started as large military camps or troop concentrations in various parts of Luzon and other islands.

Then there is the legal aspect. In 1935, when we were still a colony or a so-called commonwealth of the United States, the United States passed an act which would give independence to the Philippines in ten years, but at the same time incorporated the retention of the U.S. bases here. A referendum was held here which rejected this act precisely because of the U.S. bases provision. The act was revised, and the revision was called the Tydings-McDuffie Act, which allowed only refueling stations until the expiration of our status as a commonwealth. But immediately after the war, the U.S. government took advantage of the fact that we were so hard up economically and we needed aid so desperately. An executive agreement was made between the Philippine President Roxas and the United States government, which culminated in the signing of the United States–Republic of the Philippines Military Bases Agreement. This allowed the United States not only ninety-nine years of maintaining these American military bases but even allowed them to expand them if required for national security.

Whose national security?

Well, it was assumed that the national security of the U.S. was also our national security, which is quite an assumption. So this is why many nationalists, especially those who have a legal background, question even the legality of the bases.

The American bases here are regarded for their importance for American military operations not only in the Philippines but in the region. Historically, these bases have been used as launching pads for intervention or even aggression against Korea, against Indochina. Their role is to safeguard American geopolitical interests in the whole region. I would say that they are a psychological support for America's allies and client regimes.

And their value for Philippine security?

It is ironic that one of the major arguments given in favor of the U.S. bases here is that they are here for Philippine security. One of the reasons the Japanese invaded the Philippines was that the U.S. bases were here. They could not even protect us. In fact, they were the first things to be attacked by the Japanese and wiped out.

And their value for the Philippines economy?

As for their economic contribution, an estimated 85 percent of the income generated in the two major cities outside the bases, namely Angeles City and Olongapo City–Subic, comes from expenditures by the base authorities, apartment rentals and especially, of course, this thriving so-called hospitality industry, which a lot of Filipinos are dependent on. I don't think that any country can be proud of having an industry based on the degradation of fellow Filipinos, no matter how much income or money is involved.

The U.S. does not pay rent for the bases. There is what is called a compensation package, but that compensation package is not covered by the Military Bases Agreement but by the Military Assistance Agreement, which is a separate agreement signed only one week after the signing of the Bases Agreement in 1947. That compensation package is not in any way rent. It all depends on what the United States is willing to give; there is no fixed amount.

During the time of Marcos, the bases were used to increase the level of American military assistance to the Philippines. In the late 1970s, the Marcos government started getting a lot of very sharp criticisms, even from the U.S. government, because of its human right violations. Marcos started linking the bases with this compensation package, which was in fact already committed. But he used the bases in the negotiations so that he could ask for more.

The bases have proven historically to be major sources of smuggling. All you have to do is to go around the base territories and see the businesses that thrive on the smuggled PX goods, and so that's a lot of revenues lost for the government. And besides a lot of the drugs that have penetrated Philippine society have been smuggled in through the bases.

Aren't the American bases necessary to offset the Soviet military presence in the region?

Last year I had the opportunity to interview some people from the American Embassy and I asked them, what would it take from the Soviets for you to be willing to withdraw. You know what the answer was? The Soviets would have to close down their bases north of Japan, which is in Vladivostok, which is where the Soviet Far East forces are located. But this is ridiculous because that's Soviet territory. It's like asking the U.S. government to withdraw its forces from California in exchange for some Soviet overseas facilities.

In other words, what the Americans want is a so-called balance of forces between American forces abroad and Soviet forces on Soviet territory. In fact, even in this booklet that the U.S. Embassy came out with last year, during the Constitutional Commission proceedings—this 90-page color booklet on the bases, there's a map of the so-called balance of forces in Asia where they balance the Soviet bases on Soviet territory, plus Cam Ranh Bay in Vietnam, with American forces bases overseas in other countries.

Should there be a plebiscite or referendum on the bases issue?

That should be done. This is something that really affects all Filipinos. Of course, there is a need to have a balanced information campaign. Often times, there is misinformation in the way the issue is presented. For instance, being against the bases means you're against the Americans. Of course, people would say, I'm in favor of the bases if you equate being against bases with being anti-American.

Yes, a "snap" referendum right now, without preceding it with a legitimate educational campaign, would result in the majority being in favor. But I would say that in the past decade those who are against the bases have increased. In fact, in the last national survey that was done by an independent research organization, 60 percent are in favor of keeping the bases and 40 percent are either against or undecided. Only a decade ago, as much as 80 percent or even 90 of Filipinos were still in favor of the bases, because of the thorough acculturation of Filipinos.

Has the legal position of the bases changed under the Aquino government?

There are two items in the new Constitution that directly or indirectly affect the bases. One is in the declaration of principles. It is an item that says that in the interest of national security, the Philippines pursues a nuclear-free policy. Based on this provision we are now disallowing the presence or even the transit of nuclear weapons on Philippines territory.

Of course, the U.S. government has the policy neither to deny or admit the existence of nuclear weapons. In fact, the Seventh Fleet, most of it, is nuclear armed. And it's an open secret that the Americans are storing tactical nuclear weapons both at Clark and Subic. I think that we should not allow the entrance of U.S. aircraft carriers suspected to be carrying nuclear weapons, if they do not allow an inspection by the Philippines government. There is still a need to put more teeth into this provision in the Constitution. We need a monitoring body, for instance, to monitor whether there are nuclear weapons here or not, given the U.S. policy.

The nuclear issue is a potent one. We saw that with the campaign against the nuclear power plant in Bataan. Practically the whole province went on general strike—and that was under Marcos. That's why I think it was a brilliant move to use the antinuclear policy in the Constitution as a stepping stone for the eventual removal of the bases.

In another provision in the Constitution, it says that the Philippines will respect the 1991 agreement, after which it will be left to the Philippines Congress, by two-thirds of the Senate, to legislate a treaty. In the past, it was merely an executive agreement signed by the president with the legislature out of the way. In other words, in the Senate alone, with nine senators who are anti-bases, you can block the treaty. So I'm encouraged by the Constitution on paper, but it's a piece of paper.

In my own estimate, even if a nationalist government were to win power I do not think that they could right away force the United States to move the bases out. Even after a social revolution, it would still be another problem to remove these bases, even if the government had the political will to do so, because the U.S. really wants to keep them. Many ways will have to be utilized to eventually get rid of them.

Can you elaborate on the connections between the bases and internal Philippine politics?

I think that as long as the bases are here, they will provide some sort of a justification for the United States government to more and more involve itself, not only politically but also militarily, in Philippine affairs. This is especially true now, after the breakdown in the ceasefire and the declaration of war, so to speak, by the Aquino government against the insurgency—given the fact that the armed forces of the Philippines are almost totally dependent on the United States logistically and in training and even in indoctrination.

The United States will involve itself much, much more, both covertly and overtly, in events here in the Philippines—even more than in Central America. What makes us different from Central America is that the United States has very big facilities here. Withdrawing their bases from the Philippines would, I believe, be pyschologically a far greater defeat for U.S. policymakers than their defeat in Vietnam. Most of our ASEAN neighbors send their armed forces personnel to train at Clark and Subic. So as long as there are the bases I would easily predict a growing involvement of the United States in the Philippines, an involvement that could in a few years surpass what we have seen recently in Central America.

Richard "Dick" Gordon
Ex-mayor
Olongapo

R ichard Gordon meets with me in his office, located on the street level of a large
family house just off the "strip." The office is a photographic pantheon. Every
inch of the walls are covered with autographed ("To Mayor Dick Gordon")
black-and-white glossies of top brass and political figures, mainly Americans—am-
bassadors, fleet commanders, base commanders, Jeane Kirkpatrick, senators, Los
Angeles Mayor Tom Bradley.

*Down the center of the room runs a long wooden table, at which twenty or more
people are seated, mainly middle-aged women, seemingly all talking at once. A dozen
more are standing on either side. "They're market vendors," Gordon explains.
"They're here to tell me how corrupt the police are, what chaos the city has fallen
into." A couple dozen more people waiting to see "Mayor" Gordon are crowding the
adjacent receptionist's office.*

*Gordon talks nonstop for a couple of hours, with virtually no questions from me. The
41-year-old ex-mayor's grandfather was an American. His father, James, was also
a U.S. citizen, but chose to be a Filipino. ("I'm proud of that.") His four uncles all
lived in the United States. After World War II, his father was an elected member of
the Community Council when Olongapo was under direct rule of a U.S. Navy
commander. ("It was a town under martial law, but it was fair.") A few years after
the U.S. military put Olongapo under Philippine control, his father was elected
mayor. After his father was assassinated, his mother was elected mayor. His family
owns the local theater and a number of restaurants. ("My parents made a lot of
money here.") Some charge that the Gordons also have interests in some bars and
nightclubs, but the former mayor denies it.*

I was elected mayor in 1980. I was supposed to end my term March 3, 1986,
but Cory Aquino's rule was that all governors and mayors identified with the
KBL had to go. They said they were getting rid of us on the basis of performance,
on the basis of credibility and integrity. But what really happened was that

simply anybody who's associated with Marcos—anybody who didn't help us—get them out; and anybody who helped us, get them in. No matter if they were crooks or what have you.

You Americans like Cory because she speaks nice English, she was educated in the States, and this is a Cinderella story. Well, I've seen nine months of her as president and what's happened to my country; I see it fragmenting all over me. I've been taking pills lately. I have nightmares. I see a situation where troops wearing uniforms, not Philippine Army troops, are running around with firearms. I've got two letters here telling me that I'm on the hit list of the NPA.

If I had it my way I don't know who should be president. Right now I have a few ideas. But one of these days, I'm going to get a crack at it myself. And don't write that in your book because they're going to say I'm an ambitious young man.

It's unfortunate that I was removed from being mayor here. Sure you got prostitution and crime, and that kind of stuff, but you can change it. I said what this country needs is not a change of men, it needs a change *in* men. When we embarked on those changes in 1980, those changes were indeed dramatic. We took care of infrastructure—I thought that was the minimum we would do—build schools and stuff like that. But you see, we got the people initiative. We rehabilitated the hospital. We had volunteers in the hospital, five hundred of them coming from the poor. We color-coded the jeepneys so that both Filipinos and Americans would know how to ride their jeepneys.

We had peace and order. The whole town was fired up. "Aim high, Olongapo!" That was supposed to be our slogan. We came out with it even before the air force. I came from a Jesuit school, so I had slogans like "No lazybones in Olongapo," which means I wanted to inculcate the work ethic in our people.

Cleaning up this city is a broken record for our family. My grandfather, my father, my mother, me, we cleaned up the city of debris, physical and so-called moral debris. And we cleaned up the police.

What about the problem of prostitution?

Any place there's a military base, there's going to be crime, there's going to be prostitution. What does a guy do? He softens the hurt, and there's a lot of hurt in this town. But there's also a lot of people who are making a lot of money, who are able to send their kids to school. Is that a rationalization? Perhaps. But is that reality? Yes. Some of these girls send their brothers, send their children to school.

Jun Cañete

Mayor Richard Gordon

What do you say to people who would like to see the bases go?

Nobody can give me something better than this base. Don't tell me about alternatives. You know, I was on a TV talk show the other night. This guy, Lean Alejandro, I was on with is a very smart kid [national leader of Bayan, 28 years old, later assassinated in Manila, September 1987]. I told him, "You know, Lean, we shouldn't talk about this on television, we should talk about this *mano-mano* [man to man]." If you're a communist, if you're in the Left, I don't want to talk to you about it here. Here, let's talk realities. You say the base should get out. You say you have a study. Okay, but why should we use money, which is scarce enough in this country right now, to remove a base that is already doing something for us? The base has its negatives; it has its positives. All that we have to do is minimize its disadvantages and maximize its advantages.

Let's be realistic about this whole bloody thing. There are 432,000 decent people working inside the bases or around the bases, shining shoes, giving haircuts, making clothes, prostituting, if you will. Even the prostitute lawyers make a living out of this place. For as long as you cannot give me anything better than the bases, I'm going to say let the base stay in this town.

They say the bases treaty is an unequal treaty. Well, unequal treaties are the result of unequal bargaining strength. The relationship of this country and the

United States is primus inter pares—the Americans get the primus, the Filipinos get the pares.

If they kick the Americans out of here, who's going to be here? The Japanese—who raped my country for four years? Who's going to protect us from the Russians who are in Cam Ranh Bay? I'd rather deal with the Americans than with the Russians.

Neutrality is not reality. I'm a history and government major. World War II happened because a little corporal by the name of Hitler got away with everything he wanted. People didn't want to make war. People said, Oh, it's time for peace. A guy by the name of Chamberlain, I think, what did he say? Peace in our time. So they got Munich. They walked all over these countries. What happened to Belgium? And Luxemburg? Hey, we're neutrals, guys, don't walk over us. India was neutral, but that didn't stop China from walking all over them. Cambodia was neutral, did that stop Nixon from sending in troops to Cambodia? Come on, guys, this is a big bad world. We don't have a franchise on evil. We don't have a franchise on good.

In the January 1988 elections, Gordon was again elected mayor of Olongapo. He ran as a member of the old Marcos political party.

Father Shay Cullen
Director, drug treatment center
Olongapo

I find Father Shay Cullen, a middle-aged Irish Columban priest, in a room at the drug treatment center he runs for young people. The room doubles as his bedroom and study. When I knock on the door, he is at his typewriter "banging out a newspaper article." The center is on a hillside on the coastal road from Olongapo, heading north to the town of Subic. It has a commanding view of the U.S. naval base.

My work began here in 1974. I came to the Philippines in 1969 from southern Dublin.

Family problems are a big cause of the drug problem here. Many of the fathers working in these bases spend their money in nightclubs. When the ships are not here, the clubs are getting Filipino customers. The only people with money around are the base workers. So they go into a bar, they get a girl, they don't go home. You find the wives at the gates on Thursdays or Fridays to get the money from their husbands—the payroll ambush, as they call it here.

By the early '80s, things were getting worse in the Philippines. We were giving seminars. Even in the church, I was giving strong sermons on social justice, denouncing the disrespect for human lives, including the salvage squads. Mayor Gordon and the other local wealthy people who run the so-called hospitality industry got angry. They complained to the church authorities. I was a headache to them.

The church here goes along with the idea that there's no social problem with the bases. The fact that a quarter of a million people are supporting an industry of prostitution doesn't seem to be an issue. I fail to understand that. The city authorities, whose major concern should be the welfare of the people, are engaged in the nightclub industry.

Including Mayor Gordon?

Yes, Gordon owns hotels, restaurants, and resorts. We know that his wife and he are into the nightclub business. But because of public relations, they have it in another name.

What really gets me about Gordon is that he cries over all the injustices done to him. But in fact during his administration, he set up a salvage squad. They go out and kill women. We even know some of the names, places, and times.

I don't know how much you know about the criminal mentality, but killing becomes some kind of a thrill after a while. And where there's big money to be generated out of it, and fear to be generated, and the feeling of power that comes out of it, it's an escalating and nonstop type of death squad thing. Just like the death squads in El Salvador. They started on a killing spree and they couldn't stop it. Here, they instill fear in anyone who might cross them. We found one woman right down here thrown into a ditch. Another woman was beheaded last month; you must've heard about that. And a man was also beheaded a couple weeks before that. His head was displayed.

The local police, some of them former bodyguards of Mayor Gordon, were part of that squad. He called it a "reaction squad"—to clean up the streets. He scared the living daylights out of everybody. Anybody who would not grovel and snivel at his boots, he would kill through the squad. The bodies started showing up. Sure, teenage crime dropped—they were all dead! They made the streets safe for American sailors. And that's what he wanted: more business. The sailors can walk around this town and get away with anything, because they'd say, "I'm going to report you to the mayor." The girl would tremble with fear, so she wouldn't ask for her payment. And the sailor could rape her and get away with it.

Here's the way the police operate. They set up their own extortion rings, their own gangs, to make money. These police drive around in flashy cars, wear diamond rings and jewelry, Rolex watches. On 400 pesos a month you cannot live a flashy lifestyle.

The system works like this. There's a city ordinance that says that women who work in nightclubs and bars are legitimate, the street walkers aren't. Police pick up the street walkers. They put them in jail. They start to blackmail them. The women have to give them sexual favors. The police might even give these girls money to set up an American for robbery.

Are Gordon's activities widely known?

Gordon's car passes in and out of the base without inspection. Early in 1983, navy investigators, headed by Mr. Ryle, discovered that the mayor's car was being used to smuggle things out of the base, even things from the base restaurants. They made an investigation, but it was squashed. It did get into the papers, though.

Another thing that we uncovered was child prostitution. These children—9-, 10-, 12-, 14-year-old girls—were brought to the clinic. Eighteen of them. The girls had herpes, gonorrhea, and syphilis. They had been heavily used. Mayor Gordon found out, and he had them all locked into one room in the General Hospital where they began to have treatment. He had the children interviewed and had all the interviews videotaped. The girls said that there are many more of them on the streets being picked up by some unscrupulous local people who were selling them to the Americans for sex. They used to get from twenty to forty dollars per time. The pimps got most of the money. They were able to identify one of the Americans, because he gave one of the girls a T-shirt with his name on it, Daniel Dougherty, a navy chief from Philadelphia who was regularly taking little girls to his place down in Subic town.

The mayor investigated very carefully, so he knew the whole score. He ordered the Sisters to stay quiet about the whole thing or something very serious might happen. In addition to Dougherty, a number of names came up. But the mayor let them go scot-free; he never filed charges. Of course, he didn't fail to tell the admiral, because I think he used it to gain a lot of benefits from the base. The base gives away things as a way to improve community relations. They give them to people in the local government to cooperate with them in hushing things up.

When I discovered the children in the hospital—I was told by one of the Sisters who was almost instantly transferred for doing such a thing—I interviewed them on tape and photographed them. That night, I got a strange visit from the parish priest. He got this unusual phone call. It was from the mayor's office. The admiral came on the phone. The admiral told him, "Would you please talk to that Father there. He's a bit of a radical, you know." I told him if they call up again tomorrow, tell them they can come and see me. The next day the base chaplain came over. Again saying, "Well, we would like you to cooperate and not to make a big scene out of this." They knew I'm a journalist. I do a lot of photojournalism and I was writing exposés in the newspapers as best I could under the restrictions.

So I told him, "I'll talk to the admiral." Dougherty already had left the country. The mayor let him slip away. "Admiral," I told him, "You know where he lives. You know where your navy personnel are. So you need about five days to pick him up."

So what's the problem that three to four days later the story came out? But the mayor blew a valve. He was fuming. We went around denouncing me to everybody. The very day my article appeared in the newspaper, he brought it to a meeting of the Knights of Columbus. He got up in front of everybody and says, "This guy's not fit to be a priest, he's a disgrace to the cloth, he's disgraced our country by exposing this in the papers, has doomed these children to a disgraceful future, he's brought shame to our community." This went on. At every public meeting he was making speeches denouncing me, making all sorts of threats. The arrogance of power. When that guy is mad, boy, he changes. He looks meek, a baby-faced guy. And so convincing, shedding tears. But when he gets mad, boy!

What do you see as a solution for the bases?

I advocate a conversion plan—that the military base here be converted into an industrial complex, providing dignified work. Not an export processing zone, I don't believe in that—that's a failure and an abomination. The labor is here, and the ship repair facilities are here. There are massive installations for light industry and a trained work force.

I think the process can start in a gradual way, without causing a great dislocation. When the base begins to move its operations piecemeal to other areas like Saipan or back to Guam, many of the Filipino workers may follow them, so there'll be less dislocation. Most of these guys who run the nightclubs are foreigners. Many of them are retired navy officers. I think this can be done. Look at Thailand. They're going to build a whole new ship repair facility. The Norwegians, they wanted a warm-water ship repair facility for their ships in this part of the world. And they wanted it at reasonable rates. Financially, Hong Kong is now uneconomic. The Japanese can't compete. Their labor is exorbitant.

So there're great possibilities. An expert from the University of Texas came here and made a study. He saw the base, and he went to talk to the national leaders. He told them this is the way to go. He pointed out a study made by the U.S. Department of Defense, no less, which showed that sixty-four bases in the U.S., which were closed in the last twenty years, had a 50 percent increase in employment rates after they were converted into civilian use. I don't see why it's any more difficult here, when there's huge unemployment, labor rates are competitive, and we're very strategically located, and have all the facilities. You don't need much capital investment. Everything's there. A study has to be done much more carefully on the development of export-import light industries.

Filipinos are very, very patient, but the day comes when it snaps. One thing that's happening here that will change the attitude toward the U.S. military presence in the Olongapo is this: that the very principles which the U.S. military men come here to protect, safeguard, defend, and die for are violated by their very lifestyle. And people see that here. It's all a sham. The way the navy and air force people act and live out their lives is a total contradiction of everything that they're supposed to stand for.

Lolita
Bar waitress
Olongapo

O n the three-hour bus ride from Manila to Olongapo I get out a folder of articles I've accumulated on the U.S. military bases. One is from Playboy magazine; it's called "Why They Love Us in the Philippines." The subtitle is, "Even as a dictator fell, the more serious business of servicing the U.S. Navy went on as usual."

My first couple of evenings in Olongapo I go "barhopping" with Brenda Stoltzfus, a social worker for the Mennonite Central Committee in Olongapo who has befriended many of the women working in the "entertainment" industry. I see why Playboy would conclude that Olongapo is "a magical place ... for a 19-year-old navy kid, the magic of a place where anything is possible. And cheap."

One afternoon, I talk with Lolita in her room, in a house she shares with her cousin and several others in a shanty section of Olongapo. While we talk, with Brenda interpreting, in Tagalog, she bounces on her lap Michael, a beautiful baby boy. Lolita is 17.

I'm a waitress. I won't give the name of the bar, okay? I get paid 150 pesos a month. If the American buys me a drink—it's called a lady's drink—it costs him 30 pesos for a small one, and I get 14 pesos from that; a big lady's drink is 60 pesos, and 28 pesos goes to me, the rest to the bar owner. The bar fine is 410 pesos. From that I get 128 pesos.

What is a bar fine?

That's what a customer has to pay the bar owner if he wants to take a girl out of the bar. I have to go with the customer. If the management finds out that an American wants to pay my bar fine, I have to go with him, or they'll get mad at me.

What if you go out without paying the bar fine?

Jun Cañete

Lolita and son, Michael

If I do a sneak-out with an American, I'll be fined 500 pesos. If I'm walking down the street with an American, a policeman can ask to see my bar fine paper to show that my bar fine's been paid. If I don't have it, then I can be picked up by the police. I can be put in prison for several days. And the police take advantage of you. I know, it happened to a friend of mine.

When are you at the bar?

I have to work every day. I go around four o'clock and have to stay until past twelve at night. If I want to take a day off, they don't always agree to give you the day off. If I take it anyway, then I will have a fine of 250 pesos.

I used to be a stay-in. That's what you're called if you live in the bar. I didn't have enough money to rent a place. At the bar, bed-spacers are free. [People rent space to sleep in rooms and dormitories, called bed-spacers.] But the bar is open twenty-four hours a day; so if you're a stay-in, you can be woken up any time a customer comes and wants to have a drink with you or go out.

We are fined 100 pesos if we fall asleep at work. And if I forget to bring my

One of some 500 bars and massage parlors and a few of the more than 1,600 women working in the entertainment industry in Olongapo, a former fishing village adjacent to the U.S. naval station at Subic Bay.

straw hat [part of the get-up for the women working at this bar—a "gay '90s" motif], I'm fined 25 pesos. The bar owner has a lot of fines for us.

Who is the bar owner?

The owner is an American. He was in the navy. His name is Scotty. He must be rich. He owns two bars here. He also owns a bar in San Diego. He takes videotapes of that bar and shows them here and takes videotapes here and shows them there.

The brother of the owner is the manager. He gets angry with me because I don't want to go with one of the American sailors. Sometimes they want to force certain kinds of sex on me. If I really refuse, then he can go back to the bar and get his bar fine back. He can get his money back even if I had sex with him if he says that I wouldn't do what he wanted. And then the manager is angry with me and charges the bar fine, the 410 pesos, to me.

What I most dislike about working in the bar is that I am afraid of getting sick.

You know there's more serious sickness now. Yes, AIDS. But if you don't have any money, there's nothing you can do. You have to go to work.

Where do you go if you get sick?

I go to a social hygiene center. I think the navy pays for the center. If I go to a private doctor, I'm the one who has to pay. But I don't think I can go to the social hygiene center for all kinds of illnesses, just the ones that I might give to an American—isn't that it?

Is there anything you like about your work?

Nothing. Yes, I do have some friends among the other women at the bar. But I am never really happy at the bar. I really don't like it. Even if there were some AIDS medicine, I still wouldn't like the bar. I do it only because I want to help my mother. My parents have a big debt and that's why I'm working here.

I'm from Samar [province]. My father is a farmer. He is a tenant. We grow coconuts. Two-thirds go the landlord. The debt is to the landlord. When I was 10, grandfather got sick, and my father had to get money for the doctor and the medicines. They pay 20 percent interest each month.

I am the youngest in the family. I have seven brothers and sisters. But they are all married and can't help my mother and my father. Three are in Samar, and three are in Manila.

Maybe I could have gotten a job in Samar as a maid. Maybe. But I would be getting 150 pesos a month. Here, if there is a big ship in, like a carrier, I can make maybe 500. Then I can send 100 to 150 back home. I usually try to send something.

How did you happen to come here?

My cousin brought me here. She was already working in a bar here and went back to Samar for a visit. I was 15. I wanted to go to Olongapo and work as a maid. But the pay was very low for a maid, and my cousin said why not just work here in a bar? I wrote my family that I was working as a maid.

But then when I was pregnant I wrote them the truth. They were angry, but they also felt sorry for me because I was pregnant. Even my brothers and sisters were upset with me. They didn't like that I am working here. But the fact that I was pregnant helped lessen their anger.

When Michael was born, I had to pay for it all. From July to December I received fifty dollars from the father. From January until now [March 25] I haven't received anything from him.

The last letter I got from him was in December. He said in his letter that he would send more money, but I haven't heard from him since. In August, when I was still pregnant, he was here for two weeks. He said he would support the baby, but I don't know if he will marry me.

Would you like to marry an American?

Sure I would like to marry an American! I want to help my family. If I marry a Filipino, it will be the same; but if I marry an American, maybe it will be better. Some Filipinos beat their wives, and I don't like that. I really don't know if American men also beat their wives.

Are you currently working?

No, I'm not working right now because of the baby. I asked permission from the management to leave, so I don't have to have my bar fine paid. But I will have to go back to work soon. For a while my cousin is helping pay the house expenses and for the baby.

How do you feel about the foreign bases in the Philippines?

It's good that they're here, because they can help poor women like me. Some Filipinos don't like the bases here, because their wives work in the bars. Couples fight because the man doesn't like it that the woman is working in the bar.

Sure, if I had other work, I would like to see the bases leave. I would like to go to Samar and help my father farm. Help plant things like corn, *camoteng kahoy* [a root crop like a sweet potato]. I miss my family and my friends.

And I want to study more, because I only finished grade three. Here we can't continue our studies because of the class schedule. We don't get enough sleep. I'd like to help my father farm.

Sister Agnetta
Principal, St. James High School
Subic City

One Sunday I meet with Sister Agnetta, who is dressed in traditional nun's garb, in the convent next to St. James High School in the town of Subic. Most of the students, in the high school where she is the principal, are the children of Filipinos employed by the U.S. Navy as civilian workers.

Whenever I'm asked where I'm from, I always say Leyte and Nueva Ecija—Leyte because my father hails from that province, and for years I lived there. He is a law graduate, he works with the government in Manila. I lived also for some time in Nueva Ecija, my mother's home province. Then I entered the convent, and I've been assigned to different places in Nueva Ecija and Pampanga. Then I was sent for further studies at the University Santo Tomas. After finishing my graduate studies, I was assigned to San Antonio, near here, where the U.S. Naval Communication Center is located, for three years, and after that here in Subic to help in the administration of this school. That was seven years ago.

Of course, during these years in San Antonio and Subic, I was aware of the U.S. bases. But I was not so aware of the many implications, the consequences, until a few years back when suddenly I opened my eyes to the growing misery most of the people are experiencing in our country and sought to understand its roots. But the foundation was laid following Vatican II when our congregation started reviewing our mission. Through various congresses, we formulated our vision of our mission. Basic to our mission is that we live as a faith community of Franciscan women, professing our commitment to the local church and to the people of God with a preferential option for the poor. This preferential option for the poor is a continuous challenge, and we keep telling ourselves that we have to live as poor as they do.

I know you are opposed to the presence of the bases. What would you like to see done in the Philippines?

Jun Cañete

Sister Agnetta

In the first place we have to look at education here, both in and out of the classroom. The United States of America has subjugated our minds very systematically. I'm not even an exception to this. From the moment you open your eyes in this country, you are told that nothing is better than America, the United States of America. Our school books are from the U.S. You know, when day in and day out you hear this, it becomes difficult to change your outlook and viewpoint.

An American Navy chaplain was commenting to me about the U.S. losing millions here in Olongapo-Subic, through the smuggling out of stateside goods from the commissary by American employees, or dependents like Filipino women living with American servicemen. I told him, "Father, you can tell this to your people back home, you cannot blame the Filipinos entirely because you have conditioned our minds to think that there is nothing superior to U.S. goods. And so, no matter how poor they are, they would put in even their last penny just to buy U.S. goods." And he agreed with me. That's why, don't be surprised if many Filipinos have views different from mine regarding U.S. bases. Around here a rather high percentage of people work for the U.S. Navy, and they are receiving a higher pay than from almost anywhere in the locality. Losing the bases for them would be losing stateside goods, losing dollars, losing their bread. But they have not gone really into the root causes of our problems in the Philippines—why so many Filipinos are poor, and why the Philippines and they are so dependent economically on the U.S.

What problems do you see associated with the presence of the bases?

Prostitution and drug addiction are very prominent features of the impact of the base on Olongapo and neighboring areas. One of the consequences of prostitution is, of course, the breaking up of families—unwanted children or children who have problems, children who will later on resort to drugs just to forget the reality of who their mothers are. And these women are coming from different sections of the country where the lack of agrarian reform keeps their families poor. They have not got an elementary education, much less a high school education. Many of them are illiterates. Although, you know, some are professionals who become desperate to get a decent job in the Philippines and fall into this indecent job. And the scarcity of decent employment is a direct result of how wealth here is controlled by foreign and local power.

It's not only that these bases are rooted in the economic and political intervention of the United States in our country, and it's not only the social cost, indeed, the social pain, of their continued presence, but also the threat to all human life they pose here. Because as long as there are bases of a superpower here, we remain aligned with a foreign country, and therefore in any war another superpower will surely attack us with a nuclear strike. The very presence of the nuclear weapons that they store at these bases is dramatically opposed to the peace we are trying to achieve here and in the world.

As a high school principal, how do you deal with the attitudes of dependence on the U.S.?

A young man came here to share his views about the U.S. Naval bases to our students. He is a Manila boy who comes from a very well-to-do family, who got his college education at the College of La Salle. We invited him to give a talk to our students. It was his first time to come to the area and the first thing that he noticed were the trash cans painted "Donated by the U.S. Naval Station." And he started by chiding the students, Can you not provide your own trash cans? Do you depend on the Americans for your trash cans? The students did not argue with him, many of them were intent on listening to him, and I think some were convinced.

Young people are now beginning to open their eyes, especially in this school, maybe in other schools. Just a few days ago, there was a group of Japanese who came over here working for a ban on nuclear weapons. I invited the student council officers to listen to them, and I found them very intently listening, and they had so many questions to ask. Before I knew it, they were signing a paper in favor of banning nuclear weapons.

Do parents object to this kind of instruction?

Yes. Many of the parents of our students work on the bases, many of them. So, you can understand they feel threatened when you talk against the bases.

What do you say to parents who might call you a communist because you oppose the continued presence of the bases?

Well, it's very easy. You see, it would be very hard for them to see me as communist. Communism is linked with atheism and basically, I think, the majority of Filipinos oppose communism because they think it's godless. They know that I have given my life to my Catholic faith. No, I am not opposed to groups like the National Democratic Front, the New People's Army, the Communist Party of the Philippines, because I know their true origin. Some of them could be the closest to God. They are guided by the virtue of their love for the people—the poor, the oppressed, and the exploited in Philippine society. Even by that virtue alone, I would say that they are closest to the heart of Christ. I certainly do not fear them.

Would you say you give a balanced view to your students?

We leave our students open, we don't try to impose anything. We just educate them as much as we can. We try to give them an education that is based on justice, because that is a Christian education. Otherwise, what kind of Christian education are we giving if we don't emphasize justice as the basis of genuine freedom? We try to open their eyes. We are encouraging our students to be more analytical, more critical, and not just simply take in what is said in the papers or what they hear from others, us included. They should as much as possible widen their vision. Read, listen, and be critical.

When we had a peace rally in Olongapo City, it opened with a mass and a symposium on the disadvantages of the continued presence of the U.S. bases. The students and teachers here were free to join the rally or not. I did not even advise them in order not to give the impression that they were being coerced, pressured. I only told them that in case they were interested to join the peace rally, then we would see one another in Olongapo City. Many teachers did come, and many students, even without the permission of their parents. One student, a student leader in fact—he's a son of an engineer working on base—he told me that when he was asking permission from his father, his father said, What about me now, since I'm working on base, what will people say? So, you see, some students might not have gone more out of respect for their parents, and fear perhaps of the consequences to their parents' jobs. But this young man, he did go, and even represented the student sector in the prayer. I was surprised that he went. I was also surprised when many of the students were there, and about 85 to 90 percent of the teachers.

How did the rally come off?

Roughly two thousand people attended this rally. There were workers of the base. And this is what I can tell you from getting their pulse beats: If only our people can be assured that when the Americans pull out, they will have a sure job, that they would not be economically dislocated, 90 percent of them would not mind the closing of the base. This is the opinion given to me by workers of the base.

If only the Americans—they're a beautiful people—if only they would help the Filipino people by influencing the U.S. government to leave the Filipinos alone, we would be more than grateful. Then, we would enjoy national sovereignty and could begin to deal with each other on equal terms. As a religious person, this is my personal reflection on what we call national sovereignty. God has given us a piece of this earth, just as he has given the Americans theirs. If we simply leave this land to be exploited by foreigners, I believe that it is some kind of ingratitude toward the God that has given us this land. Maybe it would not be so bad, if our people were not suffering from deep poverty, extreme poverty, hunger, starvation, living in subhuman conditions, living without any genuine freedom like the women here in Olongapo. So as a religious person, this is my reflection: that our claim to national sovereignty is related to our commitment to the gift that God has given us.

Student Council
St. James High School
Subic City

S ister Agnetta told me that the Student Council would like to talk with me about the U.S. bases. I meet with six bright young men and women in the school's library. Their fathers are employed on the naval base. They are so eager to speak that after a few minutes they are frustrated that their English doesn't flow fast enough for them. I tell them that Tagalog would be fine since the tape will be transcribed by a Tagalog-speaking person—just give me the gist from time to time in English.

My name is Albert Payumo. I'm 17 years old and am in my senior year. Presently, I am the chairman of the student council here in Saint James. I've lived here in Subic almost all my life. My father used to be a radio operator for RCPI, Radio Corporation of the Philippines, Inc., but now he works on the U.S. base here. My mother is a housewife.

For me, the U.S. bases cannot really help the Philippines because they only place the Philippines in danger, since in case of any foreign attack on the United States, these military bases in the Philippines, and the areas around Subic and Clark Air Base, would be the first to be hit. Therefore, to me, the military bases are a threat to our security. What's more, if the U.S. bases remain here, we cannot say that the Philippines is free because of foreign domination.

Another young man picks up from Albert.

We think the advantages the people have in Olongapo in jobs and from the money spent by the sailors are small compared to the disadvantages.

Most of our parents are displeased with our views.

What I'd like to tell the American people if I had the chance is that they should look at the experience of Thailand. In the '50s, the Thai government wanted the American bases there to go. Some argued that if the bases would close, a communist takeover would happen, because at that time the insurgency was already high. But the Thai government closed the American bases anyway and the communist takeover didn't happen. The communists even decreased.

I ask for one of the two young women to tell me what they think.

I'm the vice-president of the student council. Actually, it could be good that we have the bases here. But when I see what the Americans are doing to the Filipinos, I cannot say that it is fair. What I want to say to them is treat us fairly. Because here in the bases, there is unequal pay but equal work. The Filipinos who work in the bases can't express their rights. The labor code inside the bases is worse than outside. The Filipinos are being downgraded by the Americans. My father works inside the base as a taxi driver. He receives unequal pay. We respect them, but they don't respect us. What I would like to say to the U.S. government is that it should change its policies, and to our government, don't allow them to meddle with us, don't let them use the IMF–World Bank to interfere with our economic, political, and cultural affairs. Even our education is affected by the U.S.

Another young man joins in.

My name is Froilan Ribao. You know, the Spaniards sold the Philippines to the Americans at a low price. We were like a ball passed to another country. We are Filipinos, and we want to stand on our own feet—without the help of Americans. We have the knowledge and power to manage and guard our country from another attack from other countries.

The Americans are not our enemies. We are brothers in the world. But the military bases serve as guards of American interests in our country. Our land is rich in natural resources, suitable for planting. As Filipinos, especially for us teenagers, the Americans have already broken the Filipino culture. We have only western culture.

In our books in school it says that Americans and Filipinos don't fight. It says that the Americans helped us from the Spanish colonialists. But beneath that help is the interest of the U.S. in our rich natural resources. That's their Number 1 interest. I can say that the U.S. is imperialist.

I want to dismantle the bases.

Jerome Caluyo
Social Worker
Olongapo

Jerry Caluyo, whom I meet through the Mennonite Central Committee, operates a center that works with drug addicts and street children. "I was once a street child myself," he tells me. He ran away from home when he was 12, because he wanted to go to school.

Since my older brothers and sisters were in school, my parents wanted me to work in the coconut fields on our farm. I lived on the street for a year in Iloilo [on the island of Panay in the Visayas]. For my sleeping mats, I used cardboard boxes. And when I was hungry, I used to beg from fishermen. I used to run errands for them just to have a meal.

My father died when I was 16, and I went back home. I joined the Franciscan Capuchins and stayed there for six years. For a pastoral training program, I moved out of the seminary to Antique and became involved with Basic Christian Communities, with community organizing. Then I went back to the seminary and stayed there until 1981. I found out that the theology being taught to me by Germans, Italians, and Spaniards did not really respond to social realities. So I decided to go out of the seminary. I moved here to Olongapo and started working with a center for drug addicts. Then after a while I transferred to another project, with the street children I am working with now.

How big is the problem of street children in Olongapo?

In Olongapo, there are at least 3,000 abandoned and street children. Of those, 1,852 or 1,952, I can't remember the figure, we could say almost 2,000—are the products of Americans. They are Americans.

These three thousand children live on the street, under bridges, in the parks, on the stairways of churches and nightclubs, in vacant lots, in old buildings that are already abandoned. Many work as scavengers. They scavenge on

When the pain of poverty is too much to bear a marginalized generation appears.

Help the 3,000 Abandoned & Street Children of Olongapo attain a just and humane living condition.

Jun Cañete

Jerome Caluyo

garbage, at the city dump or any garbage lying on the street. They take anything that they can use, can resell—cardboard boxes, bottles, and food. Sometimes they eat spoiled food. Many also are gathering garbage from the markets. Others work as vendors. Others are mendicants. Many boys are also into pickpocketing. They pick on pockets of Americans, not of Filipinos.

Is drug use widspread?

There is a real drug problem here. In the entertainment business, you will see a lot of entertainers taking drugs. Not because they want to take drugs, but they are placed in a situation wherein they are being dehumanized. And to save face from the process of dehumanization they take drugs—palliatives, just to forget about everything. For street children, it's the same thing. The reason why they take inhalants [sniffing glue and other solvents] and a lot of that sort of thing is because they are hungry, because they want to forget that the pavement that they are sleeping on is cold and wet, forget that the paper and cardboard boxes used as a blanket are also wet and cold during rainy season.

The center where I worked is for boys only, for drug users. These are the product of the R & R industry. Say, the mother is an entertainer and, if you will trace the family line, the mother is also taking drugs. So the children follow the steps. If you're a growing teenager, realizing that your mother is a prostitute, it really is an image of your mother—or of your sister—being shattered in your mind. So, what will you do? You cannot kill your mother, you cannot kill your sister because they are into prostitution or the R & R industry. So the palliative is to take drugs. They want to destroy. The view of these kids is very limited. They see their mother's occupation per se, they don't look beyond it. So the mothers end up being blamed by their sons for being what they are. That makes the situation complicated in terms of parent and children relationship.

Do you know much about the families the street children come from?

Starting last June, we interviewed the street children. Not all three thousand, maybe about six hundred. We found out where their parents lived. Some are from the provinces, of course. But for those children whose parents are in Olongapo, we made home visits and we really discovered the situation of the family. It's really horrible. The whole family has to live in a room, four-by-six or four-by-seven. It's worse than on the street. There's no place to even place your head, to lay down your tired body. And we discovered real malnourishment in 81 percent of the homes. The parents are jobless. The mother is sometimes sick, or the father.

So we found poverty, terrible poverty. But the problem of street children, of abandoned children, is not just a result of the social environment in the immediate area around the bases. But there is a direct link to the overall economic control of foreign interests, largely those of the U.S., in the Philippines. This is not debatable any more, this is a blunt and brutal fact.

The presence of the base in Olongapo does not correspond to the needs, the economic needs, of the people of Olongapo. This goes against what we are told to think, that the base gives Olongapo a solid economic base. If you examine the indicators of health and of education, you cannot say that the bases are helping Olongapo. Why, we have 3,000 out-of-school youth in Olongapo over and against a school age population of 24,000. And from 1981 to 1985, 51 percent of the deaths are of children. The top five causes of death—things like gastroenteritis, tuberculosis, malaria—speak of Olongapo as a city of poverty. How could you say that a community with a solid economic base would be killing its people with gastroenteritis? It's really very stupid to say that the base is developing Olongapo. Furthermore, the base makes Olongapo not self-reliant but dependent on it, and they want Olongapo to remain dependent on the base.

Now, let's go back to the point—the cause of why we have so many street children. It's poverty, and the root of poverty here is U.S. control. How do you get at this cause? We are building people's capacity to fight back. What we are doing here now is basically the same as what we used to do with people in Antique, where we formed Basic Christian Communities. We believe that we can beat the U.S., no matter how sophisticated its weapons, only in solidarity with the people, in solidarity with the poor. The people need to be empowered. We need to help make the people aware of what's going on, make the people aware of what could be the alternatives and allow them to choose. The moment the people become highly politicized, they cannot be fooled anymore. For example, I know a lot of people, even street kids, who consider the sailors dumb. Many poor people here do. Why? Because they could always make money off them. Imagine a 6-year-old kid who can pick a sailor's pocket without the sailor knowing it. Really, they consider them dumb. In interviews with street kids, they say, "Why I'm stealing from Americans is because they're stealing a lot from us." What they're saying is, "What I'm doing is bad, but what about what they're doing?"

They used to pick pockets of Americans in my presence. I don't encourage them, but I don't discourage them either, because organizing these kids, the first thing that you must not do is to preach. If you do moralize with these people, they would run away. They won't listen to you anymore. Their back has been bent because of poverty, and then here come the middle-class people telling them what they are doing is wrong. In fact, we should tell them that what society has been doing to you is wrong. What the Americans have been doing to us is wrong.

Are there American military personnel working with street children?

No. They give some dole-outs—food, medicine. They are so, so ... I want to kill them! There are some church groups, American church groups, say, the YWAM—Youth With A Mission. Everything that we build, they have the capacity to destroy in a day. Because we are training young people to be self-reliant, to stand on their own, to respond to their own needs with the resources of the community. And the YWAM is giving dole-outs left and right. Again that would destroy the stance of the people to stand on their own and would also strengthen the feudal relationship between the whites and the browns. I will not dare ask help from Americans, from Americans on base. We can do this ourselves.

The Americans with their project "Hand Clasp" went to the center and gave free medicines. One of the doctors of the city health office was really mad at them because when they came in they acted like they are the owners of the whole center, of Olongapo, of the whole Philippines. They were so arrogant. So the doctor was saying, "Okay, we welcome your medicines. We are thankful that you are giving us free medicines. But if you will not change your attitude, you can pack your medicines and go to hell." Just because you are giving us medicines, free medicines, doesn't mean you are going to treat us like dogs.

These so-called civic action programs of the military are quite obviously designed to put impressions into the minds of Filipinos that the American military are doing good service in the Philippines. I don't think it's working, because if they are successful why is the anti-American sentiment in Olongapo growing?

Larry Salasal
Ex-U.S. base worker
Olongapo

L arry Salasal is one of the "Subic 42," an informal organization of forty-two
Filipino civilian base workers fired by the U.S. Navy in the aftermath of a strike
in 1986.

I was born in Castilejos, about 30 kilometers from here. But I consider that I
grew up in Olongapo, because I got my education, my elementary, high school,
college education here in Olongapo. My father worked in the base and also
five of my brothers and my three sisters' husbands. I worked with the U.S. Naval
base for nine years. When I was fired in 1986, my position was that of ship
reproduction planner.

Do the workers on the bases have a union?

Yes, we have a union. Actually, they call it the Filipino Civilian Employees
Association. It is of workers for Subic Naval Base, Clark Air Base, Camp John
Hay, San Miguel Communications Station, and all the other U.S. military
facilities in the Philippines. There are about twenty-thousand Filipino workers.

It is a yellow union. The union is a yellow union because of its leaders. That's
one thing that has to be categorically stated. It's not because of the workers. In
the monthly publication of the union, the *Tinig ng Manggagawa* [*Voice of the
Workers*], for example, when the peso wage line was increased in 1985 by 30
percent, that was a big headline; but when two workers meet an accident due
to poor safety, and one worker is now totally a vegetable and the management
will have nothing to do with the health and care of the worker, it is never
mentioned in the publication.

The base workers are not very much enticed by political issues. If you are good
at talking with them, you can get elected. That is exactly what happened in
the election of the incumbent president, Bobby Flores. The problem is that,

Jun Cañete

Larry Salasal

when a leader is elected to the union, he becomes closer to the management rather than closer to the workers.

Can you give an example?

A clear example is our strike, which started on March 21 and ended on April 2. The issue was severance pay after resignation. Our demand was that whenever an employee resigns, he should get his severance pay. After eleven months of negotiation, they arrived at a memorandum of agreement signed by the U.S. management panel and the union panel, which included the severance pay agreement. The problem is it still had to be signed by "higher authorities," which we presume are authorities in Hawaii or Washington. The union leadership and the chairman of the U.S. management panel were assuring the membership with all their press releases, talks, and forums that everything's okay. But after three weeks, the more substantial parts of the agreement were turned down.

On March 21, Bobby Flores along with his buddies, the executive council of the union, came back to Olongapo empty-handed, and the base workers—they were about four thousand—were all agitated to go on strike. But the yellow leadership did not want to for reasons we do not know, and so the base workers went on strike without the yellow union leadership.

That evening there was a barricade at the main gate. At about ten o'clock in the evening, there were about ten marines who had a good time in town and were going back to the base. They were drunk. They were not allowed to enter. The ten marines started stabbing everybody with knives. Six Filipino base workers were wounded. It was only at that point that Bobby Flores was forced to declare that, okay, I am sanctioning the strike.

Was there any attempt to suppress the strike?

There was a violent dispersal that happened at the main gate, on the morning of April 1. That was a concrete experience for us workers that even with the Cory Aquino government in power, the democratic space that they are always telling us about is not at all realizable in Olongapo. If the U.S. military bases are at stake, there is no such thing as democratic space here. There was the Philippine Constabulary from the outside and Philippine Marines from the inside with truncheons and fire trucks—we were sandwiched.

The strike ended after that?

We realized that even if we have all the courage to continue with the strike, nothing will come of it. We decided to end the strike and continue to work to transform the union. After all, we had impressed upon our fellow workers that the main problem here, as far as trade unionism is concerned, is the leadership. There were workers who, because of thirteen days of struggles—the first time in their lives, I think—were beginning to realize that after all, what is the use of the base here if the richest employers in the world cannot give in to a small demand?

We thought that it would be very good for us to consolidate the workers who have realized that we have to topple down the regime of Bobby Flores and that we have to institute some reforms. I was one of those who formed the group—there were sixteen of us—this *Partido ng Manggagawang* Base [Base Workers Party]. There were a lot of issues that were dug out during the strike like the Toyota car of Bobby Flores, the mansion house of Bobby Flores. Where have all these riches come from?

It was not only a question of transforming a yellow union to a genuine union, it was a question of the hatred of a common worker toward graft and corruption in his own union. And so there were thousands of workers who were interested in joining the PMB. A part of our plan was to demand a special election. But all our plans were blocked because of our termination by the U.S. management.

What happened?

There were forty-two of us terminated on the morning of June 17. We were one by one kicked out from our working places without any notice. We were picked up by military personnel, and we were brought to our commanding officers. I was handed this separation paper stating that my continued presence in the U.S. military base is inconsistent with the interests of the U.S. military forces. When we turned to the base labor agreement there was the specific provision in it that the U.S. management has a right to terminate any employee whose continued presence, in their judgment, is inconsistent with the interests of the U.S. military forces. We were not given any due process, we were simply kicked out.

Now we are only demanding what the U.S. government is propagating—that it is an advocate of human rights. Give us due process and we will prove that you are wrong in accusing us of being subversives and communists. We were never given the chance to defend ourselves. We did not even say that you have to dismantle the bases. I personally am not for the outright dismantling of the U.S. bases. We were accused of that because of our involvement in working for a genuine union. Because they think we are threats to the U.S. military bases, they kicked us out. And so what is U.S. justice?

I am still dedicating myself to politicizing base workers. My main preoccupation is explaining to them that they have to understand all these laws and agreements which are not famliar to them. They are sympathetic. The base workers think we were made a sacrificial lamb.

If only the American people knew what are the effects of the U.S. military facilities here, I think that the American people would not tolerate the existence of the military facilities here. If only the American people knew what happened to the Subic 42, they would not tolerate that.

Eight:
CHILDREN OF THE
UNDECLARED WAR

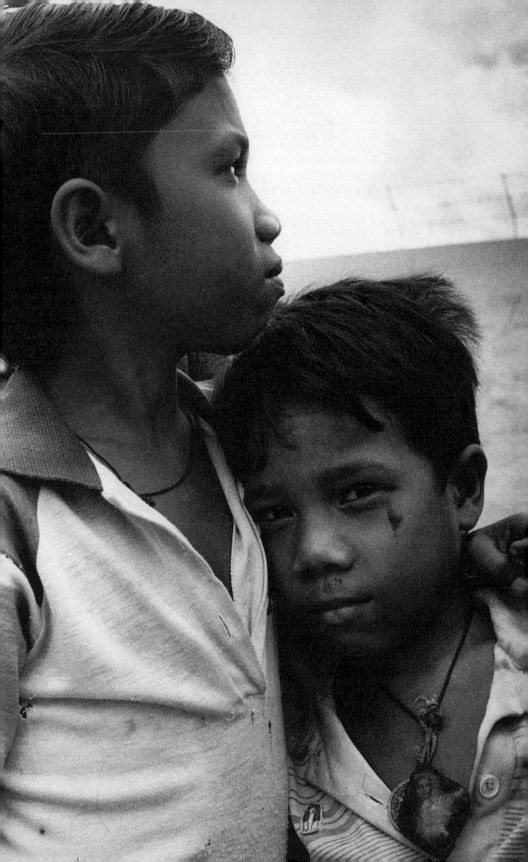

Dr. Elizabeth Marcelino
Director, Children's Rehabilitation Center
Manila

In May 1988, just as I was completing this book, I was introduced to Dr. Elizabeth Marcelino. She was in San Francisco as part of a brief trip to the United States in search of donations for the Children's Rehabilitation Center in Manila. I met her with no notion of interviewing her, but as I listened to her speak of the children with whom she works, children who are victims of political repression, I knew I wanted her voice—her story and that of the children—to join the others in this book.

In her mid-30s, Dr. Marcelino is a professor of psychology at the University of the Philippines. Her commitment to children who are survivors of human rights violations comes from the time she herself was a political prisoner.

I was not arrested, but in the course of looking for my husband the day after his arrest I was rounded up together with several other wives, parents, and children of those who had been arrested. My husband had been organizing the workers from an American wire and cable manufacturer.

This experience changed the wishy-washy way in which I went from one side of the fence to the other. It was a real tempering experience because it really made me go to the deep end, know what it's like to be on the verge of being crazy or committing suicide or something like that, because of the extreme isolation and depression. I was held in prison for only three months. They kept my husband in prison for three years.

I experienced the whole range of torment, from people not knowing we were arrested and where we were being detained to being held two weeks in isolation, and so on. Being a psychologist, I did all sorts of survival tricks; but actually they don't work as well there as when you're teaching them. I was not physically harmed because my father was a military man, and also because there was a lot of pressure for my release since I was from the university, and that made a difference compared to the common person who was arrested. It was all terrifying, but at the same time I knew my situation was not the worst. I saw a lot of people, mostly men, being dragged past my cell, really badly broken, I mean bleeding, and so on. I kept telling myself I don't know them, I don't know them, but actually they were all my very good friends. But I had to deny this, because any recognition would cost my own survival and theirs too. Of course, this caused a great deal of pain for me.

So this personal experience really brought me to my senses. And I made a promise to myself: If I ever get out of this, I promise to do something for the children. I don't know what, but I just said I will do something. I'd never really been so much involved in child psychology; it wasn't my area of work and study. But for children to be the victims of political repression was too upsetting for me.

What was life like for the children in prison with you?

There was so much neglect in terms of attention given to the children in the prison. The toilet training was very upset. Some who were already toilet trained regressed back to earlier stages. I saw so many signs of what the children were going through—a lot of nightmares, children mutilating things, and the parents yelling and hitting them hard because we had to have really good behavior in prison. When I got out, I could visit my husband at least once a week, at most twice a week. I did that for the next three years. In the beginning, I tried to develop a program for the children just so that they were not a nuisance to the prison life. These children were not really arrested, but the fact is that both of their parents were political prisoners, and therefore there was nowhere for the children to go. So the government was like washing its hands, saying, we are not arresting children and we only give you the privilege of having your children inside prison, and we are not responsible for providing for them. There was therefore no food for them, and a father would have to share his portion. Children would have a fever inside the prison, and if it was late at night there was nothing you could do until the doors opened the next day. And the children had to go through seeing their fathers handcuffed, for bad behavior or because they were going to trial, or being raided and searched in the cell, soldiers running around, police dogs barking all the time. The trauma was constantly reinforced.

Dr. Marcelino recounted one incident with the children in prison that she found particularly hopeful.

The political prisoners had some pets, including ducks, which they decided they would kill for food after they were grown—the prison food was so bad. The children had learned from their parents about rights, so one of the children said to the parents, "You're just like Marcos, you don't respect the rights of children and the rights of animals. Animals have rights too." The parents had already killed one of the two ducks. The children made small placards from pieces of wood saying something like: "Stop killing the ducks!" One boy organized a group of eight other children and had a kind of petition—which is the way it works in the prison, you get things by organizing petitions. They were in tears over this. So one of the parents who had killed the duck, said, "When your mother goes to the market and buys a chicken you eat the chicken and think it's very delicious and you don't make a protest." But the boy said, "But this duck has a name, and he's my pet; so you should ask me first if I would like to eat it or not." They held a trial right there in prison. That really struck us, that incident.

What were the circumstances of starting the Center?

In June 1985, we started the Center. That was six months after my husband was released. He was released with a lot of help from solidarity groups, particularly in Europe. We then worked together to get the Center going. Things started falling into place. We got some funding from Europe, I got some training in Denmark, colleagues were volunteering to help.

We started with thirteen children and six families. The thing these thirteen children shared with each other was that they had all spent time in prison with their parents who were imprisoned for political reasons. Six of them had been with me for the three months in prison, so they were rather special, almost like family.

What kind of work do you do with the children?

We started with just a groping method of helping. We simply asked them to tell their stories. And we did a lot of open, free activities to communicate these experiences. We felt that the initial step was simply to realize that there was a community of people who were supportive—that they were not ostracized, they were not outcast from the community. There was a very big stigma for being in prison as political prisoners. Children in school told lies about their parents, saying "My father is a busy businessman," or "He's abroad working," and so on, when his or her father was in fact in prison.

From there on it was like a chain reaction—other people knew about the Center, other parents encouraged their friends to come, and we grew and grew. Then we started receiving children of parents who had gone into hiding, children whose parents had been killed. Some children even who had witnessed their parents being killed by the military or right-wing vigilante groups.

There were different kinds of therapies. We found group therapy activities more effective than one-on-one therapy. In group therapy many things happen. Group methods are more indirect than direct, more informal than formal, more nonverbal than verbal, more covert than overt.

Let me describe the whole process of therapy work with one child. The first session would be more of a medical approach, a thorough physical examination by a professional doctor. Then there is basic play observation, a very unstructured, almost free-wheeling technique.

The second phase is to get a lot of the information, first from the parents. But the most critical part is to get the information from the children, which is not coming through the verbal process, or through any kind of testing technique using pencil-and-paper type tests or what have you—which are usually the measurement devices used in the Western context. So we would engage the children in "organized play" as we call it, or planned play activities. This usually happens once a week when a group of thirty or so children will come together.

We start with a lot of nonverbal activities like painting, drawing, the "expressive forms of art." Drawing especially is often the beginning of many of our discoveries into the child's story. They start scribbling, and then they start making shapes and forms and colors. It's amazing how they can progress from simply drawing lines and using very neutral colors—grays and blacks and whites, basic colors—to richer colors, more forms and shapes. A child might draw mountains and hills and rice fields and make a story about this is where he lives in mountains, and this is what happened to him while he was with his father in the fields, the soldiers came and killed his father, and then they ran away and now he's dreaming that he could go back to this place, and then he might draw his home. For those who refuse even to take a pencil or a crayon, maybe a brown paper-bag puppet or used clothing or whatever we can manage will be used—inverted paper cups with faces drawn on, whatever. They play with them freely and put characters on them, father, mother, sister, or whatever, and a whole story will evolve around this. Now we have developed something very systematic in theater because it embraces most of the other art forms. In theater you can go from drawing to puppetry, to singing to dancing. We have found this to be very effective in bringing out all the material data from the children and also in really realizing their potentials and skills.

The other aspect is to involve them in sports, help programs, etc., to give them a sense of worth, a sense that they have control over their bodies, that they can manage simple exercises because a lot of their experiences in their early life were extreme helplessness, lack of trust, frustration, basic uncertainty about everything. We have a boy who knows all the parts of the body of another person, and can point out the details when he's referring to another person. But if you ask him where *his* eyes are, *his* nose, *his* mouth, he cannot describe that to you. Everything is external to him. The first years are so critical to the development of self, and for so many it is lost because of the trauma.

Trusting is the most difficult thing. Sometimes simply to ask the name of a child can bring the child to tears, because they have been used to hiding their names from the military, not speaking to strangers, checking out with their parents. It has been difficult for them to know who can be trusted and who cannot. And so the program is geared to bring back trust, some kind of sense of self. Some of the older children have not had any personal property for as long as they can remember. So when you tell them that they can have this for their own toy, they cannot believe it.

We feel that the schools cannot answer the needs of such children. Therefore, we have alternative forms of trying to help the children understand the world. They are confronted with death, with disappearances, with torture, all these very broad issues of life and death, early in life. What is good and bad, what is right and wrong, what is justice and what is injustice, all these abstract things they ask.

Sometimes it is very difficult to explain the political reasons for the beliefs of their parents. For instance, in general they think military men are bad. But one day, this military man gives some candy to one of the boys and sort of takes care of him and so forth, so the child comes up to his mother and asks, "How come this one isn't bad, how can he give me candy?" Another child approached his mother asking if they were really rich now since they had gone from living in a cardboard-box house to these high walls, a room of their own, regular meals, security guards all around, and barbed wire over the walls, just like the wealthy people in Manila live. One boy lived for nine years in the prison and went to a nearby school. His school I.D. card even showed the prison address as his home address. So it was very difficult for him when his father was finally released to understand that this was not really his home at all and that this was being taken away. One girl wouldn't go to school. She would go as far as the front gate of the school and stop there. She told us she didn't like going to prison—the school somehow had this connection with prison, the big gates and walls and so forth. One 5-year-old boy had always known his parents separately, his father in prison and his mother in hiding. And when his father was released he was very confused about the relationship between his mother and father, who were suddenly living together, and there was a separation trauma as he could no longer sleep with his mother.

So all these perceptions of family life, of structures in society, of the way the world moves, are all very complicated and mixed up for a child, not to mention the children often wonder why if, as their parents claim, they are fighting for the country's poor, and oppressed people, why they can't spend time with them

Lito C. Ocampo

Children of the "disappeared" at a media conference in Manila, December 1988. Illegal detentions, torture, and murder of Filipino civilians by soldiers, police, the military, and landowner-backed "vigilantes" have been on the rise since early 1987.

and help them, why they love others so much but don't seem to love them. Why do they say they are doing good and helping the poor and yet teachers and friends all say that prisons are where bad people go? One boy wondered, "Why, after Marcos' departure and so many of the prisoners were released, is my father still kept in prison—what has President Aquino got against my father?"

All these questions, difficult even for an adult of 35 years of age, you must contend with in a very young child. Not to mention that he has to learn his ABCs, and he has to go to school, and he has to do the usual stuff. So it is very, very complicated.

Dr. Marcelino tells the story of Rodel, a boy in the Center.

The interesting thing about this boy is that he embodies in his life story the whole range of traumatized experiences for children survivors of human rights violations. His father was killed before his eyes. His mother was missing and killed. His brother is missing. He was arrested and detained. He was tortured. He ran away, escaping from the soldiers. Normally, before he came to the Center, I would have given you different cases for each experience of political repression. But this boy has it all in one package.

The story begins in July of '86—that's five months after Aquino came to power—in Cagayan Valley about eight hours by bus north of Manila, in a small, rural village where rebel soldiers were known to encamp. The boy, then perhaps 12 years old, was in the fields with his father planting rice when some soldiers arrived. His father was accused of aiding the rebels with food and provisions, and then was questioned as to their whereabouts. His father would not answer their questions or he could not understand them. The soldiers then began torturing him, beating him black and blue and shooting off their guns. The boy disappeared into the bushes nearby, watching, not wanting to leave his father alone with the soldiers. He watched for some time as his father was beaten to near death, then shot, and his body chopped to pieces. The boy described this in very great detail, how they first removed the penis, and then how they took parts one after another.

Once he realized there was nothing he could do about it and that the soldiers might be after him too, he ran away, and joined his mother. At this point the soldiers were after him, so he, his mother, and a younger brother fled their home, but with nowhere to go but into the mountains. After about a month, the boy had to go down into the town, walking long hours, to buy rice and other basic provisions for them. But he made the mistake of riding a jeepney along the way—public transportation that passed through military check-points. At one of the checkpoints he was recognized by the soldiers as the one who had seen his father being killed by soldiers. He was taken from the jeepney and detained in what the boy describes as a small hut. They then began beating him up. No questions or anything. He was held there about two weeks, frequently beaten by the soldiers. One of the most painful things that he recalls is the time they took two blocks of wood together and used them to beat him directly on the ears, over and over until he was bleeding. The boy told us that it may have been the same wood that was used to kill his father.

He doesn't remember how he escaped, but from his account it seems the soldiers may have relaxed their watch one day and the boy somehow summoned the presence of mind to begin walking away from the place. So he was just wandering on and on, eating grass and bananas for days, until he was found by a farmer who took him into his house for one day, and then asked him to leave for fear that the soldiers would come looking for him. So he moved from place to place, until someone took him to the local parish priest. The priest checked with the Task Force Detainees, which was the local group in the area, who found us and arranged for his coming to Manila. From the time his father was killed to the time he got to us was two and a half months or so.

When he got to us, all he wanted was the assurance that he would be able to see his mother again. In fact, that was his condition for his coming to Manila. So we said, Yes, we will just have you treated, your wounds, and then we'll check to see if we can send for your mother. At that time he was very confident, because the people who found him knew where to find the mother, and the mother had expressed the desire that she wanted to go to Manila, but she couldn't find a way out. So we said we would try and facilitate this, but of course, it was not that easy.

At first he would speak only to the person who delivered him, and who spoke his local dialect. He was very withdrawn. Until about a month later. We had our second case of an orphaned boy, a much lighter case, about 14 years old. And when this boy came into his life, the whole thing changed. He had a friend. He started talking, not to us, but to the boy. He started playing, moving around, in a very quiet way. His friend started telling us how he was feeling. This is when we found out about the injuries to his ear. The soldiers had broken his ears inside, and there was badly clotted blood in his inner ears. The only way we could get him to go to the doctor was by saying that when the mother comes back he had to be well for them to return together, otherwise he would have to stay longer. We had to put drops in his ears every night to loosen the blood clots, so that the next day the doctor could get in there to clean them out bit by bit. The doctor said the boy would often scream and cry and accuse him of being just like his torturers, that this was like being back with the soldiers again. But there was nothing the doctor could do to stop the pain without getting into extensive anesthesia and so on.

As December neared, he was very anxious, and we had to tell him that we couldn't find his mother. She had communicated that she would come; so we just said be patient and wait. Then December came and went and he said, "You must hurry because we have to harvest the rice." The way he said it in our language was really very poetic, something like "when the grain is golden and the wind is chilly, then it is the time to harvest." He has no indication whatsoever that it is harvest time except these signs, the cold wind, the golden grain.

He would describe the soldiers as "bad men" because they take away all our property, they took our chicken, even our plants. And then, he tells us, there are these other men, he calls them "nice people," they help my father on the farm, and so forth. So this is his description of the rebels. And he said if it were not for these nice people we could not have planted all this rice, because they were coming in the daytime and helping us do the work. So it seems he knew a lot about the things that were going on where he lived, and in part because of this knowledge the soldiers eventually came after him wanting to know where these "nice people" were.

Eventually, in February we received word that the mother was now thought to be dead. We agonized over who would tell him. Finally, a social worker on the staff went to him with the news of why we could not return him to his province. This social worker was the first to cry. The boy was just standing there and at length said: "Where's the body? I want to see the body, I want to bury my mother." We said we don't know where the body is, we'll try to find it. The social worker was sort of waiting for him to cry, but he didn't. There was this awkward silence, and then he finally went up to his room. One of the children, a younger boy, followed him up. The boy returned to us saying, "Hey, he's been up in the toilet for so long, he just keeps on washing his face over and over again." All the children wondered why he didn't cry at the news of his mother, not recognizing that he was really crying all the time he was up washing his face.

Rodel's still with us. He's very, very much better. A lot has been facilitated through this friend, whom we think was the most critical factor in his life. Now he speaks Tagalog very fluently. But he had to hurdle one trauma after the other. He had had no reading at all; so we started just encouraging him to draw. In the beginning he refused, but later when he did start drawing he would tell stories about it. He started writing, by writing his name on drawings.

He dreams of seeing his brother. He writes letters to him, even though he is missing. He gives them to us as if we could send them, but knowing that in fact we have to just keep them. And he tells his brother that probably, "If you are with me, I'll stay here in Manila, but maybe I'll go home first and see what has happened to our farm." He'll say, "Do you know that mother is dead?"

When we ask him what he wants to do, he says whatever he decides to do later, he wants to go home first. That has really been his only wish since the time he came to us, and the only wish that we cannot grant. He can't go back because it is too dangerous, the military are very active there, but still he hopes that he will.

What is the human rights situation now, more than two years after Marcos?

The situation has really gone from bad to worse, I must say. Especially in the rural areas. I think that now there is a cover because you have a popular government, seemingly wanting to do a lot of good. Sincerity is not enough, although it is necessary.

There are more political prisoners now than there were in Marcos's time—or at least the number when Marcos left has been surpassed. The only reason you don't hear about them is that Amnesty International just got into the picture lately and most of them are no-name people. I mean they are usually peasants, ordinary workers, so there is not a big fuss about them, unlike the old political prisoners who were mostly intellectuals, students. Now there are more

Jeanne Hallacy

Manila's "Smoky Mountain," a garbage dump that is home and workplace to more than 4,000 Filipino families. Scavenging is one of the many forms of work for some 10 million Filipino children under the age of 14.

Robert Gumpert

Robert Gumpert

grassroots people in prison. Another reason you don't hear so much about the political repression now is that they have distributed these prisoners to prison camps outside the Metro Manila region. Also, there has been an increase in the number of salvagings, of summary executions, meaning they are simply killed outright, no questions asked, no records. You must have heard about what we call the "symbolic assassinations" of mass leaders. A trade union leader, a peasant leader, a worker, recently a student leader, Lean Alejandro, have been summarily executed. And all that the present government has done is to create committees to investigate the crimes. There has been one committee after the other with no results. There is nothing significant going on to punish any of the Marcos people who have committed so many violations of human rights in the Philippines. Not even some kind of token example to those who are doing the same now.

With all this repression, there still is this popular aura that keeps Aquino from being criticized. And now there are the right-wing vigilante groups. The vigilantes are a creation of the government. There is a very explicit policy of support for vigilantes. And in this way Aquino is responsible. In fact, there are a lot of radio and television and newspaper quotations where she openly supports vigilante groups, as do some leaders in the Catholic Church.

Actually, there is an undeclared war going on. The one big difference between this undeclared war now and the one under Marcos is that the war now has escalated so much because of the phenomenon of vigilante groups. Whereas, before you had very clear groups fighting each other—the rebels on one side and the military on the other side—now, with the creation of so-called citizens' army, you have citizens divided among themselves. In one village, for example, you would have vigilante members and nonvigilante members. And the nonvigilantes are seen as communists, of course. I've even seen, in Davao, houses marked with an "X". If your house is marked with an "X," then you're not a vigilante and you must move, or else the vigilantes will take hold of you, accuse you of being a communist because you're not joining them. And, of course, the rebels can't retaliate with the same strength that they would if they were fighting the military alone, because there are a lot of civilians now who are caught in the crossfire.

So, based on our documentation, we have estimated 4.5 million children are direct or indirect victims of the increasing militarization in the countryside, of this undeclared war. We did this through identification of heavily militarized areas and the number of cases already that we have had at the center.

Why would anyone torture children?

Like in Rodel's case, the military or the paramilitary groups think he knows something about the rebels, or that he knows too much about what they have done. But also, children are being tortured in front of their parents, because the military find that this is the most effective way to get peasants to tell them what they want to know.

Does the Center have any support from the government?

None at all. At the beginning we had a bit of moral support. In fact, three days after Aquino came to power, I was on television appealing for the children. Then when we received this first case of torture we went to Malacañang and personally tried to convince her to try to stop the military from torturing. But unfortunately nothing came from this. We wrote four letters. We met with middlemen. But we didn't even get the courtesy of a response. The government doesn't want to admit that children are victims of human rights violations.

I must say, I'm much more afraid now than I ever was in Marcos's times. Nothing at all happened to us during the last six months of the Marcos period. Now in the Aquino period, we have the military calling us up and saying they don't want all this publicity about tortured children. Two of our staff have been under surveillance, and some of our clientele have been stopped on their way into the Center, intimidated by plainclothes men. Of course, the parents report it to us, but the next time they don't come anymore because they're so scared. Last year in October, two of our staff were arrested while doing a relief mission for children. The government labels us as subversives. The situation is getting so bad that the staff really have to think twice—do they want to work here? We have appealed over and over again that we be allowed to continue with the treatment in much the same way as doctors. We are not against the government in a political way—of course our cases are political, but I think at war or at peace we should be allowed to do our work.

Do you get help from international agencies like UNICEF?

It has proven impossible. One difficulty is the UNICEF policy of coordinating everything with the government. We had this one big project that really could have helped us work with more children, including setting up centers in several different areas in the country; it was half a million U.S. dollars. But one condition laid down by the government was that the military would come onto the advisory board. Imagine! We said, No way, not for any amount of money. So if we were to get help from UNICEF, we would not get a single child after coordinating with military people. The government wanted the military to be there in the delivery of services to promote their whole counter-insurgency campaign of image-building, using UNICEF as the entry point and us, a nongovernmental organization that is very credible at the grassroots. So the whole thing of the government is really something very sinister.

Although we focus on the individual child's problems, the problems of the children are definitely very closely linked to the structural problems of society. And I think if we do not have bold changes on that level, we will just be going in circles and presenting palliatives for the children. We simply will be saying you will just have to tolerate this war, that there's nothing we can do about it. Personally, I think there is something we can do. We need to speak out against this brutality, make our voices heard in the open.

I think also, from the point of view of the American people, they must protest the way their government handles its own foreign policy in the Philippines and other third-world countries, especially its collaboration with the military. In this way it is a global problem because the experience of the Philippines people with this undeclared war and the vigilante groups, etc., is actually similar to the experiences in many countries that also are directly connected to U.S. policies. When we see the drawings of children with helicopters and very explicit labels saying "Sikorsky" [U.S.–made military helicopters], you can really see how directly involved the U.S. is in this vigilante phenomenon, and the whole undeclared war going on now in the Philippines.

When children are tortured in any society, there is something grossly wrong with that society, and we have to be disturbed by it. Whatever effects this will have on the Filipino children will have long-term effects for the way society will be run in the future. What kind of future will it be when these children enter into society? I think we are doing this work most of all for the future of our children's children. That's the only way we can keep on going, because right now there is so much helplessness and desperation. But if you think of it in terms of the future of generations to come (which is actually the name of one our organizations helping children, *Salin Lahi*—The Next Generation) it is the only way we can be given hope. Looking at the children, battered and bruised, it seems like there's no hope. But the smile on their faces and the fact that they can bounce back seem to say that, with a lot of caring and support from the family, from relatives, from mental health workers, but most of all from the community and the world as a whole, we will have some hope for the future.

Selected Sources

Agricultural Policy and Strategy Team. *Agenda for Action for the Philippine Rural Sector*. Los Baños: University of the Philippines at Los Baños.

Aguilar, Jr., Filomeno V. *The Making of Cane Sugar: Poverty, Crisis and Change in Negros Occidental*. Bacolod City: La Salle Social Research Center Monograph Series, No. 2, 1984.

Amnesty International. *Philippines: Unlawful Killings By Military and Paramilitary Forces*. New York: Amnesty International USA, 1988.

Bain, David Howard. *Sitting in Darkness: Americans in the Philippines*. Boston: Houghton Mifflin Company, 1984.

Bello, Walden, David Kinley, and Elaine Elinson. *Development Debacle: The World Bank in the Philippines*. San Francisco: Food First Books, 1982.

Bello, Walden. *U.S.-Sponsored Low-Intensity Conflict in the Philippines*. San Francisco: Institute for Food and Development Policy, Food First Development Report No. 2 (December 1987).

Bonner, Raymond. *Waltzing with a Dictator: The Marcoses and the Making of American Policy*. New York: Random House, 1987.

Broad, Robin. *Unequal Alliance: The World Bank, the International Monetary Fund, and the Philippines*. Berkeley and Los Angeles: University of California Press, 1988.

Canlas, Mamerto; Mariano Miranda, Jr., and James Putzel. *Land, Poverty and Politics in the Philippines*. London: Catholic Institute for International Relations, 1988.

Catholic Institute for International Relations. *The Labour Trade: Filipino Migrant Workers Around the World*. London, 1987.

Chapman, William. *Inside the Philippine Revolution: The New People's Army and Its Struggle for Power*. New York and London: W. W. Norton and Company, 1987.

Collins, Joseph. "Philippine Land Reform: Cory's Broken Promise." *The Nation*, Vol. 245, No. 16 (November 14, 1987).

Constantino, Renato. *A History of the Philippines from the Spanish Colonization to World War Two*. New York: Monthly Review Press, 1975.

——————————. *The Philippines: A Past Revisited*. Quezon City: Foundation for Nationalist Studies, 1975.

—————————. *The Miseducation of the Filipino*. Quezon City: Foundation for Nationalist Studies, 1982.

—————————. *The Nationalist Alternative*. Quezon City: Foundation for Nationalist Studies, 1986 (rev. ed.).

Constantino, Renato, and Letizia Constantino. *The Philippines: The Continuing Past*. Quezon City: Foundation for Nationalist Studies, 1978.

Department of Agrarian Reform. Various documents, 1987 and 1988.

Dumaine, Brian. "The $2.2 Billion Nuclear Fiasco." *Fortune International*, September 1986.

Feder, Ernest. *Perverse Development*. Quezon City: Foundation for Nationalist Studies, 1983.

Hofstadter, Richard, William Miller, and Daniel Aaron. *The American Republic*. Vol. II. Englewood Cliffs, New Jersey, 1970.

IBON Databank Philippines. *Land Reform in the Philippines*. Manila, 1988.

Jagan, Larry, and John Cunnington. *Social Volcano: Sugar Workers in the Philippines*. London: War on Want, 1987.

Karnow, Stanley. *In Our Image: America's Empire in the Philippines*. New York: Random House, 1989.

Kerkvliet, Benedict J. *The Huk Rebellion: A Study of Peasant Revolt in the Philippines*. Berkeley and Los Angeles: University of California Press, 1977.

Kilusang Magbubukid ng Pilipinas (KMP), *Program for Genuine Land Reform*. Quezon City, 1986.

—————————. "Peasant Update International." Quezon City, various issues.

—————————. *Policy Proposals on Agriculture and Countryside Development*. Quezon City, 1986.

Lopez-Gonzaga, Violeta B. *Crisis and Poverty in Sugarlandia: The Case of Bacolod*. Bacolod City: La Salle Social Research Center Monograph Series, No. 3 (1985).

McCoy, Alfred W. *Priests on Trial*. New York: Penguin Books, 1984.

O'Brien, Niall. *Revolution from the Heart*. New York: Oxford University Press, 1987.

Ofreneo, Rene E. *Capitalism in Philippine Agriculture*. Quezon City: Foundation for Nationalist Studies, 1980.

Paez, Patricia Ann. *The Bases Factor: Realpolitik of RP-US Relations*. Manila: Center for Strategic and International Studies of the Philippines, 1985.

Poole, Fred, and Max Vanzi. *Revolution in the Philippines: The United States in a Hall of Cracked Mirrors*. New York: McGraw Hill, 1984.

Porter, Gareth and Delfin J. Ganopin, Jr. *Resources, Population and the Philippines*. Washington, D.C.: World Resources Institute, 1988.

Putzel, James and John Cunnington. *Gaining Ground: Agrarian Reform in the Philippines*. London: War on Want, 1989.

Rosca, Ninotchka. *Endgame: The Fall of Marcos*. New York: Franklin Watts, 1987.

Rosenberg, David A., ed. *Marcos and Martial Law in the Philippines*. Ithaca: Cornell University Press, 1979.

Sandoval, Romulo A., ed. *Prospects of Agrarian Reform Under the New Order*. Quezon City: National Council of Churches, 1986.

Schirmer, Daniel B., and Stephen Rosskamm Shalom. *The Bases of Our Insecurity*. 2nd ed. Quezon City: BALAI Fellowship Inc., 1985.

_____. *The Philippines Reader*. Boston: South End Press, 1987.

Simbulan, Roland G. *A Guide to Nuclear Philippines*. Manila: IBON Databank Philippines, 1989.

Steinberg, David Joel. *The Philippines: A Singular and A Plural Place*. Boulder: Westview Press, 1982.

_____. *In Search of Southeast Asia*. 2nd ed. Honolulu: University of Hawaii Press, 1987.

Third World Studies Center. *Political Economy of Philippine Commodities*. Quezon City: University of the Philippines, 1983.

"U.S. Bases in the Philippines: Assets or Liabilities?" *Defense Monitor*, Vol. XV, No. 4 (1986).

United States Information Service, *Background on the Bases*. 2nd ed. Manila: USIS, 1987 and 1988.

Warr, Peter G. *Export Processing Zones in the Philippines*. Canberra and Kuala Lumpur: ASEAN-Australia Joint Research Project, 1985.

Wynne, Alison. *No Time for Crying: Stories of Philippine Women*. Hong Kong: Resource Centre for Philippine Concerns, 1980.

Resource Guide

Human Rights

The best source of up-to-date information on the state of human rights in the Philippines is the Task Force Detainees of the Philippines (TFDP). The other groups listed serve as invaluable sources of information and suggestions for action on human rights issues.

Amnesty International
U.S. Office
322 Eighth Avenue
New York, NY 10001
(212) 807-8400

Canada-Asia Working Group
11 Madison Avenue
Toronto, Ontario
CANADA M5R 2S2
(416) 924-9351

Church Coalition for Human Rights in the Philippines
Building Box 70
110 Maryland Avenue NE
Washington, D.C. 20002
(202) 543-1094
Publications: *Philippine Witness* (monthly)
Philippine News Survey (biweekly)

Columban Fathers Justice and Peace Office
P.O. Box 29151
Washington, D.C. 20002
(202) 529-5115

Ecumenical Movement for Justice and Peace
P.O.Box 1127
Manila 2800
Quezon City
PHILIPPINES
Publication: *Justice and Peace Review* (quarterly)

Free Legal Assistance Group
55 Third Street
New Manila
Quezon City
PHILIPPINES

Lawyers Committee on Human Rights
10th Floor, 330 Seventh Avenue
New York, NY 10001
(212) 921-2160

National Movement for Civil Liberties
1186 Quezon Avenue
Quezon City 1103
Metro Manila
PHILIPPINES

Synapses
1821 W. Cullerton
Chicago, IL 60608
(312) 421-5513

Task Force Detainees of the Philippines
214 N. Domingo Street
SFI Bldg.
Cubao, Quezon City
PHILIPPINES
Publication: *Philippine Human Rights Update* (monthly)

Political and Economic Developments

A good source of news and editorial interpretations of political and economic issues and U.S.–Philippine relations is the daily *Manila Chronicle*. The Third World Studies Center has an excellent track record in researching and analyzing Philippine political and economic developments. For a reliable source of statistics and insights on economic issues, contact IBON Databank.

Catholic Institute for International Relations (CIIR)
22 Coleman Fields
London N1 7AF
ENGLAND

Conjuncture
Institute for Popular Democracy
P.O. Box SM-156
Metro Manila
PHILIPPINES

IBON Databank Facts and Figures
P.O. Box SM-447
Room 305, SCC Bldg.
3892 Ramon Magsaysay Blvd.
Santa Mesa, Manila
PHILIPPINES

Institute for Food and Development Policy
145 Ninth Street
San Francisco, CA 94103
(415) 864-8555

International Solidarity Network Desk
Association of Major Religious Superiors of the Philippines
P.O. Box 10238
Broadway Centrum
Quezon City
PHILIPPINES

KSP Filipino People's Committee
Admiraal van Gentstraat 26 bis
3572 XL Utrecht
NETHERLANDS

Manila Chronicle
371 Bonifacio Drive
Port Area, Manila
PHILIPPINES

National Midweek
2nd Floor, Mar Santos Bldg.
43 Don A. Roces Avenue
Quezon City 1103
PHILIPPINES

Philippine Agenda
1353 Leon Guinto
Ermita, Manila
PHILIPPINES

Philippine Resource Center
P.O. Box 40090
Berkeley, CA 94704
(415) 548-2546
Publication: *Philippine Monitor*

Philippine Resource Center
1/2 Grangeway
Kilburn, London NW6 2BW
ENGLAND

Third World Studies Center
P.O. Box 210
University of the Philippines
Diliman, Quezon City
PHILIPPINES
Publication: *Kasarinlan* (quarterly)

Agrarian Reform and Land Issues

The organizations listed below provide information and suggestions for action on land reform and agrarian issues in the Philippines and in Europe. In the United States, the Philippine Resource Center and the Institute for Food and Development Policy (addresses given prior) monitor agrarian issues.

Agency for Community Educational Services Foundation (ACES)
12 Eleventh Avenue
Cubao, Quezon City
PHILIPPINES

Committee for a People's Agrarian Reform (CPAR)
c/o Center for Social Policy and Public Affairs
Faura Hall
Ateneo de Manila University
Loyola Heights, Quezon City
PHILIPPINES

Kilusang Magbubukid ng Pilipinas (KMP)
88 Maningning Street
Teacher's Village
Diliman, Quezon City 3008
PHILIPPINES
Publication: *Peasant Update International*

Philippine Partnership for the Development of Human Resources in Rural Areas (PHILDRRA)
2178 Pasong Tamo Street
Makati, Metro Manila
PHILIPPINES

Philippine Peasant Institute
P.O. Box 159 AC
Dilman, Quezon City
PHILIPPINES

Philippine Rural Reconstruction Movement (PRRM)
P.O.Box 10479
Broadway Centrum
Quezon City 1112
PHILIPPINES

Philippine Program
Transnational Institute
Paulus Potterstraat 20
1071 BA Amsterdam
NETHERLANDS

Labor
The following groups provide information on labor issues and on campaigns launched by the labor movement.

KMU (May 1st Movement)
International Department
3rd Floor, Jopson Bldg.
510 M. Earnshaw Street
Sampaloc, Manila
PHILIPPINES
Publication: *Correspondence*

National Federation of Sugar Workers
5 Rosea Street
Bacolod City
Negros Occidental
PHILIPPINES

Philippine Workers Support Committee
P.O. Box 11208
Moiliili Station
Honolulu, HA 96828
Publication: *Philippine Labor Alert*

U.S. Bases and the Nuclear Issue
The following groups monitor developments and serve as organizing centers around these two front-burner issues.

Alliance for Philippine Concerns (APC)
North America National Office
P.O. Box 170219
San Francisco, CA 94117
(415) 540-5230

Campaign Against U.S. Military Bases in the Philippines
135 Haddon Place
Montclair, NJ 07043
(201) 783-4778

Friends of the Filipino People (FFP)
P.O. Box 2125
Durham, NC 27702
(919) 489-0002
Publication: *FFP Update*

Nuclear-Free Philippines Coalition
2215 Pedro Gil Street
Santa Ana, Manila 1009
PHILIPPINES
Publication: *CALL*

Women's Issues

Spearheading the Philippine women's movement is GABRIELA, a coalition of 86 organizations.

GABRIELA
P.O. Box 4386
Manila 2800
PHILIPPINES

Cultural and Minority Issues

The struggles of the many cultural minorities in the Philippines are the concern of the following organizations.

Cultural Survival
11 Divinity Avenue
Cambridge, MA 02138
Publication: *Cultural Survival Quarterly*

Episcopal Commission on Tribal Filipinos
Room 15, CAP Bldg.
372 Cabildo Street
Intramuros, Manila
PHILIPPINES
Publication: *Tribal Forum*

Moro Resource Center
P.O. Box 5468
Iligan City
PHILIPPINES

People's Action for Cultural Ties (PACT)
National Council of Churches in the Philippines
P.O. Box 1767
Manila
PHILIPPINES

Survival International
310 Edgware Road
London WC2 1DY
ENGLAND

Survival International USA
2121 Decatur Place NW
Washington, D.C. 20008
(202) 265-1077
Publication: *Survival International News*

Health Issues and Medical Support

Two organizations concentrate on generating concern for the health and medical needs of Filipinos.

Health Action Information Network (HAIN)
49 Scout Madrinan
Diliman, Quezon City
PHILIPPINES
Publication: *Health Alert*

Philippine Assistance for Technology and Health (PATH)
3524 Adeline Street
Berkeley, CA 94703
(415) 655-0933

Arts and Culture

In the 1970s and 1980s, "people's drama" and other forms of committed art were born in the Philippines. Among the renowned pioneers of political theater is the Philippine Educational Theatre Association (PETA).

PETA
1 Scout de Guia Street
Quezon City
PHILIPPINES

Travel

The Center for Global Education periodically arranges tours that bring visitors in contact with the social, economic, and political realities of the Philippines.

Center for Global Education
Augsburg College
731 21st Avenue South
Minneapolis, MN 55454
(612) 330-1159
Publication: *Global Perspectives*

Index

About the Author

Dr. Joseph Collins, co-founder of the Institute for Food and Development Policy, is a leading expert on world hunger and international development issues. His world experience began in his teenage years when he spent his summer vacations working with Catholic missionaries in city slums and rural areas in Chile, Peru, the Yucatan, Guatemala, West Africa, and the Philippines.

Collins received his undergraduate degree from Maryknoll College and a master's and doctorate from Columbia University. As a staff member of the Institute for Policy Studies from 1971 to 1975, he assisted in the research for *Global Reach: The Power of the Multinational Corporation* and co-authored *World Hunger: Causes and Remedies*. In 1975, Dr. Collins and Frances Moore Lappé, author of *Diet for a Small Planet*, founded the Institute for Food and Development Policy, a San Francisco-based research and education center devoted to exposing and eliminating the root causes of world hunger. He has written numerous books on food and development issues, including collaborations with Lappé, which began with their classic, *Food First: Beyond the Myth of Scarcity*. His articles have appeared in dozens of publications, ranging from newspapers and popular magazines to scholarly journals. He frequently is a consultant to the media, appears on radio and television, and speaks before university and civic audiences throughout the world.

About the Institute

The Institute for Food and Development Policy, also known as Food First, is a nonprofit research and education center. The Institute works to identify the root causes of hunger and food problems in the United States and around the world, and to educate the public as well as policymakers about these problems.

Institute research has demonstrated that the hunger and poverty in which millions seem condemned to live is not inevitable. Our Food First publications reveal how scarcity and overpopulation, long believed to be the causes of hunger, are instead symptoms—symptoms of an ever-increasing concentration of control over food-producing resources in the hands of a few, depriving so many people of the power to feed themselves.

In 55 countries and 20 languages, Food First materials and investigations are freeing people from the grip of despair, laying the groundwork—in ideas and action—for a more democratically controlled food system that will meet the needs of all.

AN INVITATION TO JOIN US

Private contributions and membership dues form the financial base of the Institute for Food and Development Policy. Because the Institute is not tied to any government, corporation, or university, it can speak with a strong independent voice, free of ideological formulas. The success of the Institute's programs depends not only on its dedicated volunteers and staff, but on financial activists as well. Our efforts toward ending hunger are made possible by membership dues or gifts from individuals, small foundations, and religious organizations; book sales account for about 15 percent of our income. We accept no government funding.

Each new and continuing member strengthens our effort to change a hungry world. We'd like to invite you to join in this effort. As a member of the Institute you will receive a 25 percent discount on all Food First books. You will also receive our newsletter *Food First News*, and our timely Action Alerts which provide information and suggestions for action on current issues of economic and social injustice in the United States and around the world.

To join us in putting Food First, just clip and return the coupon at the back of the book. All contributions to the Institute are tax deductible.

Publications and Resources

The Philippines: Fire on the Rim by Joseph Collins. Learn about one of the hungriest countries on earth by reading the stories of its people. This collection of interviews from left, right, and center of the post-Marcos Philippines is a good, long look at the realities following the People Power revolution. Hardcover $18.95, Paper $9.95.

Rediscovering America's Values by Frances Moore Lappé. In a lively exchange peppered with quotes from a chorus of thinkers, Lappé probes the values of freedom, fairness and democracy, airs out some musty myths and points the way toward bold, new solutions for some of our toughest social problems. The dialogue style that so effectively draws the reader into the provocative debate is also a natural format for sparking discussions in classrooms and community groups. Hardcover $22.50.

Family Farming: A New Economic Vision by Marty Strange. The author asks tough questions about the morass of farm failures, big banking subsidies, price supports, and trade agreements in order to construct a new land ethic based on American agricultural tradition. Hardcover $18.95, Paper $7.50.

A Fate Worse Than Debt by Susan George. A thoroughly researched and fascinating work on the world debt crisis and its effect on the poor. It reveals how the crisis could be an opportunity to transform third-world debt from an instrument of starvation, oppression, and misery into one of productivity, democracy, and hope. Hardcover $17.95, Paper $8.95.

Betraying the National Interest by Frances Moore Lappé, Rachel Schurman and Kevin Danaher. Why do our assistance programs—now dominated by military aid—end up backfiring, creating the very instability and undemocratic institutions they claim to check? Takes head-on the threat of Soviet influence in the third world and other strong arguments used to defend U.S. aid, revealing the flaws in both the liberal and conservative points of view. Hardcover $18.95, Paper $8.95.

Don't Be Afraid, Gringo: A Honduran Woman Speaks from the Heart translated and edited by Medea Benjamin, with photos by Susan Meiselas. Elvia Alvarado, a courageous peasant organizer, tells of the struggle to regain land taken from the poor in Honduras and how she has been harassed, imprisoned, and tortured for her efforts. Living in the shadow of the largest U.S. base in Honduras, Elvia provides a revealing account of the disastrous effect U.S. military expansion is having on her country. Paper $9.95.

Nicaragua: What Difference Could a Revolution Make? by Joseph Collins, with Frances Moore Lappé, Nick Allen, and Paul Rice. This highly acclaimed study documents the transformation of Nicaragua's food and farming system since the popular revolution of 1979. Hardcover $22.50, Paper $10.95. Spanish edition $7.95.

No Free Lunch: Food and Revolution in Cuba Today by Medea Benjamin, Joseph Collins, and Michael Scott. Based on sources not readily available to Western researchers, this examination of Cuba's food and farming system confirms that Cuba is the only Latin American country to have eradicated hunger. Paper $9.95.

World Hunger: Twelve Myths by Frances Moore Lappé and Joseph Collins. A revealing and often shocking book that shatters common beliefs about the causes of hunger and the present approaches to a solution. Each chapter is a concise, self-contained essay, written in a popular style, but with thorough documentation. An excellent introduction to a complex issue; perfect for the classroom and group discussions. Paper $9.95.

Food First: Beyond the Myth of Scarcity by Frances Moore Lappé and Joseph Collins, with Cary Fowler. This landmark study draws on a worldwide network of research to demystify such complex and vital issues as: rapid population growth, the green revolution, U.S. foreign aid, the World Bank, and agribusiness. Paper $4.95. Spanish edition $7.95.

Circle of Poison: Pesticides and People in a Hungry World by David Weir and Mark Schapiro. In the best investigative style, this popular exposé documents the global scandal of corporate and government exportation of pesticides and reveals the threat this poses to consumers and workers throughout the world. Paper $5.95.

Diet for a Small Planet by Frances Moore Lappé. This completely revised edition of Lappé's bestseller draws on more than a decade of research to explain how political and economic systems keep people hungry. 432 pages with charts, tables, resource guide, and recipes. Paper $3.95.

American Lake: Nuclear Peril in the Pacific by Walden Bello, Peter Hayes, and Lyuba Zarsky. Using previously undisclosed and formerly classified Pentagon files, *American Lake* exposes the full extent of the nuclear arms race in the Pacific and reveals the precarious state of the American and Soviet nuclear stand-off. Paper $6.95.

A Quiet Violence: View from a Bangladesh Village by Betsy Hartmann and James Boyce. A moving portrayal of village life, this books shows how the effect of economic and social forces keep people bound in the quiet violence of poverty and hunger. Paper $11.95.

Needless Hunger: Voices from a Bangladesh Village by James Boyce and Betsy Hartmann. The global analysis of Food First is vividly captured here in a single village. The root causes of hunger emerge through the stories of both village landowners and peasants who live at the margin of survival. Paper $4.95.

Alternatives to the Peace Corps: Gaining Third World Experience by Becky Buell. Updated and revised, this guide provides essential information on voluntary service organizations, technical service programs, work brigades, study tours, and alternative travel in the third world, and offers options to the Peace Corps as the principal route for people wishing to gain international experience. Paper $5.

Education for Action: Graduate Studies with a Focus on Social Change by Andrea Freedman, with Kim Berry and Mary Crain. A guide to progressive graduate programs and educators in agriculture, anthropology, development studies, history, law, management, political science, public health, sociology, urban planning, and women's studies. Paper $3.

Curricula

Exploding the Hunger Myths: A High School Curriculum by Sonja Williams. With an emphasis on hunger, twenty-five activities provide a variety of positive discovery experiences—role playing, simulation, interviewing, writing, drawing—to help students understand the real underlying causes of hunger and how problems they thought were inevitable can be changed. 200 pages, 8.5 x 11 with charts, reproducible illustrated handouts, resource guide, and glossary. $15.

Food First Curriculum by Laurie Rubin. Six delightfully illustrated units span a range of compelling topics including the path of food from farm to table, why people in other parts of the world do things differently, and how young people can help make changes in their communities. 146 pages, three-hole punched, 8 ½" x 11" with worksheets and teachers' resources. Grades 4-6. $12.

Strangers in Their Own Country: A Curriculum Guide on South Africa by William Bigelow. This unique resource introduces students to the lives and struggles of the people of South Africa using stories, poems, role plays, simulations, news articles, and historical readings. Lessons are easily adaptable for junior high, high school, college, church groups, and trade unions. $14.95.

Food First Comic by Leonard Rifas. An inquisitive teenager sets out to discover the roots of hunger. Her quest is illustrated with wit and imagination by Rifas, who has based his delightful comic on *World Hunger: Twelve Myths*. $1.

Hunger Myths and Facts. An illustrated fold-out fact sheet on the most common misconceptions about world hunger and Food First's responses to them. Succinct and powerful, this overview of the root causes of hunger is perfect for classes, discussion groups, and conferences. 20/$5; 50/$10; 100/$15; 500/$50.

Audio Visuals

The Challenge to End Hunger. Experts and activists from around the world join Food First analysts in pointing out how world hunger is linked to apartheid,

U.S. policy in Central America, the sanctuary movement, as well as to export agriculture and many foreign aid programs. 20 minutes, color. $30 VHS/$50 filmstrip/$100 slideshow.

The Business of Hunger. Examining how placing profits above people takes place at the price of malnutrition and famine, this video is certain to stimulate discussion on hunger issues and the role of the U.S. in development. Maryknoll Films, 28 minutes, color. $52 VHS.

Central America: We Can Make A Difference. An overview of the roots of conflict in Central America, this slideshow also debunks the conservatives' favorite myths: that the conflict is provoked by communist influences, that current U.S. policy will guarantee peace, and that our involvement in Central America is in our best interests. Central American refugees, union leaders, Latin American policy experts, religious workers, and Vietnam veterans tell how we can work together to change current policy. 20 minutes. Comes with audio-tape and study guide. $52 slideshow/$17 filmstrip.

Faces of War. This controversial documentary illustrates the devastating effect of U.S. military aid to Central America through the dramatic personal stories of six Americans working in the region. $25 VHS or Beta.

Four Myths of Hunger: An Evening with Joseph Collins and Frances Moore Lappé. In this introduction to four of the most fundamental misconceptions about causes and solutions to world hunger, Lappé and Collins share their discoveries and observations, focusing on the myths of scarcity, increased production, the trade-off between justice and production, and the effects of foreign aid. Filmed in cooperation with Sid/Impact Video. 35 minutes, color. $90 VHS/$110 3/4-inch videotape.

Seeds of Revolution. An award winning documentary produced by Howard Enders for ABC-TV, with the assistance of Joseph Collins. A corporate banana plantation in Honduras, destroyed by a hurricane, is brought back into full production by peasants who form a cooperative. When the cooperative decides to break from the corporation's marketing system as well, it comes under military attack. The story is poignantly told through interviews with corporate and military officials, cooperative workers, and union leaders. 30 minutes, color. $500 16mm/$315 video/$55 16mm rental. NOTE: ORDER DIRECTLY FROM: Icarus Films Inc., 200 Park Ave. South, Suite 1319, New York, NY 10003, (212) 674-3375.

Food First Books
Institute for Food and Development Policy
145 Ninth Street
San Francisco, CA 94103 USA
(415) 864-8555
800-888-3314

Name _____

Address _____

City/State/Zip _____

Daytime Phone (___) _____

Educators: If books are examination copies please check here: ___

Item Description	Qty	Unit Cost	Total

I want to join Food First and receive a 25% discount on this and all subsequent orders. Enclosed is my tax-deductible contribution of:
___ $100; ___ $50; ___ $25

Member discount -25%	_____
CA residents sales tax 6.5%	$ _____
SUBTOTAL	
Postage/15% ;UPS/20% ($2 min.)	$ _____
Membership(s)	$ _____
Contribution	$ _____
TOTAL ENCLOSED	$ _____

Payment Method: ___ check or money order

___ Mastercard ___ VISA

Name on Card _____

Card Number _____

Expir. Date _____

Signature _____

Institute for Food & Development Policy, 145 Ninth Street, San Francisco, CA 94103 (1-415) 864-8555 Toll Free 800-888-3314